Note to the Reader

Although it unfolds as a documentary, the story in this novel is science fiction. The scientific details are accurate or predicted based on sound principles. Some historical events are factual, whereas others are invented to fit the narrative.

I hope you enjoy the journey.

Christer Jansson

January, 2024

GENES OF THE PAST

A novel

Christer Jansson

To Janet

my wife and travel companion

on the journey through life

ACKNOWLEDGMENTS

This book is a work of fiction. Any resemblance between the characters in the story and extinct or extant hominins is purely coincidental.

Except when it isn't. In defining the family of the protagonist, I'm indebted to my own family for lending material. I'm also grateful for all the information about pubs and other amenities in the U.K. from our daughter in London.

I thank my family members and other people in my orbit for providing valuable edits.

Many of the recipes referred to throughout the story have been personalized to fit my own taste, but they all have an origin. I'd like to acknowledge some of them by providing links to sites from where I got my inspiration.

Farro salad:
https://www.delish.com/cooking/recipe-ideas/recipes/a43059/best-farro-salad-recipe/

Italian Eggplant Parmesan:
https://www.delish.com/cooking/recipe-ideas/recipes/a43059/best-farro-salad-recipe/

Sourdough crackers:
https://www.loveandoliveoil.com/2019/03/sourdough-crackers-with-olive-oil-herbs.html

Shakshuka:
https://downshiftology.com/recipes/shakshuka/

Finnish rye bread:
https://www.saltakvarn.se/recept/brod/finskt-ragbrod/

Hasselback potatoes:
https://www.ica.se/recept/hasselbackspotatis

TABLE OF CONTENTS

ABOUT THE AUTHOR

PROLOGUE

1967. Central Morocco.

The hominin fossil was found in what would eventually become known as "Fat Man's Cave." Ironically, neither was the site a cave nor the man who stumbled upon it fat. On the contrary, Felix Fleischmann, an Austrian car salesman and avid ornithologist, was a spindly, tall, and somewhat stooped character in his early sixties. Because of his stature, his fellow companions in the bird-watching group amicably started to refer to him as "Fat Man" when the tour bus left Marrakesh.

Fleischmann had traveled to Marrakesh as part of an organized tour to study the Moroccan avifauna. The group first spent two full days enjoying spectacular Atlantic Coast birding. They moved inland toward the desert for the third and final day to experience a different bird repertoire. They had now stopped for a lunch break in a thuja groove, which provided much-appreciated shade and a pleasant pine-scented aroma. The other twenty-three persons in the group—mainly European and American men and women, including their hyperactive tour guide and his bus driver—started unwrapping their prepackaged cheese sandwiches and thermoses filled with sugary mint tea, a local staple. Meanwhile, Fleischmann, who had become tired of the guide and his never-ending chatter of self-promoting birding escapades, caught sight of a low-flying raptor. He decided to explore the dual benefit of getting a closer look at the falcon-looking bird and getting away from the guide.

Fleischmann soon found himself astray in a stretch of bare red soil interspersed with rocks and bushes. He paid more attention to the sky and what might have been an Eleonora's Falcon than he did to where his feet landed. He hit his foot on a pile of rocks and dropped ungraciously to the ground. The small Kodak Instamatic camera he stored in his breast pocket fell and took a tumble between rocks and loose pebbles. It finally tore open a hole in the thin, dry clay layer and got lost from sight. He collected himself and took stock of injuries and other calamities: his glasses on the ground, skewed but not broken, blood seeping through a scratch on his left knee just below the shorts, gravel embedded in his otherwise well-groomed beard, and a sore left hand. He picked up his glasses and bent down on his right knee, throwing rocks this way and that in pursuit of the camera, sweating and cursing in the hot air from the zenith sun.

"Scheiße!" he muttered, using his right hand to alternately move rocks and wipe the blood from his knee while trying to shake the pain off his left hand. As he soon realized, beneath the dry soil layer, the rock pile continued underground, and after fifteen minutes of more cursing and rock throwing, he spotted the camera at the bottom of a shallow basin that had now been revealed. He reached down to grab the camera, but it slipped from his sweaty hand, and when he searched for it again, his hand touched something else, and he felt a sudden shiver propagate down his spine. He rushed to get the camera up and used its flashlight to peek down the hollow.

"Mensch—Hey, come here!" he shouted. "Hey!"

———

Later inspections and excavations of the place where Fleischmann fell exposed an almost rectangular fifty square meter-large area scattered with fossilized skeletons embedded in fine-grained calcareous sediment, all found at a depth of no more than one meter. Although the excavated area was best described as merely an indentation in the ground, the locals quickly upgraded it to a "cave" since it was close to the Jebel Irhoud cave, around sixty miles west of Marrakesh. Jebel Irhoud is well known in the archeological space, most prominently for the finds of fossils belonging to a three hundred thousand-plus-year-old *Homo sapiens*. Domestic and international newspapers followed suit, and the site was soon known as "Fat Man's Cave."

Within a week of the finding of Fat Man's Cave, an archeology team was hard at work in the area. It soon became evident that they were looking at a Lower Paleolithic site packed with animal and human remains dating back between five hundred thousand and a million years ago. It was the eye sockets of one of the human skulls that Fleischmann found his hand caressing six days prior when he was trying to grab his camera. Most remarkably, a near-complete human skeleton with an intact cranium was unearthed a little farther away from where Fleischmann's camera landed. The hominin skeleton was, in due course, dated to be around five hundred fifty thousand years old and with features placing it somewhere in the lineage between *H. erectus* and *H. heidelbergensis*. In keeping with the Fat Man moniker, the hominin species was eventually named and cataloged as *H. crassus*, although, colloquially, it also became known as "Fat Man."

What no one could possibly know at the time was that the discovery of the Fat Man fossil would reveal that our human ancestors over half a million years ago possessed a unique sensing ability unknown to modern-day humans and that this realization would come to change the world for good and bad.

CHAPTER 1

Spring 2023. The OMICS National Laboratory, USA.
Olfaction. The discovery.

It's a beautiful May morning. I'm sitting in the courtyard outside my office in Richland, Washington, coffee in hand, taking the last bite of my second scone (huckleberry cream). Starlings show off their song repertoire in the oak crowns that dominate the canopy. My mind drifts while I follow a busy squirrel's erratic movements. I see him (her?) finally settling for a spot to bury the payload—a good-looking hull-less walnut—right by an indentation in the dark green grass still steaming in the late-morning sunshine after the last irrigation cycle.

"Dude, that's a really bad spot to hide the walnut," I advise him. I point to the sprinkler and explain that once the head pops up, the walnut will get airborne like a projectile. I also take the opportunity to ask him how come he had a walnut in his mouth in the first place when there are no walnut trees for miles around, not to mention that it's early summer and a long time before the walnut season. He just sits there by the walnut and stares at me with curious, big, round eyes. I wonder what goes on in his little head. I also wonder if anyone has ever GPS-tagged an individual squirrel and the cognate walnut and tried to find out if and how often they meet. Maybe a squirrel never finds the walnut he hides. But then again, if all squirrels are equally squatter-brained, there will be plenty of hidden walnuts to go around.

Well, I didn't come out here to engage in rodent observations but to ponder tonight's dinner options. So, I finally let go of the little guy to continue his life—he's randomly rushing up and down a nearby oak tree, playing hide and seek with a friend. I return to my dinner plans—*Italian Eggplant Parmesan* comes to mind. It stays there together with *Roasted Cauliflower Salad with Halloumi and Lemon, Moroccan Jackfruit with Lemon Couscous, Farro Salad with Shaved Parmesan,* and *Pasta Limone.* A few other options fly by but don't stick. I decide to go for the Farro salad, a mix of Mediterranean and Mid-Eastern flavors I've refined over the years. I'll let you in on a couple of tricks: cook the farro in vegetable stock rather than water, and sauté shallots in extra virgin olive oil long enough to be crisp and golden brown upon drying under a sprinkle of salt. The leftover shallot-induced olive oil goes into the dressing with apple cider vinegar, Dijon mustard, and maple syrup. Assemble farro and shallots with lots of fresh arugula, a chopped Anjou pear, a handful of toasted pecans, several shaves of *Parmigiano Reggiano,* and some cut fresh parsley and basil. Drizzle the dressing on top and toss to combine. *Molto bene!*

"Symphony, what the fuck? Your meeting!"

Whoops! Okay, it's time to clarify something. A couple of things, actually. First off, this is as good a time as any to introduce myself. My name is Ludvig Bertil Thovén, or Ludvig B. Thoven, as it is simplified in my email address and on credentials such as my credit cards. However, as long as I can remember, certainly from adolescence and onwards, I've gone by Symphony. If you don't pick up on the subtext here, I won't hold it against you. I'll also give you the benefit of the doubt that you'll eventually figure this one out. I'm a Swedish ex-pat living in the U.S. since the beginning of the 1990s—thirty-plus years now. I'm sixty years old, tall (close to two meters), and slender. I'm totally bald and display thick-framed, provocatively blue glasses. When I was in my twenties and still lived in Sweden, my hair was straw blonde, and when I realized I needed glasses for long-distance vision, I decided to don blue spectacles to make a bold fashion statement. As my hair eventually went south, I still kept to blue glasses. Together with my bald head and tall stature, they give me a presence in crowds. My wife, Julie, whom I love dearly, says I'm vain. What can I say? It's hard to be humble when you're Swedish.

All this about yours truly, squirrels and dinner plans are not critical or even relevant to the story at hand. I should let you know now; I tend to wander off-topic, and that will likely happen again as we move forward. That's just who I am; I like to teach and share what's on my mind. I have a dynamic intellect. I'm also good-looking and have a pleasant personality; I'm an extremely likable guy.

Anyhow, what *is* relevant is that I'm the Director of OMICS (the Operation for Molecular Integration of Computer Sciences), a mega complex housing over eight thousand research staff in various areas of computational biology, together with managers, administrators, and other support personnel. OMICS' mission is to use the most advanced computational tools available to decipher, explore, and utilize molecular information, particularly as it pertains to genomics, proteomics, and metabolomics—all in the interest of U.S. national security. OMICS is located in Richland in south-eastern Washington, close to the Hanford site, in a shrub-steppe desert region of the Pacific Northwest. As it so happens, a desert region with plenty of water provided by the Columbia River and its tributaries, the Snake and Yakima Rivers. Richland is part of the Tri-Cities, which, in addition to Richland, includes Pasco and Kennewick. Hanford and its surroundings owe their desert environment largely to their location in the rain shadow of the majestic Cascade mountains to the west. The Hanford site, as you may know, was established in 1943 as part of the Manhattan Project. In addition to OMICS, the Hanford site is also the home to other world-renowned facilities, such as PNNL (the Pacific

Northwest National Laboratory) with the associated EMSL (Environmental Molecular Sciences Laboratory), and LIGO (the Laser Interferometer Gravitational-Wave Observatory).

When Lieutenant General Leslie Groves selected Hanford as one of the sites for the Manhattan Project in 1942, the proximity to the Columbia River as an abundant water source for cooling the nuclear reactors was a decisive factor. Similarly, but for a different reason, when OMICS was planned in 2012 by the Obama administration, Richland was attractive as a construction site because the Columbia River provided cooling water for OMICS' supercomputer, Sirocco. Sirocco is currently the most powerful supercomputer in the world, allowing for challenging and complicated simulations with many variables that are the bread and butter for much of the research at OMICS. Although Sirocco employs a state-of-the-art water-saving cooling method, it still requires nearly one million gallons of cooling water per year.

Sirocco and the entire OMICS were made possible by a commitment and targeted effort by the Obama administration and the private sector to establish a unique organizational structure for computational molecular biology with a two-pronged focus: national security and national health (NSNH). The NSNH concept was conceived in a political environment of escalating international terrorism and conflicts and recognizing that disease control is an integral part of bioterrorism defense. In 2021, when OMICS was fully operational for several years, domestic terrorism and insurrection were added to the NSNH model and incorporated into the OMICS mission and vision statements by the Biden administration.

OMICS' main sponsors are DHS (The Department of Homeland Security) and NIH (The National Institutes of Health). There is also sizeable buy-in from pharmaceutical corporations and other industry stakeholders. These entities afford long-term core funding for much of OMICS' diverse research portfolio and operational expenses. Additional funding for individual research projects or programs comes from competitive grants or special scientific focus areas issued by DHS, NIH, DOE (The Department of Energy), and other agencies or industries on a regular basis. OMICS is also funded by paleontological research institutes and The U.S. Department of Justice for forensic genomics of cold cases. More about that later. Due to its exceptional expertise, OMICS can also be exploited for outside researchers, such as universities. This is offered by competitive grants, where successful applicants can utilize OMICS staff and equipment infrastructure free of charge.

I should also point out that it was my Admin, my Administrative Assistant, Hanne, who called. She'd come out to remind me about a meeting. A meeting I was well aware of, but that had been pushed to some hidden alcove in my brain by squirrels and dinner plans. Hanne is one of those rare jewels that combines a no-nonsense attitude with a charming and disarming demeanor. She is a short and petite Afro-American woman in her mid-fifties. What she lacks in stature, she makes up for in boldness. She swears like a sailor, and she often calls me a moron. Others probably do, too, but she's the only one who does it to my face. That's okay. I know I'm a very popular and likable guy among my colleagues and staff. And to be fair, Hanne also calls me pretty boy every so often. So, it's all good.

"Oh, sorry, I'll be right there." I'm clearing my head of pecans and farro, brushing scone crumbles from my pants, and trying to erase a huckleberry stain from my left shirt sleeve with the napkin. It doesn't work. Oh well… I grab my coffee and walk inside.

———

"Okay, Noa, what do you have?" I'm at the meeting now, sitting at a rectangular table together with ten other scientists. Noa Malka, an Israeli postdoc, shares her screen, and we look at her presentation on a big monitor on the wall.

"Okay, the background is familiar to most of us. But I see some new faces here, so to get us all on the same page, let me start with a brief introduction. Give me just a minute." Noa locates files on her laptop and inserts a few more slides into her presentation.

The new faces are luminaries from DHS—two men and one woman— who came from DC specifically to attend this meeting. Noa is aware of that, and what she made look like an impromptu amendment to her presentation was probably well rehearsed.

"One year or so ago," Noa continues, "we received a cranium from Max Planck Institute for Evolutionary Anthropology in Leipzig, Germany. The cranium belongs to a five-hundred-fifty-thousand-year-old fossil of a male hominin found in Fat Man's Cave in Morocco some fifty years ago. Informally, we refer to the hominin as Fat Man. Scientifically, he is designated as *Homo crassus*—crassus being Latin for fat—and represents a new branch in the human evolutionary tree."

Noa shows a diagram of hominin evolution that depicts *H. crassus* close to *H. heidelbergensis*. She then flips to another slide with a picture of the Fat Man fossil, a closeup of the Fat Man cranium, and a reconstruction of the head.

"One reason the Max Plank team was excited about Fat Man was the relatively large amount of soft tissue in the nasal cavity." She zooms in on the cranium. "And, obviously, the possibility to extract DNA, or even proteins, from a hominin fossil this old must have been exhilarating. The only lab that conceivably could pull this off is OMICS, so that's how the Fat Man cranium ended up with us."

Noa advances her presentation, displaying spectra and tables from MS (that's mass spectrometry) runs. "We started this project—the Crassus Project—last spring. Within a month, we extracted what now seems to account for nine fully intact proteins from the lower nasal cavity of Fat Man. This is in addition to a lot of fragmented proteins. The amino acid sequence obtained from MS data of one of the proteins suggests that it belongs to the G-protein-coupled receptor superfamily, most likely an olfactory receptor, or OR for short, given the location. It contains seven transmembrane-spanning domains with a total of three hundred forty-one amino acids. And we now have MS data for all nine proteins." She shows a slide with models of the novel Fat Man olfactory receptor proteins together with models of several other sensory receptors for smell, vision, and taste from humans and other animals.

"Now, as you can see, these extracted proteins from the Fat Man cranium certainly look like some kind of olfactory receptors, but they are clearly distinctly different from any olfactory receptor we know of—or, indeed, from any sensory receptor at all." Noa pauses and looks at the DHS contingent. I can tell she's getting excited. "And, if we focus on the Fat Man receptor," she moves the cursor around the slide, "you see that all of the nine receptors are similar, but there are between seven and eleven amino acid substitutions at an extracellular cavity that distinguish the receptors from each other. Based on the structure of known ORs, we assume this is the ligand-binding site, the site where odorants bind. This amino acid sequence and 3D-structure of this cavity deviates significantly from the binding site in other receptors."

She pauses and brings up a slide with a large, fat, red question mark and cartoons of stereotypic scientists in white coats scratching their heads and looking bewildered. People start chuckling because the characters are obviously supposed to be some of us OMICS folks in the room, including me: a tall, bald guy with blue spectacles. I'm sure our Graphics Department had a field day making this slide.

Noa lets the cursor rest on the question mark and waits until the people have their act together. "So, it seems like we're dealing with something unknown. If these proteins truly are olfactory receptors, they probably were receptive to a different set of odorants than we are used to today. Another thing is that we found the ORs in the lower nasal region. But, of course, for all we know, that could be where Fat Man and other Crassus individuals had the bulk of their ORs. I should also point out that, as we'll hear from Mike," Noa indicates Mike Baker, another postdoc, "Fat Man also had 'normal' olfactory receptors."

Noa looks around, a broad smile on her face. "So, the million-dollar question is: why did these hominins five hundred fifty thousand years ago have these extra olfactory receptors, and what were they used for?"

This rhetorical question incited an exciting discussion. One of the ideas that popped up was that Fat Man could have experienced odorants that no longer exist, such as scents from now-extinct plants or animals.

"That's an interesting idea," I say, although I don't think so. Well, the idea is certainly interesting. What I mean is that I think it's an unlikely scenario since the binding site—the site where odorants bind—in Fat Man's ORs is so clearly different from that in other ORs.

"We definitely have an intriguing mystery in our hands that we will try to solve," I summarize to end the discussion. "If we are ever fortunate enough to receive samples from well-preserved *Homo heidelbergensis*, or other ancient hominins, we may be able to find out when these enigmatic receptors evolved and when they were lost, and maybe get an understanding for their purpose."

I look at Noa. "Another aspect of Fat Man's ORs is the signaling transduction pathway. What do we know or suspect here?"

"Well, that's interesting, as well." The G-protein binding site is similar to binding sites for other olfactory-specific G-proteins, but there are some noticeable differences. We don't know what G-proteins or adenylate cyclases were involved."

Now, olfaction biochemistry may not be your day-to-day discussion topic, and the scientific jargon here may fluster you. Fear not. We will touch on these aspects repeatedly, and they'll become more familiar. But, being the thoughtful person that I am, I'll summarize olfaction in plainer language before we move on

When you smell a rose while strolling in your illustrious backyard garden or a glass of wine in your library as you relax for the evening—say a Ridge Lytton Springs Zinfandel from Dry Creek Valley in California—volatile organic compounds (VOCs) from the rose or the wine travel up your nose and bind to your olfactory receptors (ORs). These receptors are proteins on the cell membrane (plasma membrane) in cells located in the nasal cavity. The conclusion that hominins (humans) that lived around five hundred fifty thousand years ago had an extra set of ORs that differ from the ones we know of is fascinating. It suggests that these hominins could sense VOCs or other compounds that we cannot do. The binding of the VOCs to the ORs is the first step in the signal transduction pathway that makes you sense the floral fragrance from the rose or the blackberry, plum, and cherry scents from the wine. G-proteins and adenylate cyclase are other components in the signaling pathway. Like other proteins, olfactory receptors comprise a sequence of amino acids with an N-terminal and a C-terminal end.

"Thanks, Noa." I turn to Mike Baker. "Okay, Mike, what do we have on the genomics front?"

"Well, we have complete or partial sequences for close to three hundred genes from surface fragments isolated from the temple region of the cranium. We looked for OR genes and found thirteen of them. Eleven are normal OR genes, similar to OR genes in modern humans. Two others clearly represent the novel ORs Noa just talked about. In fact, one of them matches exactly to one of Noa's ORs, but the second one deviates in several amino acids." Mike points to sequences in his presentation.

"What does that tell you?"

"Well, it tells us two things. First, Fat Man had both normal—unsurprisingly—and the extra type of ORs. Second, the family of Crassus extra ORs, or Crex-ORs, as we call them, is larger than the nine we've found; we have protein sequences for nine novel ORs and genomic sequences for one more, so the Crex-OR family contains a minimum of ten members. Also," Mike brings up another slide. "We have quite a bit of five prime sequence for the gene encoding 'Noa's OR,' enough to suggest that the protein carried an N-terminal signal peptide and was synthesized co-translationally. It also seems as if the promoter and regulatory elements weakly resemble those of many known ORs, but that's preliminary. —Oh, I almost forgot!" Mike brings up another slide, "As opposed to normal ORs, including Fat Man's normal ORs, the Crex-ORs seem to have introns; there is one intron in each of the Crex-OR genes. Each between fourteen and sixteen kb."

Again, let me rephrase in plain English: Like other proteins, OR receptors are encoded by genes embedded in DNA molecules. We measure the length of DNA or a gene in base pairs. One kb is short for kilo base pairs, that is, one thousand base pairs. A gene, just like a protein, has two ends: an upstream or five prime (5') end—which harbors most of the controlling elements in gene expression—and a downstream or three prime (3′) end. Introns are segments in a DNA molecule that generally do not encode proteins and often interrupt genes. When Mike said that the protein (the Crex-OR) is synthesized co-translationally, he meant that it's being inserted into the cell membrane (the plasma membrane) at the same time as it's being synthesized. —See how nicely I explain things so you don't get irked!

The meeting lasts for another forty-ish minutes with questions and more comments from Noa, Mike, and me. I ask Mike to push the envelope on the sequencing effort, particularly on "Noa's OR," and try to get more 5′, or upstream, sequences. DHS has had a heightened interest in ORs ever since the success of the Olfactor Receptor Chip, or ORChip, technology. I'll tell you about this ORChip story in a while. At any rate, DHS has become very engaged in the Crassus Project and the Crex-ORs. Indeed, at the meeting, we learned from the three top-level DHS folks in attendance that DHS recently imposed a continued moratorium on the Crassus Project for as long as needed. This means we will not be able to publish any results from the research. Later that day, I asked Hanne to schedule a meeting with Rosy Boyd, our administrative point of contact at DHS, to get some clarification. I don't like Rosy Boyd. I might as well tell you that right away.

CHAPTER 2

*Fall 2023. The annoying Rosy Boyd. My friend and
chess opponent, Bryce Vogel.*

The summer falls into fall—pardon the pun—and I'm busy with other projects, travel, and vacation. So, it's not until early November when I take two of the senior Crassus Team members, Ron Chakraborty and Laxmi Singh, with me and go up to Washington, DC, for the meeting with Rosy Boyd. Noa and Mike were supposed to come as well. However, Mike came down with a cold, and Noa had a sudden change of plans due to her fiancé's work schedule. Rosie Boyd had promised us one hour of her time, which she wanted me to understand was a great favor on her part when I called her to confirm.

"We're very grateful for your taking the time, you pathetic old cow," I told her on the phone. No, I didn't. But it was close. Rosie Boyd is younger than I am by a couple of years, but she's still an old cow. I've never liked her. She used to be an assistant professor at Colorado State University, Fort Collins, but she didn't manage to get tenure. Instead, she climbed the ladders at DOE and then DHS. When OMICS was formed, Rosy became the administrative head of OMICS at the federal level. Dealing with her has always been a struggle. She has the urge to show that she's in charge. I've never liked her—I said that, right? I suspect she has had a chip on her shoulder ever since the involuntary abortion of her academic career.

When we arrive at Reagan National Airport, it's afternoon. It's snowing and freezing cold. When I reconnect my phone to the internet, I see a message letting us know that Rosy will not be able to make it after all due to other commitments. Someone will call us soon to provide more information. I'm neither disappointed nor surprised. She often sends underlings to do her business. Although, as I'm about to find out, that was not the case this time. She had asked Bryce Vogel to meet with us, and he called me within five minutes. Where Rosy is the Administrative Head of OMICS, Bryce is the Scientific Head. However, Bryce's primary position with the DHS is Head of Domestic Terrorism. Bryce and I go way back and know each other well. We're about the same age and have had similar careers. When I was a professor and the Head of the Department of Computational Biology at the University of California, Berkeley, Bryce was a Senior Staff Scientist at the Lawrence Berkeley National Laboratory, and we overlapped by several years. I was recruited to lead the OMICS at about the same time Bryce accepted the position at DHS. He took the pay cut to be closer to his wife's elderly and frail parents in Virginia.

Bryce and I also share many of the same interests. We're both Christians, and, as scientists, we're fascinated with integrating faith and science. Also, we're foodies; we like to eat, explore, and cook food. And we are avid chess players. We often play whenever we meet, but mostly, we play via a chess app, d4c4, that one of Bryce's sons invented. If you're into chess, you might get the meaning behind the d4c4 name. If not, let it be a challenge to ruminate on. It's good for your brain. Our chess games can go on for weeks. We're very well-matched. Of course, I play with my left hand, so that gives him a handicap. —Yes, I know, right? I'm not only popular and likable; I'm also funny. I'm right-handed, by the way.

Since it's late afternoon, closing in on dinner time, Bryce suggests we meet at Fiola Mare in Georgetown instead of his office. Bryce and I have eaten there a few times, as have Julie, my wife, and I. I enjoy their seafood. I'm happy we're meeting with Bryce and not Rosy. For one thing, I very much like Bryce, and I very much dislike Rosy. For another, if we had met with Rosy, for sure, we wouldn't be sitting at a restaurant, let alone at a fancy one; we would be in her office, she at the head of the table and we as peons on the side. I really dislike that old cow, you ought to know that by now.

Bryce is there when we arrive. The place is packed, but Bryce had secured a table in a secluded area close to the open fire. Bryce stands up when we arrive. We all shake hands. When you see Bryce, you think jovial and squashy. He is jovial, and he looks squashy; medium-build with a round, open, smiling face with warm brown eyes and a little extra fat all around. He is a person you'd want to embrace and, halfway, expect to find your arms springing back in motion when you let go. He looks that soft and squashy. Everyone seems to like Bryce, and he gets along with even the most obnoxious and difficult people. I think this could be another reason why Rosy asked Bryce to take the meeting; we're about to hear some bad news, and she wants Bryce to be at the dispensing end instead of herself.

Yesterday, I added a chess move for Bryce in the d4c4 app, not knowing that we would meet today: *Nc6*. I've just threatened his queen. As we sit down, he smiles—a jovial smile but with just the slightest hint of pomposity.

"I'll add my move tonight or tomorrow morning. You're not going to be happy." I try to bring up the board in my head to see what he's referring to, but, of course, I can't.

We make small talk, look at the menus, and order food and wine. We get some eggplant and *burrata antipasti* and a couple of bottles of their Pinot Noir to share. Laxmi, who doesn't drink alcohol, ordered a spritz. Ron and Laxmi have been a couple for quite some time now and live together. I know that Ron, out of support, also doesn't drink alcohol at home and that he savors it when he gets a chance. He looks a little sheepish at Laxmi when he joins the toast. She just smiles. They're adorable together! Visually, they make an interesting comparison; they're both from India, and Ron is short and sturdy with a round face and a shock of curly black hair, while Laxmi is taller and slender with straight black hair.

Julie and I rarely cook or eat meat at home; it's either vegan, vegetarian or seafood. That doesn't mean I don't eat meat. Every now and then, I enjoy a quality piece of beef as much as the next guy. Tonight is such a time. I'm not sure why, but it could be Bryce's looming chess move that made me want red meat. Maybe my brain tries to tell me I need extra iron and B12 to plan my next step. So, I order the wagyu from a local ranch specializing in pasture-raised cattle. I have wilted spinach on the side. Bryce looks at me and raises his eyebrows. He has chosen Fiola Mare because he knows what I usually like to eat. Bryce gets the lobster — an excellent choice. That's what Julie and I had last time we were here. If you come to Fiola Mare for the first time, I highly recommend you try their lobster. Ron and Laxmi decide to share a mixed seafood grill selection.

While we're eating, I let Ron and Laxmi briefly present the Crassus Project. They had prepared a PowerPoint slide deck, which they would have used had the meeting been as planned in Rosy's conference room. I had previously looked at their presentation and made a few edits to sharpen the message. They had their laptops and were considering hauling one of them up, but I suggested that, in this more intimate setting, they merely describe the project in a low-key manner. Bryce is familiar with the general outline and results of the work, but he doesn't have all the details.

"Bryce, what the hell is going on," I request, taking over the baton from Laxmi after her concluding remarks. "Where does this continued moratorium come from? We're about to write this up for a publication, several publications, actually. DHS has already had close to two years to decide on this. Besides, this is a collaboration with Max Planck in Leipzig. We can't just dodge them."

Bryce takes a sip of wine and shakes his head. "I'll bring it up with Vanessa to see what she thinks. I've got a pretty good idea, though." He's referring to Vanessa Ashby, the DHS Secretary. He continues, "If there's even the slimmer of a chance that these Crex-ORs might recognize some hitherto unknown volatiles, DHS will want to add those to the existing repertoire. The consensus at DHS is that the Crassus Project stays classified until further notice."

As Head of Domestic Terrorism, Bryce is part of the upper strata of DHS, so I assume he shares that sentiment. Something he soon confirms.

"And I agree," Bryce says, taking another sip of the Pinot.

I start to say something, but Bryce produces one of his jovial smiles and interrupts. "Symphony, in a way, this is your own doing. If the ORChip technology hadn't been so successful, this continued moratorium would not have been an issue."

———

Okay, I owe you an explanation of the ORChip business. So, let's do this now. This is an idea I'd nurtured for some time. After I started as the OMICS Director in 2014, I used my momentum as a newly hired Director and addressed DHS and NIH with a white paper describing the general outline, salient features, and the potential applications of the ORChip for the NSNH (that's National Security and National Health) mission. DHS and NIH bought into the idea, and I assembled a group to write a high-risk/high-reward grant proposal for thirty-five million dollars over five years that was quickly awarded. This was a project that could only be carried out at OMICS with our physical and intellectual expertise in genomics and proteomics, in this case, specifically protein expression and proteogenomics. It was a great challenge: transformational research with many obstacles and a need for cutting-edge innovations. We needed to make some excellent hires along the road—this is how Noa, Mike, Ron, and Laxmi got onboard—and by the end of 2019, we had essentially accomplished what we set out to do.

So, what exactly did we do? Well, as you learned before, ORs (olfactory receptors, remember) are members of the G-protein-coupled receptor family, more specifically Class A rhodopsin-like G-protein-coupled receptors, which are the initial players in the signal transduction cascade, leading to the generation of nerve impulses transmitted to the brain and resulting in the detection of odorant molecules. The primary sequences of thousands of ORs are known from the genomes of more than a dozen organisms. As you may or may not know, dogs are tens of thousands of times more sensitive to the perception of different odorants or other volatile organic compounds (VOCs) compared to humans. Dogs have around nine hundred genes encoding ORs, and elephants have nearly two thousand. Humans have less than four hundred OR genes. Animals such as dogs and elephants also have several million more ORs than humans. However, recent findings suggest that the human olfactory system is more advanced than previously assumed.

So, the idea I had was that people who are nervous or apprehensive—something you might expect from, say, a terrorist trying to get through security at an airport—or who have diabetes, cancer, or many other diseases emit specific combinations of VOCs, and that these VOC fingerprints can be detected by OR-containing chips, just like dogs can be trained to sense an oncoming diabetic shock. The first step would be to express an extensive portfolio of dog and elephant ORs and then mount them topologically on a chip such that the odorant-binding sides are all on one side, the transducing sides on the opposite side, and where each OR is linked to an electronic sensor system. When a VOC binds to the cognate receptor(s), a signal is transmitted and recorded. Different combinations of VOCs will elicit unique readouts. By exposing ORChips to people expected to be nervous or apprehensive—which was done covertly—or known to have diabetes or cancer, the ORs responsible for binding the corresponding VOCs were identified. Second- and third-generation ORChips were then made with millions of copies of specific ORs, for example, to detect people who emit VOCs in response to being nervous. The chip technology was developed in-house as part of the DHS grant.

That was the basic idea, and we were successful! ORChips and associated analyzers have now been secretively installed at strategic places at major airports. Once DHS lets go of the moratorium and when patent procedures are taken care of, the ORChip technology will also be rolled out at medical clinics. Meanwhile, DHS continues "training" the chips for a suite of different NSNH applications.

———

I apologize for this lengthy lecture, but I wanted you to know about the background here. First, to show you how smart I am—truly!—but also to understand what Bryce Vogel alluded to at our DC meeting. DHS obviously sees the Crex-ORs as a potentially valuable complement to the existing receptors in the ORChips.

The fact that these receptors differ from any other ORs we know of makes them even more interesting. We left that meeting well-nourished and a little frustrated. I also had an off taste in my mouth after the beef that I tried to rinse out with the last glass of Pinot but to little avail.

We took an Uber to our hotel, and I'd been in my room less than an hour when I got Bryce's chess move on the app. I had to wait until I had the chess board in front of me to digest the situation fully. I had a travel chessboard in my luggage but was too tired to unpack it.

———

When I get back home the following day, it's early afternoon. The weather is much better than in DC, a typical East-of-the-Cascades November, relatively mild, with no snow. Juniper, our dog, greets me at the front gate. She's been in the garden where Julie is cleaning up the raspberry patch. She jumps all over me and starts licking my face—I'm talking about the dog, by the way, not my wife. Jupiter is a shelter rescue. We had her DNA sequenced, so we know she is mostly Britany and, to lesser degrees, German Shepard, Husky, Lab, and Collie. She is a genuinely gentle soul but with a somewhat twisted personality.

"It's about fucking time you got back," she tells me. Well, she can't talk, of course, but I have an uncanny ability to know what she's thinking. That also goes for most other dogs.

"I tried to make it as short as possible," I respond.

"Sure, you did!" She wanders off.

I know she loves me, but she does have an attitude.

Julie is a veterinarian. She is from the U.S. We met when I did a postdoc at Michigan State. She fell in love with me, of course. We got married, and after my postdoc, we moved to Sweden, where we stayed for twenty-plus years. She is a beautiful person, Julie, inside and out. Medium-built with thick auburn hair and captivating, rather cold-looking green eyes that contrast with her warm personality.

Julie has to take care of emergency surgery on a dog at six p.m. tonight, so we're skipping our dinner routine. Typically, we start with "wine time," where we have a glass or two of wine (red for me and white for Julie) while taking stock of what's happening around us and in the world. We also compare notes on what we heard from our kids and Julie's parents. Our three grown children have all been on their own for several years. Before the glasses are empty, we bring them to the dinner table, where we enjoy the rest of the wine with our meal, which is all prepared at that point. Julie and I both like to cook, but I'm the designated chef in the household. Partly because I really enjoy cooking and baking and exploring food and also because I have more time on my hands than Julie. I'll be fully transparent here and, on a side note, let you in on the fact that considering my hefty salary and excellent benefits package as the OMICS Director, I probably spend less than sixty percent of my working hours doing actual "work." For the rest of my time, I spend a considerable amount thinking about food and planning meals. It's not uncommon that I go shopping for ingredients or swing by the house in the middle of the day to prepare dinner. I'm telling you this about my work ethic without any qualms since I know I'm very good at what I'm doing for OMICS, and others know that, too. As I mentioned, I'm a very popular and likable guy.

So, anyway, our regular dinner routine is off the table tonight—pun intended. Julie cannot drink because she must perform surgery, and we're kind of rushed since she needs to leave soon. We make it simple. We have pasta with pesto. For a side dish, I massage some Swiss chard and kale that Julie just brought in from the garden. To do this, I add some extra virgin olive oil (first cold press), fresh lemon juice, and a little sea salt to a bowl. Then, I drop in the Swiss chard and kale and use my hands to squeeze the leaves hard for a few minutes. I pretend I have my hands around Rosy Boyd's neck when I do it. No, I don't. Well… kind of. We have a nice dinner, chitchatting about this and that. I vent a little about DHS' stance on the Crassus Project. While Julie has a kombucha, I pour a glass of an excellent Syrah. —Okay, I know, right? Maybe I should have opted out of drinking wine since Julie can't have any. But I didn't, so judge me! Julie doesn't.

With Julie gone, I put away the dishes and walk into my home office to study the chessboard. I bring up Bryce's move from the app. Yep, the weasel outmaneuvered me. He took a bishop, which also put me in check. I'd been so focused on my offense that I didn't pay enough attention to my own part of the board.

After Julie got back and while lying in bed waiting to fall asleep, I brought up the chessboard in my head, projected it on the ceiling, and started laying out a strategy by moving pieces around. —Kidding! You really thought I could do that? No way, Jose! I've seen The Queen's Gambit, though. No, what I was really thinking about was something else, someone else, rather. Someone who might be able to shed some light on the Crex-ORs.

CHAPTER 3

Spring 2024. The very, very annoying Rosy Boyd. The missing Derek Tyne-Callaghan.

I'm in my office after a morning with back-to-back meetings. I'm pondering again whether I should set up a chessboard at work and replicate the score on the one in the app. And, again, I decide not to. The risk is that I would get comments and suggestions from all sorts of people visiting my workspace. Bryce and I have a gentlemen's agreement that we are not asking people for advice. We want to improve by just playing. Since our meeting in DC, Bryce has won two games in a row. In our current game, where I'm white, I have a slight advantage by having captured one of his knights and two pawns against his capture of three pawns.

I'm reviewing the week's agenda that Hanne has given me. As the Director of OMICS, I oversee many programs and operations. In addition to Hanne and other admins, I have strong support from the Chief Operations and Chief Science Officers, who take the brunt of administrative and management issues, so I can focus on big science questions, where my strength lies. I'm unusual as a Lab Director in the sense that I'm almost like an informal Principal Investigator for some of the research projects. None more so than the Crassus Project. Another move I've made is to divorce myself entirely from the NIH aspects of OMICS and assign a Deputy Director to handle that part.

My CSO (my Chief Science Officer), Kirsten Anjou, is the one who needs to deal with people like the old cow Rosy Boyd, and she is very good at it, no-nonsense but polite. Kirsten and her husband were in Italy on their thirtieth wedding anniversary last November when we went to DHS; otherwise, she would have come along to wrestle down Rosy Boyd. Only, we never met with Rosy, as you may remember. So, in that case, it didn't matter.

One OMICS program that stands out from the bulk of our research is what we refer to as "cold cases." Because of OMICS' world-unique ability and expertise in extracting and analyzing DNA, proteins, and other compounds from minuscule amounts of material, we now and then receive fossil samples from paleontological institutes and natural history museums. That's how the *H. Crassus* cranium landed in our lap. Another example of cold cases is forensic genomics of evidence material from decades-old or even older unsolved homicide investigations. Cold cases have rather low priority in terms of staff and machine time, but we do attend to them on a regular basis. They are not integral to the OMICS mission, but separate agreements and funding mechanisms are in place that allow us to devote some time to these cases. However, now, given DHS's strong interest in olfactory receptors and the Crassus case, I wouldn't be surprised if we get a decree urging OMICS to re-prioritize old cases with hominin samples.

It is now late February, and spring is around the corner. The Crassus Team has extracted and sequenced a little more protein from the nasal cavity. They found one more Crex-OR. The rest is mostly collagen, which holds less interest. The new Crex-OR does not match up with either of the two Crex-OR genes we found previously. So, we now know that the Crex-OR family is at least eleven members strong. I have called for another meeting next week with the Crassus Team, some additional OMICS folks, and two invitees from DHS, Scott Krasinski, and Brad… something— I forgot his last name. Scott and Brad are Program Directors at DHS. I haven't made up my mind whether or not I dislike Scott

Krasinski and Brad Something. I've heard they have a posture as if they pull the threads for anything and everything of importance at OMICS. It's become a little of an issue for some of the staff. If that continues, I need to sit down and talk to them. They are both new at interacting with OMICS, so I'll give them some time.

I'm composing a Happy Birthday text to my younger brother, Lennart. Or, Lelle, as some of us call him, a diminutive he detests. So, I use it as often as I can. *Hej Lelle*, I start when Hanne calls. "Rosy the-fucking-Boyd is in town," she declares without preamble. "She's here for the Women with Power event in PNNL's Discovery Hall. She indicated that she was going to look you up before the symposium. I told her, you're busy all week, but… well, you know her. So, I thought I should give you the heads-up in case you'd want to go in hiding."

"Thanks, Hanne!" I'm certainly not in the mood to try and reason with that old cow. But no sooner am I getting ready to escape than I hear hoof stomps and Rosy Boyd the Annoying is poking her muzzle through the door. "Good, I see you're not working," she observes and sails into the room with a strong scent of jasmine and orange. "We need to talk about the progress reports."

I say nothing but nod at the visitor chairs. She shakes her head and remains standing. "I don't have much time."

"The progress reports are getting too sloppy," she continues. "There are standards to follow, but they are ignored. The reports are the most important product coming out of OMICS, and they need to follow proper formatting. There are standards—"

"Let me correct you right here," I interrupt. "The primary product from OMICS is the research, not the reports. The progress reports are something we are required to submit, and we oblige. We have streamlined the process to save time. There are boxes to check and spaces for short explanatory texts. DSH and NIH are free to request additional information as needed. This format works just fine."

She ignores me. "As I said, there are standards. The font should be Times New Roman, the size should be twelve points, the text should be double-spaced, and specific topics must be addressed. Therefore, I have set up a Review Board to evaluate the reports. The Board will work with your staff to ensure the submitted reports follow proper standards."

"This will just add an unnecessary layer of bureaucracy and rob our staff of valuable research time. I haven't heard any complaints about the progress reports from the Departments before."

"Well, you have now. I repeat, there are standards, and they are there not as garnish but to be respected and followed."

"You can take the standards and shove them up your bony ass," I suggest. But by then, she had left the office, leaving the Coco Chanel fragrance lingering in the air. I shake off my frustration and make a mental note to ask Bryce if he can help us get Rosy Boyd out of our orbit.

———

"I know we're all tired of meetings," I say by way of starting off early Tuesday morning the following week. "We've certainly had our fair shares since returning after Christmas. But I want to bring everyone up to speed with Crassus, and then I want to talk about something that's been on my mind since last November."

I walk back and forth in the room while talking, hitting my head on an overhead light on the first lap, which brings down a chuckle. I'm used to hitting my head on a lot of things. Partly because I'm tall and partly—according to Julie—because I have no self-awareness of my body.

"We now have eleven unique Crex-ORs. They are vaguely similar to human and other ORs, with notable differences regarding the ligand-binding domain and some other areas." I poke at the monitor with my hand. "There are a few crystal structures of ORs available. Together with our new protein algorithms, we have generated computational models of ORs, including the Crex-ORs. That's the kind of model Noa has been showing at previous meetings and one of those we see here. As Noa has also pointed out, according to this model, a major difference between the Crex-ORs and so-called normal ORs is the ligand-binding site. And that's also where the differences between the Crex-ORs are found. So, they have different binding specificities."

"Now, this is all fine and dandy," I continue. "But we still don't know *what* these Crex-ORs bind or what they *do*. DHS has asked us to up our efforts." (Here, I glance at Scott Krasinski and Brad Something, who nod and look important.) "So we organized the Crassus Workshop just before Christmas. Most of you were there." I'm referring to a workshop with invited scientists from the U.S. and overseas with expertise in various areas of G-coupled receptor signaling. The pretext here was to discuss G-coupled receptors in general and in the context of how they differ between humans and animals. We did not mention anything about ORChips or the Crassus Project.

"Well, that was rather worthless, if you ask me." It's Steve Bailey, and from the nods and soft chorus of supportive mumbling he picked up around the table, he seems to sum up what most of us think.

Ron chimes in, "It was a very nice workshop, though, with plenty of nice talks. And good food and lots of scones. We laugh. "But I agree," he added. "We didn't learn anything new."

"Right!" I sit down. "So, any suggestions on how we should proceed?"

"How about we make chips with the Crex-ORs and challenge them with various compounds?" It's Noa, and she suggests something I've already decided we should do. But I wanted someone else to come up with the idea and feel proud. I'm nothing if not a magnanimous mentor!

"That's a great idea, Noa," I say. "Let's make some Crex-ORChips, throw the kitchen sink on them, and see what sticks." That sounds very flippant, I know, and you may think that making these chips is a day's worth of work. In fact, designing and manufacturing ORChips is a very complicated and tedious procedure, and it'll be a few months until we have them ready to test. That's why I will set the process in motion right after the meeting.

"Any other ideas?" I look around and wait for a while.

"No, okay, that brings me to the second bullet point for this meeting." I stand up again and start pacing the room, avoiding the light fixture. "Does the name Derek Tyne-Callaghan mean anything to you?" No, that doesn't seem to ring a bell with any of them. This does not surprise me; most of the folks in the room are younger than I am by ten years or more. Also, Derek's scientific career was short and made little impact.

"I've met Derek once. This was in the early eighties, and I was a graduate student still in Sweden. In that life, I studied photosynthesis, and I went to a photosynthesis conference in Halkidiki in Greece. Other symposia were going on at the same time, so when people gathered for lunch and tried to find a seat, you often ended up in a very mixed crowd."

I continue to describe my meeting with Derek Tyne-Callaghan. One lunch—or, I think, it was the closing ceremony—I came to listen to a guy who obviously had had too much to drink and was in the midst of describing his research topic to some people who looked as if they'd rather be somewhere else. He was kind of stocky with short brown hair and sporting a goatee. I predicted his age to be forty-plus. His crooked nametag read DEREK TYNE-CALLAGHAN, UNIVERSITY OF MICHIGAN, ANN ARBOR, U.S.A. I thought his ranting—as well as his accent that gave him away as British—was interesting. He must have noticed that because he turned his attention to me. Also, I was junior compared to the others, so I was an easy target. With Derek's focus on me, the others took the cue and moved on to greener pastures. But others gradually joined instead, and we were a group of around five people who chatted with Derek. —Well, I mainly listened.

I learned that Derek had just started as an Assistant Professor at University of Michigan. His research angle was speech development in hominins and how that correlated with the reduction of olfaction. This was not at all in my wheelhouse at the time, but I found it quite fascinating. He went on to explain that he was working on a manuscript, a kind of perspective, where he postulated that given enough time, we would eventually find fossil evidence for hominins equipped with a different set of perception receptors—this was the term he used, "perception receptors." The manuscript would present an evolutionary timeline for when you would expect to find these kinds of receptors and how the development of speech fits in. He mentioned something about convincing arguments that would support his claims. He was very excited about this manuscript, and you got the feeling he assumed it would stir up the scientific community and result in a flurry of discourse with him at the forefront. This would be his claim to fame. We asked, of course, what these receptors were supposed to be perceiving. Derek said he was not going to disclose that. We had to wait until his paper was out. I asked—and I think this is my only question— where and when it would be published. He said he was currently negotiating with an editor. There were some detailed questions regarding the nature of these hypothetical receptors and his convincing arguments. But Derek suddenly got subdued, and it felt as if he thought he had let on more than he intended. He gave us his card. We were welcome to contact him for details later on.

"So, this is the one time I met with Derek. I kept looking for that paper of his for a while, but I never contacted him. Unfortunately, I later learned that he had a sordid exit from academia." I sat down. "Apparently, he was involved in sex plays with two fourteen-year-old girls. It wasn't rape or anything violent but some kind of lewd behavior. He was caught with his pants down, literally. I'm not entirely sure what happened next. He seems to have been extradited from the U.S. and sent back to the U.K. I don't think he did any jail time here. Whether he did in the U.K. is not clear to me. Someone told me that after a few years, he actually got a teaching position at his Alma Mater, the University of Reading."

I continue, "This is where the traces of Derek Tyne-Callaghan stop. I hadn't thought about him until one night a couple of months ago when I lay in bed trying to go to sleep. It suddenly dawned on me that there we have a guy who predicted a novel kind of perception receptor, to use Derek's terminology, in early hominins, and here *we* have what seems to be a novel kind of olfactory receptor extracted from the Fat Man fossil. I would very much like to talk to Derek and find out what his hypothesis and reasoning were. However, we can't find him. I've asked Hanne to do a search. She also contacted Reading. Derek had, indeed, a short stint as a Lecturer there, but that was many years ago. They don't know where he went after that. Hanne and her team also looked in the White Pages and other online databases, in obituaries in local newspapers, as well as in what is called the General Register Office for death certificates in England and Wales. No Derek Tyne-Callaghan there or in any Google searches."

I get up, pacing again. "So, I've decided to go to Reading and try to find him. I've cleared this with DHS, so we have federal support." I look again at the DHS folks. Brad Something nods pretentiously, almost sanctimoniously. From the look of him, you might think that he just bestowed me a Papal blessing. If I'd been Catholic, that is. Which I'm not. I'm Lutheran. Anyhow… pompous brat! "Of course, we don't know if he still lives in the U.K., assuming he's alive. He might have moved back to the U.S., for all we know. A general Google search yields close to four thousand Derek Callaghan and close to two thousand Derek Tyne hits but no Derek Tyne-Callaghan, neither in the U.S. nor anywhere else. We've looked at all the Derek Callaghans and Derek Tynes, but none fits our guy."

The meeting continues with discussions and guesswork about what Derek Tyne-Callaghan might have been up to. Did he refer to G-coupled receptors? Where on the body would they be found? When, during hominin evolution, would they be expected to be found? And, maybe most importantly, if he was such a sleaze bag, is he worth paying attention to? Don't know, don't know, don't know, and yes, are my answers to these questions.

"Just because he was morally corrupt doesn't mean he was a bad scientist. I'll give it a week. If I can't find him by then, I'll give up."

"You're just hungry for old-fashioned English scones, is what I think." That's Joe Buchanan, and he receives a round of giggles. My appetite for scones is a well-known fact at OMICS. Scott Krasinski and Brad Something hasn't been here long enough to understand, and they look confused. Good!

Despite any ulterior motives I might have for my trip to England—which I don't deny, by the way—I honestly think it has merits. Derek seemed to have a theory for why early hominins had a class of perception receptors that later got lost during evolution. If I can find him and extract that information, it might explain the function of the Crex-ORs. And it's the only lead we have so far.

"Do you know if Derek's manuscript was commissioned or if he was writing it on a whim, hoping it would be accepted somewhere?" It's Brad Something, and that's actually an excellent question.

"No, I don't know. He just said he was talking to editors."

"So, for all we know, his idea might just have been utter bullshit that wouldn't be accepted anywhere." It's Steve Bayley again, no mincer of words, that Steve.

"Yep, it could be. But he might also have been on to something. As I said, I'll spend a week on this. If there's nothing, at least we've tried."

I adjourn the meeting. I look at my phone and check the time and my agenda. I decide to go to Whole Foods and get some *Mozzarella di Bufala Campana.* I assure you, it really makes a difference to use water buffalo mozzarella, believe me. It's so much creamier and tastier than mozzarella from cow milk. I'm planning on making an Italian eggplant lasagna. I pick up two large eggplants as well. I drive home—everything in the Tri-Cities is within a twenty-minute drive. I cut the eggplants lengthwise into quarter-inches slices, brush both sides with extra virgin olive oil, arrange them on two baking sheets, and sprinkle the top side with salt and black pepper. Then I roast them in the oven. To assemble the lasagna, I layer tomato sauce on the bottom of a baking dish, cover with the eggplant slices, and sprinkle on mozzarella, then repeat this twice more, and finally top with

Parmigiano Reggiano. I cover the lasagna and put it in the fridge. While we have wine time tonight, I'll bake it in the oven until the top is golden. I check the wine storage. We don't have a wine cellar, as opposed to some of our colleagues; we just keep a few bottles at a time. We're almost out, so I'll pick up a bottle of Albariño for Julie and Syrah for me on the way home from work later today.

I drive back to work to attend two more meetings. OMICS is about to request funding for a second and upgraded 21 Tesla for our mass spectrometer park. I've been arguing that we need this to maintain our position as the leader in protein and metabolite analyses. This will require me to go to DC a couple of times in the coming months to socialize the idea at the federal level, which means that my trip to the U.K. won't be until mid-summer.

Meanwhile, the manufacturing of the new chips with the Crex-ORs is moving forward. We might have some results before my U.K. visit.

CHAPTER 4

Summer 2024. Dinner at Anthony's.

What I didn't announce to my colleagues regarding my plans to find Derek Tyne-Callaghan is that I would use the trip to the U.K. to visit our youngest daughter, Jessica, who lives in London. Jessica owns and runs a Swedish bakery, Kringlan, with her husband, Lars, close to Finsbury Park. The last time Julie and I were there was over a year ago, so I'm very much looking forward to seeing them in person again. Unfortunately, Julie can't join me since the Animal Clinic is very busy due to the backlog after the recent K9 Type A flu pandemic, and she is the Chief Veterinarian.

I will be leaving for London on July fourteenth, which is Sunday next week. I've been FaceTiming Jessica and Lars to discuss logistics. Lars has offered to be my driver for the whole week. He knows I don't like to drive in the U.K. I very much appreciate it, and I tell him so. However, I decline the offer. I don't know how much time I might spend just hanging around waiting for something to happen, and that wouldn't be fair to him. Also, with two young girls, Jessica being pregnant again, and a bustling bakery on top of that, I think Lars is needed on the home front.

So, the new ORChips, or Crex-ORChips, are coming off the belt. I'm in my office talking to Noa. She is going on vacation soon with her fiancé, so I wanted to talk to her before she leaves, although the testing of the chips has not yet started in earnest. By the way, she makes for a striking appearance, Noa. She is short and fit. She has dark, almost black, curly hair against a fair complexion, green eyes, and an aquiline nose. I know her genetic heritage is all over the place, but a large proportion is Ashkenazi and Italian.

"Well," Noa says. "So far, we've only tested a few VOCs, and there is no reactivity."

If you've forgotten what VOCs are, it stands for volatile organic compounds. These are compounds emitted as gases at room temperature. Odorants, for example, that bind to olfactory receptors, or ORs, for short, are VOCs. There! Now, you don't have to go back to figure out what Noa is talking about. Call me considerate!

Noa continues, and she almost loses her laptop as it flies off her bouncing knee. Whenever she's sitting down—and especially if she's nervous or excited—she has the annoying but somewhat endearing habit of bouncing her right leg up and down.

"We've spiked the chips with some of our previous ORs, and they test positive, so we know the chips are fine. "Funny thing," she says. "There are what seems to be random signals every now and then. But they don't seem to correlate with any VOCs or anything else in particular."

"Okay," I say. "So, you'll go on testing our larger VOC panel, including non-biological compounds. Please make sure everyone knows what to do before you leave." Although Noa is a postdoctoral fellow (postdoc), fresh off her Ph.D., she has quickly become the lab lead for the whole Crassus Project. She is very competent, enthusiastic, and easy to work with. I want to promote her to a staff position in the near future.

The rest of the week goes on without too much hassle. The 21 Tesla mass spectrometer procurement now has federal approval, so we're working on the practical ramifications of adding this piece of equipment. We need to extend the west section of OMICS with a new wing, and the whole section will be repurposed to house our entire suite of mass spectrometers.

———

The night before my departure, Julie and I decided to dine out. We go to Anthony's, our favorite local seafood place. It's a beautiful evening and not too hot, so we're sitting outside, looking out over the marina. We've just started sipping on our wines—the house Merlot for me and Sauvignon Blanc for Julie—when Julie's phone rings. There's an incoming emergency surgery, a dog hit by a car, and she needs to run. She just had time for one sip of wine, so she should be fine. She tells me to stay and enjoy the outing without her. *"There's no dinner prepared at home anyhow."* So, I do just that.

I'm starting to look over the appetizers when I feel a tap on my shoulder. I turn around, and there is Joe Buchanan and his wife, Nancy, whom I met a couple of times before. Right behind them is Brad Something, with whom I assume is his wife. While I stand up, Joe looks at me and raises his eyebrows. "Howdy, Boss, you're alone!"

"Hi, Joe; you're astute as usual."

"So, did Julie finally leave you?" he continues. "I knew it would happen sooner or later. I just wonder what took her so long."

I take his hand. "Yes, she left me, not for another man but for an emergency dog surgery."

Joe drops the funny face; they also have a dog.

"Oh, sorry to hear that."

I shake hands with Nancy, who's been rolling her eyes at Joe's tirade, and then with Brad and his wife, whom he introduces. Her name is Isabella. Joe asks if it's okay if they join me since I obviously haven't started eating yet. I say sure, and I mean it; I wasn't particularly looking forward to dining alone in a place like this. Joe and Brad talk to a waiter, and they add another table and some more chairs.

It turns out to be a nice dinner. We share some appetizers. Then we all go for the Day's Special, which is Seared Steelhead with Potato *a' la Gratin* and Roasted broccoli. We share a few bottles of Merlot. Yes, you *can* drink red wine with fish, I promise. I truly enjoy the company. The trout is excellent, and so is the rest of the food. During the conversations, I start to feel I've been misjudging Brad Something—actually, I know now that it's Brad Johansen. In this setting, he is very pleasant and humble, even gentle. I notice that the way he nods is just something he does, even to Isabella. We stay off the topic of work for most of the time. Then, Brad surprises me with a question about Rosy Boyd, and for the first time this evening, he seems agitated. He turns to me.

"Symphony, we've been meaning to get a meeting with you to see if you can put some pressure on DHS to get Rosy Boyd off our hands."

He continues, "Ever since DHS started to show an increased interest in the Crex-ORs, interactions between DHS and OMICS have shifted significantly towards allowing science to proceed without too much overreaching administrative bureaucracy, something we wholeheartedly support. However, because of this, that scorpion Boyd feels threatened, and she comes up with all sorts of nonsensical training and reporting requirements that she pesters DHS program managers with for approval. So, if we could have a chat about this sooner rather than later, that would be great."

Wow, Brad called Rosy Boyd a scorpion. My opinion about him just flips a complete 180. Anyone who calls Rosy Boyd a scorpion must be in the right frame of mind. I suddenly love this guy! I told him I would discuss this issue with Bryce when I'm back from the U.K.

The dinner lasts almost two hours. When we depart, Joe and Brad wish me safe travels. "Godspeed," Brad says by way of leaving and waves his hand. I looked at a text from Julie that came while we were paying the bills. She says she sees from the tracking app that I'm still at Anthony's, so she will be home before me. She will take Jupiter inside. Jupiter has been roaming the fenced-in front yard like she always does when we go out in the evening or when we go to church. When we're at work, she is usually at a kennel. Come to think of it, 'roaming' is a strong word here. She mostly sits and waits for us to come back. It doesn't matter if it's one hour or a whole evening; she just keeps looking for us. When we come home, she is exhilarated and jumps all around the car. So, we have to take extra precautions after opening the gate and drive very slowly until she is up by the car, dancing around it. Then we go out and let her into the car, get licked all over the face for fifteen minutes—*"About fucking time you got back, people!"*— and then drive on.

So, Julie telling me that she will take Jupiter inside lets me know that I don't need to be paranoid when I drive through the gate. She also tells me that the surgery went well. Finally, she mentions that we're out of dishwashing liquid. —Now, a weaker intellect might have taken this last piece of information as just that—information, nothing more. My brain, however, equipped with razor-sharp acuity, interprets this information to mean that not only are we out of dishwashing liquid, but I should also pick up some on my way home. That's what I call deductive reasoning! With such talent, finding Derek Tyne-Callaghan should be an easy undertaking. If you've ever read about the gentleman detective Lord Peter Wimsey journeying the English countryside, that'll be me.

When I get home, it's close to nine p.m. It's too late to FaceTime Jessica and Lars. Or, too early, rather. Jessica and Lars don't need to get up at the crack of dawn to get to the bakery anymore. They have staff that starts up the baking at night and in the morning. I have an evening flight from Minneapolis to London Heathrow tomorrow, but I need to be up and running before the rooster crows anyhow since I need to grab an early morning flight from our local airport to be in Minneapolis in time. So, I finish my packing tonight. Julie will still be in bed when I get up tomorrow; she had a long day with intense surgery. So, we'll say our goodbyes tonight before turning in.

Jupiter, hypersensitive as ever, takes the cue from my suitcase and the way Julie and I talk and looks deflated. She knows something is going on and that she doesn't like it. She hates it when one of us is leaving for a trip.

"You and your fucking travel. You should prioritize us here at home!"

I try to formulate a response but give up. I take her out for a late evening walk around the neighborhood instead to console her. While we're strolling, I tell Jupiter about my business trip to the U.K. and Derek Tyne-Callaghan's hypothesis about perception receptors, whatever that might be. This is when Jupiter decides to take a poop. Honestly, I believe that's more out of necessity than a reflection of her opinion on my comments. I pick up the poop, and we head back home. Our property is just by the Columbia River, so before going inside, we go down to the riverbank and take in the view. The sun is long set, but there is a warm glow shimmering on the tranquil water surface. The air is still. The ospreys, eagles, pelicans, and herons we often see scouting the river have settled down for the night. I imagine Chinook Indians drifting down the river in their canoes hundreds of years ago, casting their nets for salmon. The musty river scent is combined with a typical smell of agriculture lingering in the air; think manure from fields half a mile away, together with the sweet aroma of Concord grapes from a nearby vineyard. Throw in the balsamic fragrance of laundry softener from our dryer, and you have an oddly pleasant VOC concoction. I bet this is a bouquet the ORs of my imaginary Chinooks on the river would never have experienced. I stay for a while and ponder life. I decide it's good. Jupiter looks at me. Before she can devise an insult about me staring at an empty river, I nod in agreement; it's time to go inside.

Before I go to bed, I walk into my office and, enter *Bc6* in the d4c4 app and shoot it off. I smile. *Chew on that, my friend!*

CHAPTER 5

Summer 2024. London, U.K. Jessica and Lars.

I arrive at London Heathrow around lunchtime. I flew First Class, so I'm fairly rested. I also had a meal during the inflight, so I didn't need to stop for lunch. Per my instructions, my Hertz rental—a Toyota Highlander—is waiting for me close to the Terminal 3 exit. At prior visits, Julie and I have used the ride-hailing service FREENOW to get to Jessica and Lars' home, but this time, I need my own wheels. I enter the car with some trepidation and start the process of familiarizing myself with the interior. I set the GPS for Jessica and Lars' address. They live in Highgate, a residential area close to Hampstead Heath. As I alluded to before, I don't like driving in U.K. I've done it before, not in London but in Oxford and Cambridge, so I have some experience. The left-hand traffic is bad enough in its own right. But what really scares me is left-hand traffic in combination with roundabouts. As if that's not bad enough, in a stroke of genius, the U.K. Department of Transport has invented roundabouts *within* a roundabout, with bi-directional traffic, so-called 'magic roundabouts. One of those is Hatton Cross, southeast of Heathrow, which I'm now approaching with utter terror and confusion. I have no idea what to do. My brain can't convert the GPS instructions to actions. Then, just in time, and as a lightning flash from a clear blue sky, I get an idea—possibly through divine intervention: I will focus on one car and follow that through the roundabout until I'm out. So, that's what I do. I target a red Mercedes-Benz and hang on to it like a leach into the roundabout, through some completely irrational maneuvers inside, and then out the exit, hoping that it's the right one for me. Of course, it's not. The GPS redirects me—I think—and I'm once again by the roundabout. I use the same strategy as before and with the same result. The third time, however, I got out on the right exit—I'm brilliant!

There are seven more roundabouts that separate me from Highgate. They are less threatening than Hatton Cross, but I use the same "follow-the-leader" tactics in three of them. For two, I need to re-enter the roundabout, but for the third, I'm redirected after the first try to a shortcut that avoids the roundabout altogether. By this time, my brain and the GPS are better synced. The remainder of the roundabouts, the last four before I get to Jessica and Lars, I can manage on my own, mainly due to less traffic. I arrive at two-thirty p.m. A trip that, according to the GPS, should require around fifty minutes took me twice as long. But I'm not complaining; I'm quite proud of my newly acquired navigational skills. I text Julie just to let her know that I've arrived safe and sound.

———

I have a very nice time with Jessica and Lars and my little granddaughters, Kristina and Linnea, nine and eleven years old, respectively. It's Monday, but summer term has just ended, so the girls are out of school. Lars is soon taking them to soccer practice, but he and Jessica have time for some back and forth with me before they leave. I tell them about my victory over Hatton Cross, and they laugh. They know my business here and have made some inquiries of their own but haven't found anything that adds to the story. They have other news, though; they are in final negotiations of setting up a second Kringlan Bakery in London, in Kensington in West London. The building is finished; an old pub that has been renovated and repurposed, and they are in the process of hiring staff. That's exciting news, and I'm glad for them.

While Lars and the girls are gone, I help Jessica with the pizza crusts. Yes, we're having pizza! Jessica is wearing an oversized Stockholm T-shirt that she uses as a baking apron. She is at the beginning of the third trimester, and her face is glowing. This time, it's a boy. She and Lars have already made the dough balls, and we're taking them out of the fridge and start rolling them out. We reminisce about Sweden. We speak Swedish. All three of our kids, Jessica, her twin brother Richard, and older sister Inga, were born in Sweden. They moved with us when Julie and I accepted job offers in the U.S. While Richard and Inga have remained in the U.S., Jessica early on jumped at an Apprentice Baker opening in London and relocated her life to England. She met Lars, who was working at a nearby pizzeria. Life happened, and after one year, they were married. Meanwhile, they had worked together and won several rather prestigious baking competitions. They also sold their baked goods at Farmers Markets. So, later on, when they approached financial institutions and venture capitalists for funding, they were able to present quite convincing applications. They said that their wedding gift to each other was to agree to follow their passion and set up a bakery together, which they did.

We're topping the pizzas and baking them on the grill. I gross everyone out by putting pickles on my pizza. I try convincing the others to try it, but no takers. The girls think it's downright disgusting. I, on the other hand, really enjoy it; it provides a pleasant saltiness and crunch. It's not my own invention, by the way; there's a whole community out there that puts pickles on their pizzas. Pickles, or no pickles, we're eating outside in their backyard. It's cloudy, and there's drizzle in the forecast, but the temperature is pleasant: lower twenties—that's in centigrade, as I think you figured out. The girls take their pizzas inside to watch TV. We're discussing my trip tomorrow. I'm going to the University of Reading. The university has five campuses: one in Malaysia, one in South Africa—I'm assuming that's not where Derek was—and three in Reading. In fact, I know from Hanne's investigations that Derek went to the main campus, both as a grad student and for his Lecture position. So, tomorrow, I head out to the main campus, which is the Whiteknights campus. I've emailed ahead of time and scheduled a meeting for the day after tomorrow with Professor Emeritus Julius McIntosh, who seems to be the one with the most insight into Derek's whereabouts. It turns out that Reading is less than fifty miles away, so I decide to leave early tomorrow afternoon.

After dinner, we FaceTime Julie. While we're at it, I am contemplating FaceTiming Richard and Inga and their families as well. Julie and I usually FaceTime the kids on Sundays, but since I was traveling, I missed out on that this week. However, they'd be working now, so I chose not to. It's after eight anyhow, and my eyelids are getting heavy, so I say goodnight and see you tomorrow.

I skip breakfast in the morning since we're all going to the bakery for early lunch or brunch. I'm looking forward to seeing Kringlan again. When I say that Kringlan is a bakery, I should add that it's a sit-down bakery with a dining area where people enjoy breakfast or lunch, plus an outdoor patio.

There is a vibrant feeling in the bakery. As I enter, my olfactory receptors go into overdrive to take in the plethora of scents that hit me like a warm, aromatic airwave. I know that one of the key components my receptors detect is diacetyl. But I will not say that; it doesn't convey the olfactory sensation I want to describe. I'll say instead that what meets me at the door is the irresistible fragrance of newly roasted coffee and the sweet, buttery, crusty, and somewhat yeasty and mouthwatering smell of baked goods. —Sounds better, right?

It's a typical Tuesday morning, but the thirty tables in the dining area are almost all taken. Jessica and Lars are taking care of some business, and the girls have brought some friends, and they are eating away on the patio. Kringlan—and I realize I should have mentioned earlier that *kringlan* means "the pretzel" in Swedish—offers several Swedish specialties. Some of the most popular are Swedish open shrimp sandwiches, orange and cardamom pretzels or rolls, and Swedish pancakes rolled up with butter in the middle and eaten cold. Lars is American, and he moved with his parents to England when he was a teenager. However, all four of his grandparents came from Sweden or Norway. So both Jessica and Lars are invested in keeping a Swedish and Scandinavian theme and atmosphere in the bakery. You'll find ample evidence to that effect if you look around the bakery. For example, four iconic Carl Larsson reproductions are hanging on the walls. If you have a keen eye, you can find a fifth Carl Larsson, partly hidden behind a line of round, large, flat crispbread (*knäckebröd*) with a central hole and threaded on a horizontal pole. Classic Swedish tiled stoves (*kakelugnar*) occupy two corners in the sitting area. They are round and white with several ornated tiles and almost reach the ceiling. I know from experience that these stoves are more than decorations; they provide a welcome balminess on cold and rainy days.

I start my brunch by ordering a couple of Swedish shrimp sandwiches. They are made of rye bread topped with shrimp, lemon slices, dill, and avocado oil mayonnaise. I follow up with a hefty slice of their famous red current pie. The marriage of tart and sweet is almost a spiritual experience. I take a second cup of coffee and top it off with one of their equally famous blueberry scones. They're made with blueberries—no surprise there—and soft goat cheese, another heavenly creation. Julie would have told me that I was eating too fast and too much; I don't need to have a scone after eating pie. And she would have been right on both accounts. I've promised myself, on various occasions, to start eating slower. But I don't seem to learn. It's never too late, though. Maybe I'll start tomorrow. Anyhow, Julie isn't here, so I bite into my scone.

I'm proud to let you know that I've learned that one of my own contributions to the bakery menu has become very popular. I'm talking about my sourdough crackers. When I feed my sourdough starters—which I do on a weekly to bi-weekly basis—I do what many other sourdough bakers do: instead of discarding sourdough, I use it for baking. You can make sourdough pancakes or pizza crusts, which I do. But my favorite is sourdough crackers, rolled out to thin oblongs and topped with fresh rosemary and sage, garlic powder, dried onion, Harissa, Zaatar, or pepper flakes. You can also add Maldon Sea salt. When they make these crackers at Kringlan, they use a big pasta maker to produce large rectangles that they cut into sections.

While I've been eating, I've texted Julius McIntosh to confirm our appointment tomorrow morning. He tells me to meet him at Park House Bar, an eatery at the university, at ten a.m. and includes directions. *Look for a prominent red beard,* he tells me. I've looked him up, and I think he'll be hard to miss; bald, like me, but with a massive red beard.

It's time for me to leave, so I go out to the patio to say bye to the girls. I'll visit them again on my way back, so that feels good. I find Jessica and Lars in their office, and we say our goodbyes there. On my way out, I stop at the counter and consider whether to get a pancake roll or another blueberry scone for the road, but then think better of it since I've already had enough. When I get to the car, I stop, look at the busy street, and contemplate life for a bit. I decide it's good. Then I go back into the bakery and get a blueberry scone.

CHAPTER 6

Summer 2024. Reading. The Crown Caversham.

I embark on the journey to Reading in good spirit, confident that if I could defeat Hatton Cross, I should very well be able to conquer most of the British road network. The weather is nice, overcast with a light breeze and around twenty-five degrees. I set the GPS. The trip turns out to be quite pleasant, through lush landscapes and only three, not too intimidating roundabouts. The drive takes less than two hours, and I arrive in Reading at one-thirty p.m. Hanne has reserved a room for me at the Crowne Plaza close to the university. It's too early for check-in, so I boot up my laptop in the lobby and take care of some emails and work-related business. I text Julie, Jessica, and Hanne to let them know I've arrived.

Turns out that Hanne, who knows my preferences, has booked me an Executive King Room with a balcony overlooking the River Thames—good girl! After I check in, I unpack and take the laptop out to the balcony to take care of some more emails. Noa has sent data on the Crex-ORChips, basically showing that none of the VOCs in our panel elicits any response. There are still these seemingly random signals. I look out over the river for a while. There's a boardwalk with some ducks arguing over a potential takeover by the Labour Party from the Tories in the next election. I listen in for a while but abstain from offering my opinions. I check the time; there is an OMICS meeting today. I said I would try to zoom in if the timing worked out. This would be six p.m. my time. However, I'm getting hungry, so I decide to skip the meeting. Instead, I take a shower and prepare for dinner. I'll bring my briefcase with the laptop in case I change my mind and log in to the meeting anyhow.

Instead of asking the receptionist for recommendations, I feel adventurous and opt to take a stroll and look for some good dining options. I'm in the mood for some genuine pub experience. I walk over the bridge to the other side of the riverbank. Just one block further, I see a pub that looks promising, THE CROWN CAVERSHAM, it says on the building. They have a nice outdoor garden, but it's completely packed. I also see that several patrons have their dogs with them, which immediately makes me like the place. I walk inside to discover that also here, all tables seem to be taken or reserved. A friendly waitress tells me to wait while she cleans off a table in the back corner. While I'm pulling out the chair, I hear some old timers at a table next to mine order Doom Bar, which looks like a crafted and savory beer when they take their swigs. When my server comes, I ask her for the same, trying to look as if this is what I order all the time. She asks me if I want it warm or cold. When she sees my face—all pretense of being a beer connoisseur evaporated—she explains that Doom Bar is an old-school amber ale that some people prefer served warm, although it's equally popular cold. I go for cold. I'm not disappointed; Doom Bar is very good, with a touch of bitterness. I also order Fish and Chips. On the newspaper wrapping, I read local news from 1947. This reminds me of Derek Tyne-Callaghan. If he was in his forties when I met him in Halkidiki at the beginning of the 1980s—I remember now that it was 1983—he should have been born sometime in the 1940s.

I continue to think about Derek. I make room on the table for my laptop and bring up my "Derek folder." I have downloaded the only two publications I've found from his work. They're from his postdoc period at the University of Michigan. I haven't seen any published papers from his graduate studies. Derek is the sole author on both publications, and they're compilations of metadata, written more like perspectives or reviews rather than based on his own research. I've read them before, and I find them interesting. Both publications deal with the evolution of language in humans and how it coincides with reduced—or modified—olfaction. They basically say the same thing in two different journals. Derek presents two tenets. As the first, he argues that although the anatomical capability to form contrasting vowels likely existed more than twenty-five million years ago, the cognitive ability to use speech to converse with each other developed much later, somewhere between one hundred fifty thousand and three hundred thousand years ago.

As the second tenet, Derek posits that the evolution of advanced language occurred at the expense of olfaction and the reduction in ORs (olfactory receptors, remember?) This notion seemingly contradicts recent findings, concluding that we as humans have a much more sophisticated sense of smell than what has been previously assumed. First off, humans have olfactory bulbs—the part of the brain that receives signals from ORs—organized in clusters that allow for a higher degree of processing of OR signals than in animals such as dogs, elephants, or mice. Second, a large fraction of what has been annotated as OR pseudogenes in humans apparently codes for mRNA and ORs with unknown functions. However, this doesn't necessarily mean that Derek is wrong. Early hominins may very well have possessed ORs for specific VOCs that were lost during evolution as the ability for advanced speech developed.

I found out from University of Michigan at Ann Arbor that Derek did his postdoc at the Museum of Paleontology, jointly with the Department of Earth and Environmental Sciences, and that he started his tenure-track position at the Museum in 1982. I was puzzled by Derek landing an Assistant Professorship on such low productivity—just two publications. The Head of the Museum at the time, as well as Derek's postdoc supervisor, passed away. However, I managed to get a hold of the former Department Head of Earth and Environmental Sciences. He was kind enough to arrange for me to get Derek's CV from his Assistant Professor application. I learned from that, and also from speaking with some former colleagues of Derek's, that he spent the six years prior to his postdoc position traveling. He went to East Africa, the Middle East, and Israel, studying old East African languages, as well as Greek, Hebrew, and Aramaic. He apparently also took part in some volunteer work as a guide and translator for tourists visiting the Judaean desert. One of his colleagues remembered that Derek's talent for mastering multiple written languages was phenomenal, and she thought that was one reason he got hired.

While I'm thinking of Derek, I realize that my eyes have been resting on a chessboard tucked away on a shelf by the dart area. I disconnect my brain from Derek and go and grab the chessboard. I pull up my phone and the d4c4 app. I was pleased with a recent bishop move; I was planning on putting Bryce in check in two steps. But that strategy became null and void when I saw his move: *0-0-0*, a queen-side castling. I should have foreseen that! I set up the chessboard from the d4c4 display and add Bryce's castling. Now, suddenly, my bishop is threatened by his rook. And, not only that, if I move it, I'm in check. So, I can move my king and lose the bishop, or… I stare at the chessboard. It's now seven p.m., and I feel a little guilty that I'm sitting here playing chess rather than logging in to the OMICS meeting. Just a little, though, not enough to tip the balance. I start to see an elegant gambit strategy taking shape; I will move my king to avoid check. If Bryce then takes my bishop that I offer up, which I hope he will, his rook will be out of the way, presenting me with an opportunity to eventually put him in check with my queen. I feel proud; it's a long shot, but it might be worth the risk. I enter *Kf2* on the app. But I don't click "Add move" yet. I start to wonder if he will be aware of the potential threat and opt out of taking my bishop. A malicious thought pops up in my reverie, unbidden. It's around one p.m. in DC. If I send Bryce the move now, he will check it out when he gets home, maybe even on his chess board. When you send a move in the d4c4 app, you get a ding, a notification signal, so Bryce will know that he has a new move to look at. If he gets it now, he will have time to ponder his move. I know that he has a Thursday to Friday DARPA executive meeting in San Francisco, leaving early Wednesday morning, which is tomorrow. DARPA is the Defense Advanced Research Projects Agency, which is responsible for the development of emerging technologies for the DoD (the U.S. Department of Defense). So ... if I hold off with my move, and Bryce gets it later, say after dinner and wine and while packing and going over things with Lucy, his wife, then he will be less lucid and feel rushed. In this case, he might just follow through with his plan of taking my bishop and be done with it. I reflect on this. Should I really be this devious and calculating? I realize I'm not that lucid myself after two Imperial pints of Doom Bars, so maybe I should sleep on this. Or just do the right thing and send the text now. Also, it's not very Christian to trick a friend like this. I should be ashamed of myself, shouldn't I? Well… I set the timer on my phone to wake me up at one a.m. to send off the move.

I said I'm a Christian, not necessarily a good one.

CHAPTER 7

Summer 2024. The pursuit of Derek Tyne-Callaghan.
Julius and Molly McIntosh.

I eat my breakfast in the hotel. They have a very nice breakfast bar, but I had oatmeal with oat milk. Now, I'm having my coffee and a blueberry scone. Not nearly as good as the ones Kringlan makes, but good enough, although a little stale. I see a waiter coming by with a tray of scones that smell wonderfully and that are obviously freshly baked. I don't see those on the breakfast buffet, and I ask him about that. He says there's a real estate pitch at the hotel every morning this week until Friday, from nine to eleven a.m., and that those scones are meant for that event. He puts them on a small table hidden behind the piano and covers them with a towel. Hm…

I didn't sleep much last night. I usually need to go to the bathroom several times at night, courtesy of an enlarged prostate. This is not uncommon in men my age, but last night, I must have been there every thirty minutes, thanks to the beer consumption, no doubt. I have no headache, though. So, other than being tired, I'm fine. At one of those bathroom breaks, I sent the text to Bryce. I must have ignored the alarm, so it ended up being closer to two-thirty than one a.m. This means that Bryce would not have received the text until after nine p.m., so he might already be in bed. Serves me right, I guess.

I see on Google Maps that Park House is just a twenty-minute drive from the hotel, but I decide to leave at nine a.m. to make sure I get my bearings and a parking spot.

————

I arrive at Park House at a good time. The Park House Bar is in the middle of the campus and looks more like a castle. I learned later that it is one of the former houses of the Whiteknights Park Estate. I start looking for the entrance when I spot a red beard on a chair in the outdoor seating area. The beard gets up, and I see that it's attached to a big hunker of a man. Julius McIntosh looks to be in his mid-seventies and is almost as tall as I am and twice the size all around. From his handshake and the look of him, I suspect his weight is almost all muscles. He has a friendly face with dimples and big, curious blue eyes. He completely dominates the space, so much so that I first don't notice the woman sitting next to him, let alone that she's in a wheelchair.

"This is my wife, Molly. My love and partner in crime."

I bend down to shake her hand. "Nice to meet you, Molly."

Molly is the same age as Julius, possibly somewhat younger. She is as small as Julius is big. Of course, she's in a wheelchair, which makes the contrast even more noticeable. She has thick silver-gray hair and a face full of wrinkles but with distinct features and clear, piercing, brown eyes. For some reason, I think of her face as something you'd encounter in Santa Fe, a face that embodies both ethos and a frontier spirit. When she speaks, the Santa Fe vision is gone in a flash; she has what I would call an upper-class or posh English accent. "Well, you make quite a presence, Dr. Thovén. You're at least as tall as my Jollipolli here, but you carry less cargo." She smiles and pats Julius' wide frame. I smile, too, and tell her to please call me Ludvig.

"Well, have a seat, won't you, Ludvig." Julius indicates a chair. "I'd recommend one of these." He raises his glass and points at the one by Molly. "It's a local craft beer with a marvelous malty taste."

Ten in the morning is a little early for me to drink beer, but what the heck, I can't say no to these nice people. Julius waves a waiter over.

"One "Happy Dog" for our American friend here," he says and taps my shoulder. It's a friendly gesture, but his hand lands like a sledgehammer, and I almost fall off my chair. "Molly and I come here on Wednesdays, which we call 'Beersdays,' to celebrate our wedding anniversary." He turns to Molly and strokes her arm gently. And I mean *gently*; this time, his hand is like a feather. The affection between these two is palpable.

I chuckle. "So, you celebrate your anniversary once a week; that's a clever idea." I'm thinking I should mention this to Julie. My beer arrives. I admit it's very tasty with a sweet, nutty taste, almost like caramel.

We clink glasses. "Cheers," I propose. "And, Julius, thanks for seeing me; I really appreciate it."

"Well, Ludvig, I must say, I'm quite intrigued by your detective mission here." He pulls up my email on his phone. "Derek Tyne-Callaghan, hm... I do remember him, but I'm not sure how much help we can offer. By the way, my Molly here wonders if... or rather, she assumes that it hasn't escaped your notice that your email address carries a... how should I call it, musical connotation?"

I smile. "Yes, most people in my orbit call me 'Symphony.'"

"*Symphony*!" Julius' colossal body erupts in rumbling laughter that makes the grounds quake in a quarter-mile radius around the bar. I wouldn't be surprised if it was picked up by the nearby seismic station in Swindon. "Well, then allow me to do the same if it's okay with you."

"Absolutely, I'd be honored."

"So, I do remember Derek," Julius repeats. He looks at my email again. "He came back here in 1986. This was his Alma

Mater, you know. He went to Uni here (he means university) at the Department of Languages and Cultures. I wasn't at Reading then, but I checked him out in the roster, and—"

Julius stops and looks up. A waiter is coming out with a bowl. "Here's some water for Prince Charles," he says. I then realize there's even more to the scene than I first perceived. A huge St. Bernard gets up behind Molly's wheelchair.

"This is Prince Charles." Julius massages the back of the dog, a magnificent animal with a brown-white-black coloration. "He doesn't drink beer, so he mostly hangs around Molly to make sure that no covetous bachelor is coming by to snatch her away. But, of course, they would have to go through me too, ha, ha." Another bellowing laughter, not as high on the Richter scale this time, but certainly impressive. I notice that people in the bar are well familiar with the McIntoshes; they smile and nod knowingly when Julius laughs, and new guests that arrive wave and say hello. While Prince Charles drinks from the bowl, a little Dachshund comes over and wants in. Prince Charles just moves around a little to let the newcomer in—a friendly, sharing soul. I feel surrounded by a very pleasant atmosphere, and I get an urge to have a picture taken with these folks. I ask them if that's okay. "Sure thing!" So, we have a waiter snapping a few photos of us with my phone.

I look at Julius. "So, I take it that Derek would have been enrolled at the university in the late 1960s?"

"Well, from 1969 to 1973. I believe he took a gap year or two in there sometime. I learned that his folks had a cider mill somewhere between here and Bath, and Derek used to work there on and off. When his dad got cancer—prostate, I believe—Derek went to work there full-time for a while. His dad got over it, though, and Derek went back to Uni."

"His Assistant Professor position in Ann Arbor started in 1982," I say. "And it was terminated the following year."

In my email to Julius, I hadn't mentioned any details about Derek's departure from Ann Arbor. I just said he was let go.

"Derek was apparently caught in some sex play with minor girls, and he was subsequently fired," I explain. "I'm not sure what transpired after that, other than that I heard he was extradited back to the U.K."

Julius nods. "Yes, he said as much when we interviewed him; he was quite forthcoming. I was a professor at the School of Archeology, Geography, and Environmental Science at the time. I was the Head of the Geography and Environmental Science Department. It was Nancy Hale, who was the Head of the Archeology Department, and I, who arranged a position for Derek. But he was never a Lecturer, as you say in your email. A Lecturer is a competitive position, more like an Assistant Professor in your system. We hired Derek as a Teaching Assistant… or Teaching Fellow, I guess you could say. He told us quite candidly about what had happened in the U.S. and that he had spent one year at Ashfield upon return to England. It's a prison in Pucklechurch, close to Bristol west of here." As he points with his arm, Molly grabs it and turns it around. "West is this way," she says.

"Oh, right." Julius chuckles. "My gyro is not working properly. Molly here is the navigator, and I'm the driver; that's our perfect teamwork." (Yes, Julius actually *chuckled*, an uncharacteristically low-decibel sound coming from him).

Then Julius gets serious again and sighs. "But we couldn't keep him long; he was obviously bright and helpful, but his drinking problems overshadowed all of that. He spent most of his time after work at home, drinking, or at the town library. Molly here was the Head Librarian at Reading, so she can tell you more about that later. We tried to help him get out of his house and get involved in activities such as rugby. He played for a while. I played rugby, you see." Julius slams his chest, sending vibrations across the county. "I was a Tighthead Prop for the R.F.C., the Rugby Football Club." Molly, who sees my blank face, explains that a Tighthead Prop is positioned in the frontline and has the important role of preventing the team from being pushed backward. A Tighthead Prop needs to be very strong and compact and take pleasure in head-to-head competition. She points to Julius when she says this. I glance at him. Just the mere thought of trying to force a frontline with Julius in it makes me shudder. I'd rather suggest declaring a walk-over on the spot.

"Yes, the Tighthead and Loosehead Props take a hit or two," Julius says. "We didn't put Derek there, of course, but on the Openside Flanker or even Left Wing. These were not in league or tournament formats, mind you, but just training and playing for fun. He played for a while but never really took to it. Same thing with other activities like martial arts. By the way," he says and hands me a photo, "here's the only photo we have of Derek from this time. It's from one of the rugby games."

I look at the photo of Derek. I can easily recognize him. He's still kind of stocky but not nearly as I remember from when I met him in person in the early 1980s. No goatee. He looks unkempt and very uncomfortable on the rugby field. "Thank you, this should be useful. And, if I may," I say, "how come he was hired in the first place? I mean, given the history? It's very kind, of course, but were there other reasons?"

"Ah… yes, I don't think Derek would even have tried to get back to Reading, hadn't it been for the fact that the Chancellor at the time, Lord Cordengroove, was a friend of the Tyne-Callaghans. They were part of the same parish at St. James and St. William right over here." Julius starts pointing, then grins and looks at Molly, who takes his arm and corrects his direction slightly. "Close enough," she says.

"Yes," Julius continues. "Lady Cordengroove and Derek's mom were both heavily involved in the church with Sunday school and bible studies. Also, I've heard that Derek's mom saved the life of the Cordengroove's dog at a dinner party they hosted, the Cordengrooves, I mean. Apparently, the dog had gotten a big knot from a rawhide chewie in the wrong tube and was suffocating. Derek's mom noticed and grabbed the dog—a big Bullmastiff—got it upright on its hind legs and performed a Heimlich maneuver that made the piece of rawhide come out."

"So," Julius concludes, "there were obvious bonds here, and the new Chancellor wanted the university to give Derek a chance. Which we did but to no avail. His drinking problem was too obtrusive. Not that he was violent or vulgar or anything; he just couldn't perform his duties."

I look at my watch and realize it's close to noon. We've been sitting here talking for almost two hours. I've long finished my beer, and I'm getting hungry.

Julius takes notice. "My Molly here, and I usually stay for lunch. He gently squeezes Molly's shoulder. "That way, we can have another beer to celebrate our anniversary," he adds and bursts out in one more of his thunderous and contagious laughter. I find myself smiling.

"How about something to eat?" Julius suggests and asks a waiter for menus. "We really enjoy their blood pudding. It comes with fried apples and bacon. That too strange for you?"

"Actually, no. I originally came from Sweden, and I used to eat blood pudding as a kid. We had it with lingonberry jam and coleslaw."

I haven't had blood pudding for over thirty years. It's very hard to come by in the U.S., and with Julie and I eating mostly vegan or vegetarian, I haven't been looking for it. I can only remember one occasion when I saw it in stores, and that was in San Francisco. They had something called *biroldo*, which is an Italian-American version. Although I call myself a preferred vegan or at least vegetarian, I relish the thought of having blood pudding again.

"Sweden, ah?" Julius smiles. "I thought I could discern a foreign twang, but I'm not familiar enough with American accents to be sure. Well, if you're game, let's get some food going."

We order the blood pudding and a round of beers. The blood pudding is good, although not exactly what I remember from Sweden. While we're eating, I continue to explain a little more about my background, Julie, our kids, and the work at OMICS. We eventually circle back to Derek Tyne-Callaghan. Molly recalls her encounters with him at the library.

"As Jollipolli mentioned, I met Derek routinely when he came to the library, which was often. He borrowed and ordered a significant number of books about archeology, mostly in the context of human evolution. He could, of course, get some of that material from Uni. But this was in the 1980s, and online searches were not as seamless and straightforward as they are today." Molly speaks eloquently and with an almost aristocratic accent. It's very pleasant to listen to. I wonder about her background.

"And I agree," she says, touching Julius' arm. "He was always nice and friendly, albeit somewhat reserved, and I enjoyed conversing with him. But, of course, I would be remiss if I didn't concede that he most often was under the influence."

"And you mentioned," Julius says to Molly, "that he told you he was interested in starting up his own cider production."

"Yes, this was by the end of 1988, when he realized that his career here—such as it was—was over."

"And he had money," Julius adds. The Tyne-Gallaghans were in good standing in society, not only through their friendship with Lord and Lady Cordengroove but also on their own accord. They had a successful cidery, and they were also big in real estate, owning several businesses and apartment complexes. Like the Cordengrooves, they were known for their generous charity through St. James and St. William and through other channels.

"They passed away, Derek's parents, that is," Julius continues. "Within a year of each other in the very early 1980s. His dad suffered from a heart attack, and his mom from lung cancer; she'd been smoking heavily in her younger years, and I guess that caught up with her. They were both in their 80s by then. They died just before Derek's derailment from academia, which, I guess you can say, was fortunate. He was the only child, so he certainly had the means to start a cider mill or some other business if he wanted to."

"So, maybe that presents a way to find him," I say. "Is there a record of cider producers in the U.K?"

"We have the National Association of Cider Makers," Julius says. "There must be close to five hundred cider producers in the U.K., and not all might be affiliated with the Association. But, of course, if he is registered, then looking for someone who started after 1988 seems like a good opportunity."

"Problem is," I say. "We've had people looking through public online databases and local newspapers, and there's no Derek Tyne-Gallaghan to be found, dead or alive."

"One possibility is that he changed his name to escape his disreputable past," Molly says.

"Hm… that's a thought," I agree. "What would that entail?" I don't know the protocol or requirements for a name change in the U.S., let alone in the U.K.

"Not sure," Julius says, and he brings up his phone and starts googling. Meanwhile, I'm pondering how one would go about trying to figure out what names people choose in these situations. What name would Derek take, and would he change both his first and last name?

Julius looks at his phone. "Well, seems like all you need to do is present a case for a judge and maybe pay a fee. There doesn't appear to be any specific approval process. So, fairly easy to do, I guess."

"I assume that changing your last name to your mother's maiden name is a common case," I say. "That might not apply in Witness Protection Programs, but for a guy like Derek, that might be what he would do. He could just say that he doesn't want to be associated with his father's name anymore—not that he would need any reason at all, as it seems."

"That begs the question," I continue. "Do you know Derek's mother's maiden name?"

"No," Julius shakes his head. "We can ask around and see if we can jog someone's memory."

"How about marriage certificates," I ask. "Are they public? We used the General Register Office to look for death certificates. I guess they also have copies of marriage certificates?"

"They do," Molly says. "And I can help you here. I'm still affiliated with the library, and it has registrations for the GRO and many other portals. I can log in from home and conduct a search."

"That would be great. Thank you!"

It's now after two p.m., and I'm getting concerned I'm overextending the McIntoshes' hospitality. They probably have other things to do. I thought we would be chatting for an hour at the most. And here we are after four and a half hours.

"Well, thank you both so very much!" I say. "This has been very helpful, and I'm afraid I've taken more of your time than you expected."

"No, no." Julius shakes his head. "It's all gravy. As I said, we're fascinated by your mission. In fact…" Julius looks at Molly, who nods—a kind of telepathic communication that also Julie and I have developed. "What are your plans for tonight?"

"Well, I need to go back to the hotel, the Crowne Plaza, to do some work and FaceTime my wife before she heads off to the clinic. Then I was planning to go back to the pub where I went for dinner yesterday, The Crown Caversham; I enjoyed that place." I don't mention that another reason I want to go back there is to grab the chessboard again and contemplate various alternatives once I get a move back from Bryce.

"Ah, The Crown. Did you try their Scottish egg?"

"No, I had fish and chips that I washed down with Doom Bar."

"Oh, you have to try the Scottish egg. It's not enough for dinner by itself, but it goes with almost anything else. The Doom Bar is a good ale. —*But*, what I was going to say, for tonight, would you like to come over to our humble abode for dinner? We live like twenty minutes from your hotel. Our son Rufus and his wife are coming over with their twins, and I think you would enjoy talking to them. Well, at least with Rufus and Rachel, his wife. You labeled yourself as a foodie a couple of hours ago. Rufus and his wife, Rachel, have a goat farm in the countryside, and they specialize in producing goat milk kefir. I really think you would find that interesting. *And*, there's an apple orchard next to their goat farm that Derek visited a few times. Not sure what his specific purpose was. While he was there, Rufus and Rachel always invited him over for lunch. So, they might have some information on Derek that could be useful."

"Thank you. Yes, I would be delighted to join you if it's not too much extra work." I look at Molly to make sure she's on board. I must seem concerned because Julius pokes her gently. "Oh, don't you get fooled by Molly's wheelchair? She can bounce around like a flea bug once she gets her mind to it." He smiles and strokes her shoulders.

"It's the arthritis that comes and goes," Molly says. "It started in earnest five years ago. It's hard for me to walk or stand for long periods of time. When we're out, I take advantage of Jollipolli here and his muscles."

I get directions from Julius. It is indeed close to my hotel. We decide on six p.m.

CHAPTER 8

Summer 2024. Dinner with the McIntosh family.

I arrive fashionably late at six-ten p.m. It's my experience from hosting parties that having guests who arrive too early is a nuisance. You may not be fully prepared with food and whatnot, and then you also need to converse with the newly arrived. Too late is, of course, not good either. Between too early and too late, I'd rather err on the side of being late, and I think ten minutes is an acceptable margin. —How about instead arriving just on time, you ask. Well… yeah, there's that.

Anyhow, I'll be there at six-ten p.m. The McIntoshes live in an unassuming but nice, two-story granite and red brick house. The front yard is spotted with a lot of flowering plants and bushes, some of which I recognize. For example, there are hollyhocks and hydrangea surrounded by a hedge of boxwoods. Julius opens the door. "Hi there, Symphony!" he exclaims and gives me a hug, which is as unexpected as it is suffocating. Molly is there, without the wheelchair. I walk over and, taking the cue from Julius, give her a hug.

"Thanks for inviting me," I say. I hand over a couple of Washingtonian gifts: a bottle of Barnard Griffin Syrah and smoked Chinook salmon from the Columbia River.

Four other people are there as well. One is a younger version of Julius, but with a full head of thick, unruly, red hair, whom I, with my remarkable deduction abilities, conclude is Rufus. Next to him is Rachel, his wife. She is a robust woman with a ruddy complexion, blond hair, and brown eyes. Which, all together, looks quite attractive. I say hello to both. "This is Roy," Rachel says, pointing to a teenage boy. Her voice is soft but commanding. "And this is his twin sister Rita." I have a keen ability to discern patterns, and I see one here. I say hello to Roy and Rita, whom I take to be around fourteen years old.

"Why did Grandpa call you Symphony?" Rita asks.

"Well, let's see if you can guess by looking at my email address," I tell her and point to it on my phone. Rufus, Rachel, and Roy lean in and look as well. Rufus and Rachel smile but don't say anything.

"Ah!" Rita says eventually. "Ha, ha, that's so funny! So, do you play the piano?"

"No, unfortunately, I don't. I wish I could, but I've never learned. Our son is trained as a classical pianist, so we had a lot of piano music at home while he still lived there."

I spend some time talking to Rufus and Rachel, filling in some details from what Julius told them about 'my case.' While we're talking, I overhear Rita explaining the "Symphony thing" to Roy, who didn't get it. After a while, Molly ushers us to the dining area, and we sit down. Julius and Rachel are hustling around in the kitchen and start putting food, beer, and wine on the table. Rachel also brings out a glass bottle of a milk-looking beverage that she pours for Rita and Roy. She also pours a glass for me. "This is for you to try, Symphony," says Julius, looking in from the kitchen. I assume this is the kefir Julius mentioned earlier.

"This is excellent," I say. Kefir is a fermented milk product, and I've had it several times before. In fact, I often have goat kefir with my breakfast cereals, but nothing that lives up to this. It's a very pleasant combination of creamy, sour, and sweet.

"So, I take it this is from your goat farm?"

"Yes, we have a small goat milk kefir operation in the countryside towards Streatley, just twenty kilometers north of here," Rachel explains.

"At home, I have goat kefir several times a week, but I guess that's not made the same way?"

"No, I don't think kefir made with kefir grains is commercially available in the U.S. Here in the U.K., we only know of one other company that makes kefir with kefir grains, and that's the Chuckling Goat."

"Milk kefir grains," Rufus explains. "Are a kind of *scoby*, which stands for symbiotic cultures of bacteria and yeast, held together by a matrix of proteins and polysaccharides to form gelatinous grain-like knobby structures that look a little like mini-cauliflower florets." I know this already, but I don't interrupt him. It's quite an interesting story. He continues to mention that kefir is an ancient fermented milk drink and that the microbiome (the microbial composition) of the kefir grains vary depending on where they come from, what kind of milk, what temperature they grow in, and how they're stored.

Julius and Molly have made a Sheppard's Pie that we eat with boiled carrots and sweet peas. It's all very good. The pie is made with minced lamb meat, which I would normally not eat, but when in Rome… By the way, I should let you know that I've made vegetarian Sheppard's Pie quite a few times. I don't mention that to Julius or Molly.

All of us adults opt for beer; we're drinking a robust local ale—a stout, to be precise—that pairs excellently with the pie. The discussion moves organically between a variety of topics. I talk some more about myself and Julie, our kids, our grandkids, and our jobs. Julius and Molly are part of a combined whist-playing and book club group. They meet weekly, and Molly describes how they decide on the different places to meet; they often reserve a space at a pub or other eatery. "So we can feed the intellect and the body at the same time," Julius comments.

Of course, beer is involved. "Usually after the whist game," says Molly.

I learned that Rachel is a freelance writer for several environmental-oriented magazines and that Rufus has his own tax attorney firm.

"My firm specializes in representing clients in various tax controversy matters before the HMRC—something like the IRS in the U.S.," Rufus explains. They can both do a lot of their work from home. However, their kefir production is growing, and they find themselves devoting more and more time to the farm. Rita and Roy talk about their rugby teams and how they often help out on the farm. They have named all the goats—or at least thirty-two of them—based on their personalities, and we get a kick out of hearing Rita explain some of the names; Lay-Z-Boy, *"Because he's always the last one to come when we round them up,"* and Throughput, *"Because she eats and poops at the same time."*

Rachel and Rufus have brought a goat kefir cheesecake for dessert. I'm somewhat of a cheesecake connoisseur; I grade cheesecakes I eat on a scale from 1 (low) to 10 (high), where 10 is an asymptote. The best cheesecakes I've ever had are the ones Jessica makes. They are classic New York style. My top pick is one with a twist of jalapeno; it has secured a 9.6 score on my cheesecake scale. —Why not 10? you may ask. Well, what would I do, then, if I tasted one that was even better? That's why 10 is an asymptote. You see, I got all this figured out. I go back and forth in my mind about the kefir cheesecake but eventually land on 7.5. That's a pretty good score in my book.

While we're eating and chatting, I'm looking out over the backyard. It's roughly the same size as the front yard, maybe a quarter of an acre, and is also surrounded by a boxwood hedge. I see Prince Charles strolling around, sniffing here and there. There are two apple trees and a big red current bush loaded with red berries. My eyes come to rest on a red porta potty in a far-end corner of the lot. Julius follows my gaze.

"Ah, that's my hog!" he exclaims, and everyone is smiling knowingly except me. Molly looks at me.

"I'm not sure how I can be delicate about this," she says. "But, as you can see, Jollipolli here is a big man. When he goes about his business on the toilet in our bathroom, he unloads more than the plumbing system can handle."

"I got sick and tired of having to spend hours with the plunger and often have a plumber come out," Julius says. "So, I decided to build an outhouse, but I haven't gotten to it yet. In the meantime, I use the porta potty." I smiled. The more I learn about Julius, the more voluminous he seems, and the more I like him. "It's a dry flush system," he adds, "So there's no smell or mess."

I look at Rufus and Rachel. "So, Julius told me that Derek—the guy I'm trying to track down—visited the apple orchard next to your farm. Do you have any intel about what he was doing there and whom he was talking to?"

"Yes, he was over there one year, five times, and always on Thursdays," Rachel says. "The apple orchard, Winston's Farms, is known for organic farming, and it's open for visitors on Thursdays. The first time he went to Winston's, he came by our farm for directions. We told him to come over for lunch afterward. Which he did, and that became routine; he spent from nine to eleven a.m. at Winston's and then came over to us for lunch. Then he went back home."

Rufus nods. "He was always very nice. He didn't say much, and most of what he did say was condensed. But, as I said, very nice. Sometimes, you could tell that he'd had a drink or two. But he was never brusque or incoherent."

"I'm not sure who all he talked to at Winston's," says Rachel. "But I know that he had some discussions with the owner, Hugh Winston, at least once."

"Hey!" says Rachel. "Since you seem to be interested in kefir production and curious about Winston's, why don't you come for a visit? What are your plans for tomorrow?"

"Nothing special. I need to do some work. I was going to go for a run and maybe combine that with some sightseeing in Reading." I had marked out a running path yesterday morning that went by the Ruins of Reading Abbey. "But the running can wait. I would like to come. What time would work for you?"

"How about around ten? And then we can invite you for lunch, and we'll invite Hugh as well," says Rufus. "If he, for some reason, can't make it, I'll let you know, and we can reschedule."

"Okay, thanks. That sounds great!"

"You'll get some sightseeing on the road," Molly says. "You'll drive through a beautiful area of rural Berkshire, and it's just forty minutes away from here, maybe a little longer from your hotel."

Rufus gets my phone number and texts me directions. "By the way," he says. "How does it feel to drive on the 'wrong' side of the road?"

"I'm coping," I say. "And I'm getting better. My major challenge is your roundabouts." I recount my cerebral moment at Hatton Cross that led to the follow-the-leader strategy. This brings out another explosive laughter from Julius. The others are laughing as well, but it's drowned out by Julius' outburst. I can see from Rita and Roy that Julius' eruptive nature is all too familiar to them; they don't bat an eye. I think it's like living close to an active volcano—you get used to it.

It's after eight p.m., and I'm anxious to leave before sunset. I don't see that well at night, so I don't like driving in the dark, let alone in unfamiliar territory, not to mention on the left side of the road. Rufus and Rachel are also ready to leave. While we're carrying dishes to the kitchen, Molly summons me over to one of the counters.

"I used our library accounts to log in to the GRO and NACM databases—NACM is the cider makers association—as well as some other portals. I compiled pdf files and sent them to your email address, and I have printouts here." She leafs through the papers and points. "Here's the marriage certificate and Derek's birth certificate." I Look at the copies of the documents. Paul, Philip Tyne-Gallaghan married Mary Florence Freeman on June second, 1938, and Derek Philip Tyne-Gallaghan, their only child, was born on November fifth, 1941.

"In public databases, there are eighty-one Derek Freeman and sixty-eight Philip Freeman in England and Wales," says Molly. "Not all of them have the age listed, but those who do are all too young to be a fit. So, we're down to one hundred fifteen potential Freemans." She has highlighted those in yellow. "In checking through NACM, which has four hundred eighty-six registered cider makers in the U.K., there seems to be sixty-four that started up production after 1988, although this information is not straightforward to extract. I find no Freemen or Tyne-Gallaghans associated with any cideries. Of course, Derek might still be the owner, but list someone else as the front person."

"Also," Molly continues. "I looked some more into the legal process of changing your name in the U.K. As Julius mentioned this morning, it's not too complicated. It's done through what is called the Deed Poll Service. And—and I think this is important—in the U.K., birth certificates are considered historical documents, and, at least in England and Wales, there are only a few instances when they can be changed, such as gender dysphoria or changing a child's first name, none of which would apply to your Derek."

"And I guess these Deed Poll Service documents are not public," I say.

Molly shakes her head. "No, unless, for some reason, you want it to be known, which I surmise would not be the case for Derek here." That is a fair assumption, I think.

"So, what happens then if someone with a name change needs to show a birth certificate for official documents like passports?" I ask.

"Yes, then you show both the birth certificates and the Deed Poll document, which overrides the birth certificate," Molly says.

"Thank you so much, Molly!" I say. "This is great and very helpful." I sound more upbeat than I am. The information I received from Molly is valuable. However, that's only the case if Derek did indeed change his name to Freeman, which is pure speculation on our part. He may have changed his name to something completely different. Or, he may not have changed his name at all, just totally gotten off the grid. Or, he may have moved to Ireland—or Scotland, or Albania, or Lithuania. He may be back in the U.S., but I guess we checked that. Anyhow, I'm now armed with some information that merits a follow-up investigation.

I say goodbye to Julius and Molly, and I suddenly get melancholic. I feel that we have, in a very short time, become good friends; it's like I've been included in a very warm and loving family. And I sense that the feeling is mutual. I say, see you tomorrow to Rufus and Rachel and their kids. I wave to Julius and Molly, and I jump in the car. Well... you know, I don't really *jump*; I merely sit down in the car.

CHAPTER 9

Summer 2024. The R Farm. Goats and apples. A possible lead.

It's Thursday morning. Rufus had texted me last night to confirm the visit to their farm. I decide to go for a run after all. It gets light at around five-thirty a.m., so I head out a little before six. I run the loop I laid out with Google Maps the other day, and that takes me by the ruins of Reading Abbey and Forbury Gardens Park. I stop by the Abbey and poke around. I step into what used to be the Chapter House. I've read up on the Abbey, and I know it was founded in 1121 by Henry I and was dissolved and destroyed, together with most monasteries in Britain and Ireland, in 1538 by Henry VIII during the Protestant Reformation. Apparently, the last abbot at Reading Abbey met a horrible fate during this process: he was hanged and chopped up into four portions. I wish I had never assimilated that latter piece of information because I now have a gruesome image of the former abbot in my head as I run toward The Forbury Gardens. In the park, I stop and stretch for a while and clear my head.

————

I'm at the breakfast lounge. If you knew that there most likely were freshly baked scones hidden in a basket by the piano, would you go and grab some? That's what I thought! I do the same. I make my way toward the piano, look around casually and bend down as if looking closely at the piano—Yamaha, by the way— and scoop up two raspberry scones.

I put the scones under my napkin and dig in on the oatmeal with oat milk. As I eat, I look through the pdf files Molly sent me. The one hundred fifteen potential Freemans are located all over Great Britain. Hm… this will be a lot of travel with a poor prospect of finding anything useful. I need to apply some more filters, like previous addresses, jobs, photos, or other members in the household, to see if I can eliminate one or more of the Freemans. I hesitate to bother Molly, but I do it anyhow. She will have a better chance of finding additional information through her library affiliation than either I or my folks back home will have. So, I text her and explain. I wish I could consult Rachel Walling—the FBI Special Agent and profiler from Michael Connelly's Harry Bosch series—but even without her, I'm inclined to dismiss all Philip Freemans. Why? Well, if I were Derek and I decided to change my last name to avoid being tracked down, I would still keep my first name as Derek since that's what I'm used to being called, and it's common enough so as not to be a giveaway. *What do you think, Special Agent Walling?*

I'm on my second raspberry scone while I ponder life a bit. I decide it's good—life, I mean. Well, the scone, too, for that matter. It's delicious—much better than the blueberry scone I had yesterday. I start up my laptop and open my emails.

I triage and work through some of the emails. I wish Julie were here. She would tell me not to go and grab a third raspberry scone; I would get too full, and then I would complain afterward. But she's not, so… It's black, by the way, the piano, and it has three pedals. There's an email from the church. I forgot that I am supposed to be part of a bible study (Luke's Gospel) on Saturday morning. I doubt I'll be back by then, so I let them know I'm traveling and won't make it. Speaking of Julie, I got a text from her when I got back last night. All is good back home, except they're experiencing day temperatures of up to forty-five degrees, which seems to be getting normal for the Tri-Cities area in July. I like warm weather—my optimal temperature window is the mid-twenties, which is a little warmer than I get here in England, but I don't complain. Jupiter has been asking where I am, and she's looking for me from her vantage point on the upper floor. Julie keeps telling her I'll be back in a week, which for Jupiter doesn't mean much; I could be gone for an hour or a decade, and she'll be just as happy when I return. I miss them both. Even Jupiter's vulgar attitude.

I'm still munching on my third raspberry scone while I'm looking at the website for Rufus' and Rachel's goat farm. THE R FARM it says in green letters—I told you there's a pattern! The website is rich in information. You can read about the history and many benefits of kefir. They have lists of the microbiome analyses of the kefir grains, and the kefir itself carried out at the University of Reading. There's also a comparison between bovine (from cows) and caprine (from goats) milk. For example, did you know that beta-casein, which is the major protein in milk, exists in several genetic variants in cows, the major ones being A1 and A2? A2 is considered the original version; A1 arose through a mutation several thousand years ago. Bovine milk allergy in humans is caused by the digestion of the A1 beta-casein protein; the A2 variant is easier to digest than A1. The A2 variant in cow's milk protein is more comparable to human breast milk, as is milk from goats, sheep, and buffalo. That's why people with milk protein allergy can tolerate goat's milk.

I also learned about how practices at the R Farm—a small-scale operation—differ from mainstream goat farms and kefir producers through their Animal Welfare Program. They have a herd of British Saanen goats, forty of which are used for milk production. The goats roam free, and the does are not inseminated but get pregnant on their own accord. Also, the kids are not separated from the does but share milk with the farm, where milking is done by hand. Because of this, the volume of milk produced at the farm is low. Although, it's not as low as one would think because the increased demand for milk stimulates lactation in the does. The forty does, and their kids are held separately from the rest of the herd.

Another aspect of the farm's Animal Welfare Program is that the goats are not slaughtered. Goats who die of old age or occasionally have been euthanized because of disease are sent to a tannery for the production of Moroccan leather. A large fraction of grownup kids is sold. I'm impressed by what I read. However, I also think that since the farm is only six years old, the sustainability of the entire operation has not yet been fully tested. I also wonder what happens to the goats that are being sold. Are they equally well treated?

So, why am I telling you all this? Well, I think it's interesting. And I warned you; I'm a wanderer when it comes to storytelling. So, bear with me here. *But,* I might as well tell you right away; the visit to the R Farm was instrumental in my success in locating Derek Tyne-Callaghan. Yes, I *did* finally find him. I thought you might be happy to know that.

It's time to get moving and prepare for my visit to the R farm. I looked at the instructions I received and laid out the trip on Google Maps—only two roundabouts. As I go by the piano on my way out of the restaurant, I think to myself—should I feel bad that there are three fewer raspberry scones for the prospective real estate buyers today? Really, should I? Well … you know, probably. But do I? Nah!

———

Molly was right. The drive through rural Berkshire County is beautiful; I would say pastoral. The route follows the Thames and takes me through wood pastures, meadows, and occasional parkland. The riverbanks are spotted with small villages. I get the same feeling I've had before when driving outside of London with Jessica and Lars; like I'm James Herriot in *All Creatures Great and Small*. The English landscape is so… *English*!

The drive is smooth. I put on a condescending smile when I fluidly navigate the roundabouts. After a fifty-minute drive, I enter a valley and see a by-road with a ranch-style signpost saying WELCOME TO THE R FARM in big green letters. I continue, and after half a mile, I find myself flanked by pastures, some with goats. Up front is the farmhouse, a rather big building in red and white brick. The farmyard contains several buildings as well as shelters and pens for the goats. I see more pastures with goats in the distance. The end of the road gives way to a surprisingly expansive parking area with white parking lines. I park and am greeted by a beautiful Border Collie. I can tell by just looking at the soft brown eyes that it's a female. As I get out of the car, she asks me what business I have coming here. I tell her that I'm visiting Rufus and Rachel. She licks my hand and lets me know that it's okay; I can move on.

"Thank you, Regina, Rosebud, Ruth… Rebecka?" I say. I walk up to the farmhouse, and I'm about to knock on the door when it opens, and Rachel comes out.

"Welcome, Symphony," she says, and we spontaneously hug.

"Thanks for inviting me." I hand over one more of my Washingtonian gifts: a jar of huckleberry jam. "It sure was a beautiful drive getting here," I told her I felt like James Herriot.

"Ha, ha, yes, Berkshire may not be Yorkshire, but there is something about the rolling landscape around here that we find soothing." She looks at the Collie. "I see you already met Sabina."

"Sabina, huh? I would have bet a year's salary that her name would start with an R!"

"Ha, ha, yes, it most likely would have if she hadn't been used to Sabina as a puppy. So, we decided to keep it."

"Sabina is our master goat herder. Aren't you Sabina?" she says and ruffles the dog's ears.

"Rufus will soon be out," she continues. "He's in a Zoom meeting for his consulting business. Rita and Roy are out camping with some friends."

When Rufus is off his meeting, he and Rachel show me around. I see the fermentation vessels in temperature-controlled rooms, the pasteurization and bottling pipeline, and the testing rooms and other laboratories. I'm impressed by the cleanliness and neatness of the operation, and I tell them so. When we're back outside, I'm surprised to see a bus parked not far from my car and a group of mostly children and a few adults listening to one of the several farm staff I've seen before while she leads them to one of the goat pens. I look at Rachel and Rufus.

"Ah, yes. I forgot to mention," Rachel says. "Just like Winston's, we often have organized visits to the farm, mostly from schools and daycares. Even now, when school is out, we have at least one visit per week, usually Thursdays, which works best, logistically, since many people want to visit both the goat farm and the apple orchard."

I see that the group has stopped by the pen, where two does are being hand-milked. This seems so archaic to me like I'm back in the nineteenth century.

"So, I have to ask," I say, turning to Rufus and Rachel. "I read on your website about hand milking and how you share the milk with the calves. I mean, it's really impressive and laudable and everything. But how can you make this economically viable?"

"Yeah, that's what we asked ourselves when we started out six years ago," says Rachel and looks at Rufus. "We were doing fine with our other jobs. Well, actually, we were doing more than just fine, especially with Rufus' tax attorney business. At the time, I was working on a piece about precocious dairy animals for the Good Housekeeping journal, and that got me thinking about the dairy industry and, you know, how cows are forced to be pregnant all the time, and the calves are removed from their mothers. At the same time, Rufus had a Polish client who unwilfully had messed up disclosure of foreign bank accounts back home in tax returns going back several years. Rufus helped him get out of a huge penalty and straightened up his returns." She nods at Rufus to continue.

"Yes, so that client of mine, Szymon Kowalski, owned this sixty-acre parcel of land where our farm is. He was going to develop it into a golf course. But then he decided to move to the U.S. to join his brother-in-law's real estate firm in Miami. This was seven years ago, and by then, Rachel and I had gotten serious about setting up a small-scale alternative dairy production. So, one thing led to another, and we bought this land from Szymon for a very, very good price. We didn't want to have cows, so we decided on goats." Rufus throws his hands in the air. "And, voila! Here we are."

"But…" says Rachel. "You didn't ask about how we started; you wanted to know if it's profitable." She looks around. "You'd be amazed," she continues, "what impact our Animal Welfare Program has. Ever since we got a Defra certificate for humane and organic production—Defra is the U.K. Department for the Environment, Food, and Rural Affairs, like your USDA—three years ago, the demand for our kefir has been growing exponentially. Our biggest customers are schools and daycares, but we also sell to select restaurants and bakeries and to a lot of people who've heard about us on social media. For example, there's a blog, *'Goats and Oats'*, where there are a lot of features about the R Farm. Or simply by word of mouth. We now have a distribution network covering a large portion of Southeast England."

"And, of course," says Rufus. "For some people, the fact that we use milk kefir grains instead of starter cultures is an important part."

"Also," he continues, "while we focus on kefir, we sell milk to other dairies that make cheese and other products. The Saanen goat breed is high-yielding, so we get enough milk to spare."

"So, all in all, the farm is doing much better than we anticipated," says Rachel. "Actually, to the extent that Rufus is considering selling his practice to join a boutique tax controversy firm in London."

"There's another thing I wanted to ask," I say. Since you don't' slaughter any goats, it must mean that you end up with more and more goats—by the way, how long does a goat typically live?" I look at Rufus.

"Fifteen-plus years," he says.

"So, you must already have increased your herd size quite a bit, right?"

"Not a whole lot," says Rachel. So far, three have died, and they went to a tannery in Mortimer. Then, we sell goats not only to other goat farms but also to people who use goats for brush control, in livestock shows, for open-air museums and zoos, and as companions. I'm not saying it's status quo, but the herd expansion is slow. And we need more does anyhow since the demand for our milk and kefir is increasing."

We talk some more while we're milling around the farm. I get to meet some of the goats. Rachel points out Throughput. He does indeed eat and poop at the same time. But so do several other goats as well, I notice. "Oh, you should get a kick out of this," she says when a goat covered with black spots comes up to us. "It's Lilla Gubben," she says in Swedish pronunciation. "You know from *Pippi Longstocking*. Rita named this one." This sure brings back memories to me. I understand if the connection here is lost on most of you. If so, I recommend you read Astrid Lindgren's *Pippi Longstocking* books, at least the first one. Or *Pippi Långstrump* if it so happens that you're fortunate enough to know Swedish.

We're having lunch outside on their porch. When we get there, I see Hugh Winston. I know it's him because it's written on him; he wears a worn-out, white T-shirt with "HUGH WINSTON: NOT CUTE BUT STRONG" in blue capital letters on the front. Hugh is a tall guy in his upper fifties with dark hair and a mustache. He's lean and seems altogether to be an affable chap. We shake hands.

"I got this from our kids on my fiftieth," he says when I'm laughing at his shirt.

Rachel introduces us, and Hugh chuckles when she explains why I go by Symphony. We make small talk. Turns out Hugh has a Ph.D. in pomology from Reading. He started his farm sixteen years ago on a piece of land his parents owned, and that had been in fallow for the last fifty years, with no herbicide or pesticide applications. He took advantage of that and set up a certified organic apple orchard in 2008. He specializes in high-quality apples for eating. He never sells to fruit companies or supermarkets, only to select retailers and Farmers Markets, and for direct deliveries to various corporations, venues, schools, and households.

I ask him why he ditches supermarkets, seeing as they would comprise a large market share. Although, I think I know why.

"If you eat an apple from a supermarket, chances are you're biting into a fruit that's a year old. They want the apples when they're slightly unripe, treat them with a ripening regulator, 1-MCP, that's 1-methylcyclopropene, wax them, package them, stack them on pallets, and keep them in cold storage warehouses for an average of nine to twelve months. I'm very concerned about my reputation, so I'm picky as to whom I sell our apples. But, yes, I take a pay cut in the process. But not as much as you would think. Just like for Rufus and Rachel here, it's amazing these days how efficient marketing is over the internet. If someone is interested in finding high-quality, organic apples in the area, they'll find our farm, and some others, from blogs, social media, or various other web portals."

We chitchat some more while Rachel sets the table. She has made a soufflé from goat cheese and kefir. It's heavenly and delicious!

I eventually steer the conversation to the crux of this lunch meeting. I tell Hugh about my visit to the U.K., including visiting our daughter and her family, and about the bakery, Kringlan. I then describe my efforts in trying to find Derek Tyne-Callaghan and that I heard from Rufus and Rachel that he visited the Winstons on occasion.

"Thanks for taking the time," I tell him.

"Well, I take any excuse I can to have lunch with these folks," he says, glancing at Rachel and Rufus.

"I can certainly understand that. Now, I know that Derek was interested in starting a cider mill production. That would have been in the late 1980s, 1988, or later. We have looked, or rather, Rufus' mom has looked at the NACM, the cider makers association, for any possible leads. But nothing there points to

Derek setting up a business. So, I wonder if there's anything he told you or anyone else when he visited your farm that could provide any clues as to what he planned to do?"

Winston nods. "After Rufus called me yesterday, I asked around. We usually have a lot of visitors on Thursdays, at least from spring to fall, and we interact with many of them, so it's hard to remember any one specific. But your Derek was special; he came several times, but just in one year, 1987, I think," he looks at Rufus, who nods. "And I remember him from Rufus' description." He smiles sympathetically.

Hugh takes another bite of the soufflé before continuing. "He said he was interested in starting an organic apple farm for cider production, and he wanted to know how we took care of our apples throughout the year. I told him that, you know, our business is culinary apples—apples you eat—not the cider varieties. Cider apples are very tart; they have less sugar content, higher tannin levels, and lower acidity than culinary apples. So, our practices might not necessarily apply to his setup. He said that was fine; he wasn't planning on using 'true' cider apples anyhow. So, I gave him the rundown of our ritual, which is basically to tend to each individual tree on a regular basis, to keep it weeded, mulched, and pruned. And to be very cognizant of early infections and discard infected branches as soon as they appear. I gave him our protocols and told him he could come back any time to watch how we operate. He never did, though."

I thank Hugh, and we talk some more about organic and sustainable farming while we put dishes away and help bring out coffee (not tea) and a scrumptious gooseberry pie that Rachel has baked. It's slightly tart with a subtle sweetness that makes me think of a lemon orchard. Julie isn't around, so I take an extra big second slice.

CHAPTER 10

Summer 2024. The Checker girls from The Crown Caversham.

I'm planning my afternoon. I'm thinking of going back to the Crown Caversham for dinner. I'd like to try that Scottish egg dish Julius mentioned. Before then I have some work to do. In my absence from OMICS, I have four delegates for different parts of my duties. Laxmi Singh is my delegate for the Crassus-related issues. I have an email from her asking for advice. I'm in the middle of responding to her when I get an email from Molly. She has performed wonders! She's been roaming around in databases of local newspapers, event information, and other published data for all the different cities where the Freemans reside. She found pictures, including wedding anniversary photos, scoreboards from sports activities, political assignments, and job descriptions. Through this laudable effort, Molly has managed to discount all but four candidates, one Philip and three Derek Freemans. She also found home phone numbers plus mobile phone numbers for the Dereks. I'm thinking, I need to find a way to thank her.

I look at Google Maps to locate the addresses of the Freeman candidates. Philip Freeman lives all the way up in Carlisle; one of the three Derek Freeman lives outside Birmingham, one in Liverpool, and the third in Newport, Wales.

I do my best thinking with a cup of coffee and a scone, but even in their absence, I manage to devise a plan. I'll wait until after five p.m.

———

"Good afternoon. My name is Arthur Freeman. I'm from the U.S., and I'm here in the U.K. for a conference. And, while I'm here, I thought I should try to tie up one missing link in my family tree on Ancestry. On my father's side, there is a Derek Freeman in England that I cannot locate. He should be around eighty years old by now. So, I'm now calling all the Derek Freemans I can find in the U.K. on the off chance I might get a hit."

"Oh, sorry, old chap. I do feel old, but I'm still in my fifties."

"Okay, thanks. Sorry to bother you."

"No problem, man. Good luck with your search."

"Thank you."

See there! A well-executed plan, and I can now eliminate Derek Freeman from Wales. Birmingham Derek answers neither a home phone nor a mobile phone. But I can wipe out Liverpool Derek from the list because the clear voice of a little girl declared, *"Daddy is not home; he's playing at the soccer game today. Do you want to talk to Mommy?"* I didn't.

As I suggested to Special Agent Walling before, I was inclined to dismiss Philip Freeman. But now, when we're down to only four suspects, I'm thinking—why not? So, I call him up. His wife answers and tells me that Philip is at the hospital, not as a patient, as it turns out, but as a cardiothoracic surgeon.

I'm about to leave for dinner when Birmingham Derek calls me back on his mobile phone. "I see you tried to call me; what's this about?"

From his voice, I can tell that this guy is most likely in his early to mid-forties, which he confirms when I do my spiel.

Time for some advanced inferential statistics. The probability that our eighty-one-year-old Derek Tyne-Callaghan is an active soccer player or a practicing heart surgeon is low to non-existent.

The probability that he is now in his forties or fifties approaches zero. So it seems like I'm back at square one.

———

Have you ever had Scottish eggs? I'm eating one now. It's a deep-fried, hardboiled egg in a ring of sausage, covered with breadcrumbs, and served cold. I like it. It pairs well with the Black Dog I'm drinking, a savory dark ale with notes of chocolate and toffee. I have beans and a salad on the side. While eating and drinking, I'm ruminating over my path forward to finding Derek. My remaining lead is the cider angle. Apparently, Derek was interested in setting up an organic cider production outfit. I need some more inroads to that path. I will need to bother Molly once more. I text her asking if there's anything else Derek told them that could be of potential value. I also ask her to tell Julius I'm eating the Scottish egg. Molly responds almost immediately. She will let me know. She also sends a thumb-up from Julius.

I'm looking at the chessboard. It's back where I put it the day before yesterday, and it seems to have the same arrangement as when I left it. I'm tempted to fetch it and do some more strategizing. I have a chessboard in my luggage that I could put up in my hotel room at any time. However, there's something very appealing about musing over chess moves in the cozy pub atmosphere. I probably won't hear back from Bryce until Saturday at the earliest, so there's really no rush. Also, if I should do any strategizing, I ought to focus on finding the elusive Derek Tyne-Callaghan, not playing chess.

Well… I make room for the chessboard on my table. I pretend to be Bryce and move his black queen to take my bishop. I'm taking stock of my situation on the battlefield when two young women on their way out stop and look at the chessboard. I look up. They seem to be in their mid-twenties. One of them, the taller of the two, with both arms covered in black tattoos and with thick, beautiful red hair, looks at me with a serious expression on her face. She turns to her friend. "What do you think, Sophie? If I were white, I would be concerned, *very* concerned."

Sophie, also tattooed but with short blonde hair, nods in agreement. "Mister," she says. "There's only one way you can avoid being checkmate in three moves, and that is to sacrifice your remaining bishop to block black's queen. That way, you open up a space for your king to avoid getting in check."

I'm not sure if they're just pulling a prank on me or if they really know what they're talking about. Red Hair sees my confusion. "Let me show you." She bends over and slowly moves the pieces around on the board. My ORs (olfactory receptors, remember?) perceive a faint scent of flowery perfume. "This is what happens if you don't block black's queen. See, it doesn't matter what you do; black will have you checkmate before you can say 'Jack Robinson'."

"Of course, depends on how good your opponent is," says Sophie

"It's a friend back home in the U.S.," I explain. "We're about even, so since I didn't see this coming, he might not either. It's his turn, and I think he will move his queen to take my bishop." I point to the bishop on the table.

I feel funny sitting while they're standing, so I stand up to shake their hands and present myself. They both laugh when they see how tall I am.

"Wow, mister, you're a tall guy," Red Hair says.

Red Hair is Margie. Turns out they're both members of the University of Reading's chess club, the "Checkers." We keep talking chess for a while. I then mention, without much detail, my search for Derek Tyne-Callaghan, which they find amusing. I look at them while they're leaving; they look so young and vibrant. I'm thinking of our own kids who are now already in their mid-thirties with their own families. I suddenly feel old. But most of all, I feel conflicted in my chess game; should I or should I not follow Margie and Sophie's advice? I'm thinking, I need to clear my head. I'm thinking a dessert might do the trick. I look at a sign hanging over the bar disk. It says *Something Sweet,* and below is a list with *Sticky Toffee Pudding, Dark Chocolate Brownie, Bramley Apple and Rhubarb Crumble, Orange and Lemon Posset, Selection of Ice Creams, and Sorbets.* I don't know what a posset is, but I'm confident that the crumble would be a good companion to the beer I have left. And it is; the sweet and puckery taste of the crumble pairs nicely with dark beer, just like dark chocolate with red chili pairs well with red wine — in my opinion, anyhow. I start to feel better. I think about life. I decide it's good — and that getting old is better than the alternative. As for my chess conundrum, I remain undecided. Bryce and I have a deal not to be influenced by external sources. But it's not as if I solicited the advice; it just landed in my lap. Well, I'll have to wait and see what Bryce does; he might not take my bishop after all.

———

Back at the hotel, I text Julie, and we schedule a FaceTime meeting during her lunch hour. I've just sat down to watch BBC on the TV when I get a phone call from Julius.

"Hi mate, is this a good time?" he asks.

"Absolutely," I say. "How are you guys doing?"

"Wicked! How did you like the Scottish egg?"

"I liked it a lot. It complimented the Black Dog I had."

"There you go! Well, I chatted with Rufus last night, and he filled me in on your meeting with Winston. And, related to that,

Molly and I have been scratching our heads, and there's one thing Molly remembers that Derek told her when he mentioned his desire to set up a cider production. After his fresher year at the Uni, Derek took some time off to help out at his parents' cider mill when his dad was hospitalized. Derek told Molly that he tried to persuade his folks to start growing old-fashioned heirloom apple varieties for their cider production instead of mainstream cooking apples, like Bramley and Grenadier. But his dad was not interested, saying that heirloom apples would be too low-yielding and that it would take several years for the trees to mature. So, Molly got the understanding that Derek was keen on setting up an artisan cider production with truly old English apple varieties. She thinks he also said something about organic farming."

"That's great information, Julius."

"Yeah, at least it's a thread to pull. Molly remembers that Derek borrowed several books on English heirloom apples. — And now, when I think about it, I recall that he often went to the National Fruit Collection Department. You see, The University of Reading is responsible for the curation and maintenance of the National Fruit Collection. This is a longstanding collaboration with the Brogdale Farm, a couple of hours east of here, close to Canterbury, and Derek went there quite often during his latter months here."

————

After the phone conversation with Julius, I Facetime Julie. Everything is okay back home. It's still hot, though. I tell Julie about my escapades. I tell her that my search for Derek is now focused on finding a small organic cider mill specializing in old English apple varieties. I also tell her that visiting Rufus' and Rachel's goat farm has given me an idea as to how to proceed. I ask how Jupiter is doing. Julie says, "Well, you know, as soon as she gets home, she gets up to her vantage point and sits there looking for you." I feel a twang in my heart. I miss her invectives.

CHAPTER 11

*Summer 2024. The Brogdale Farm. Heritage apples.
Another lead.*

The serial number is 2110505. —On the piano. It's printed in the lower right corner. And it's vanilla cream in the hidden scones today.

I'm having my usual breakfast. I was planning to go for a run first, but it's raining, so I decided not to. I go through some emails on my laptop. I'm waiting to see if Noa has some more news about the Crex-ORs, but there's nothing yet. I respond to emails from Laxmi and Hanne. Then I sit back with my coffee and think about life. It's good, I decide. Julie still isn't here, so I'm munching on my third vanilla-cream scone while formulating a new strategy for my "Find Derek" quest.

———

"This is McKenzie Blains."

I've been on the phone for over thirty minutes with Brogdale Farm. They've been trying to find someone working there in the mid to late 1980s who might remember talking to Derek Tyne-Callaghan. They finally came up with Dr. McKenzie Blains, who was the Head Tutor at the farm at that time. She's long retired but still lives on the premises in one of the staffing accommodations. I reach her on her cell phone.

"Good morning. I got your name from Susannah Kinsley at Brogdale Farm." I briefly explain my background as the Director of OMICS. "I'm trying to find information about a distant colleague of ours, who, as I understand, visited the Brogdale Farm quite often in 1988. He was interested in heirloom apple verities for potential cider production. I wonder if this rings a bell at all?"

"Now, young man," (*Well, thank you!*) "most people who visit the farm ask about our heirloom apples, so that by itself is a poor selection criterium. Apples are part of the English heritage, as you may know, and there's a lot of interest about old varieties not only from horticulturists, pomologists, and apple farmers but also from historians and environmental scientists."

"Yes, I understand. This is a shot in the dark, but I want to try. His name was Derek Tyne-Callaghan. And, if it might be of some help, he might have come across as… what should I say, disheveled. He might even have smelled from alcohol."

"And he was a colleague of yours?"

"Well, not really. He was a scientist, and he claims to have made some predictions that might explain research results that we have obtained. We don't know what these predictions are, and I want to find him and ask about that. We have not been able to find any Derek Tyne-Callaghan in phone directories or any databases in the U.K., or anywhere for that matter."

"Well, he may have died. People do that, you know."

"Yes, I've heard about that scenario. And that could very well be, although we haven't found any indications of that in databases either. So, I'm gambling on the assumption that he's alive."

"Well, I can use some excitement. At eighty-eight years old, not much of that comes around anymore. Tell you what, young man, I'll go to the farm and peek through old archives to see if he might have ordered some cuttings. What was his name again — or can you text me his name? And text me your phone number as well. I'll call you back later."

I thank McKenzie Blains. I text her my phone number and Derek's name. I have a copy of the photo I got from Julius McIntosh on my phone, and I also sent that to her.

I bring my laptop and walk out on the balcony. It's covered, and the temperature is in the mid-twenties, so it's quite nice despite the rain. The Thames looks like it is boiling from the heavy raindrops splashing down. I work for an hour. Lastly, I check the recording of the Zoom meeting I missed last Tuesday to see if there's anything I feel I need to act on. There isn't and I'm about to head down to the hotel restaurant for lunch when my phone rings. It's McKenzie.

"You're in luck, young man!" is how she starts out. 'I found our man in the records. On October fifteenth, 1988, he ordered twelve cuttings for one very particular apple variety, the Flower of Kent, with origin certifications. He then came back in 1990 and ordered twelve more. Have you heard of the Flower of Kent?" I said I had not. "Well then," she continued, "the tree that Sir Isaac Newton sat under when one of its apples fell to the ground, and which led him to discover gravity—well, I guess he didn't *discover* gravity, but that led him to explain several concepts of gravity—was a Flower of Kent apple tree. That very same apple tree, planted sometime around 1620, is still alive today. It fell over in 1820 but rooted successfully, so the tree is still there today. This is in Woolsthorpe Manor in Lincolnshire, where Newton was born. The orchard at Woolsthorpe Manor is the custodian of the tree. Cuttings from Newton's apple tree are available at some orchards, and this is what your colleague, or acquaintance, or whatever he was, wanted."

"Thank you, McKenzie; this is both very interesting and helpful. How did he transport twelve cuttings, or did he have them delivered?"

"These were small cutting, just two to three decimeters tall, so I assume he could just put them in his car. But I'm not sure about this. And before I forget, he also wanted to order the Decio apple variety. It's a very primitive apple compared to modern varieties, but its appeal—and that's what seemed to interest your friend the most—lies in its history. You see, it emanates from Roman times. We couldn't provide him with Decio varieties having the certificate of origin he requested, so we suggested he contact various orchards. I don't know what came out of that."

After I finished talking to McKenzie, I realized I should have told her that Washington State, where I live, is also famous for its apples. Over sixty percent of all apples sold in the U.S. come from Washington, and apples are Washington's most important agricultural product. I'm contemplating calling her back and letting her know but I decide not to. I don't want to dilute her pride in seeing the English countryside as the proverbial center of pomology. Besides, I have other things to do. First off, I need to finetune my game plan from this morning. Then I need to set it in motion.

———

It stopped raining, so I ventured out in pursuit of an eatery. It's only ten a.m., but I'm hungry. I walk over the bridge again, which I now know is called the Caversham Bridge. I see a sign, GRIFFIN, that seems to indicate a pub. Yep, it is. It's crowded, but I get a table right away. I start with Feta Open Flatbread, followed by Mushroom and Ale Pie. It's too early for beer, so I have just one pint. Excellent lunch!

The steel-grey clouds have given way to a sunny sky when I get back outside. I walk for an hour, pass the hotel, and into the Abbey and Forbury Gardens Park while mulling over my new strategy for catching Derek. Back at the hotel, I work for most of the afternoon. At four p.m., I FaceTime Julie before she heads to work. Then I text Jessica and ask if this was a good time to talk. She calls me a few minutes later.

"Hej gumman," I say. I tell her what I've found out so far about Derek. I then tie this in with my visit to the R Farm and how important social media and blogs are in spreading the word about their goat kefir business and their neighbor's organic apples. I explain that this has inspired me to use the same tools in finding Derek. I asked her if she thinks Kristina and Linnea would be interested in helping out by searching through their favorite social media space for anything and anyone that might be relevant, using specific keywords that I will send her. I let her know those keywords, for now, are *cider, heritage apples, heirloom apples, Decio, Flower of Kent, Newton,* and *organic.* I tell her that as a reward, I will treat Kristina and Linnea to whatever size and flavor they want of Udderdelicious ice cream. Jessica says she's sure the girls will be delighted to help regardless of the reward but that the ice cream certainly will be appreciated. However, the size of the ice cream will be supervised by their responsible parents. She says she and Lars will also be searching through their portals.

That I'm enlisting my young granddaughters is not only because I think they can help, which I think they can, but also because I'm such a good mentor—you know that by now, right? I think they will experience a sense of fulfillment by helping their grandpa, whom they think (correctly, I might add) is a hotshot scientist, in his work. I'm sending an email to Hanne telling her to put a crew together and do the same search from their end. They're allowed to ask their children for help.

I will also ask Molly to once again employ her library connections and use the same keywords in searching through newspaper articles. I'm hesitant to bother Molly again, considering how much she has already done for me, but I will do it anyhow. "All's fair in love and war," isn't that how the saying goes? Of course, this is neither, but... anyhow. Molly, as I expected, is game and says she's happy to assist. Again, I think I must come up with a way to thank her later.

Having sent my spies out prowling cyberspace and thinking I have cast a wide enough net with different age groups and across two continents, I lean back and realize I'm hungry.

————

I'm dining in the hotel tonight at the Riverside Restaurant and Bar. I have experienced the pub atmosphere a few times now and opted for a more elegant establishment. I have a table overlooking the River Thames. I'm sipping on a glass of Italian Primitivo. I usually consider Syrah my favorite grape, especially when it renders the wine a butterscotch-ish finish. However, I have more and more come to appreciate the spice aromas of a good Zinfandel, and this Primitivo from Puglia is an excellent example.

The Chateau Briand with garlic butter and browned mashed potatoes looks delectable. I'm looking at it as the waiter puts it down on a table not far from mine. I could have that. I'm a preferred vegan, but, as you must have noticed, depending on the occasion, I appreciate most kinds of food. I could have the Chateau Briand. I won't, though. Instead, I settle for South Indian Curry Cauliflower with added scallops, a side of Confit Tomato, and rustic bread that I dip in olive oil and enjoy with the Zin. Sort of like Communion. Speaking of which, I'll have you know that due to my well-known sourdough-baking credentials, the Church Council last year asked me if I could provide my Finnish one-hundred-percent rye bread for Communion, which I did. Right after that introduction, church attendance increased eightfold.

No, it didn't, but the bread is highly appreciated. I haven't been asked to suggest a wine pairing, but if I am, I'll go for a medium-bodied Zinfandel.

I make space for my laptop and, just for fun, make a simple Google search with Cider and Newton. I get several hits, one for cider in Russia of all places, but none seem useful for my purpose. I have my troops out raiding the internet, so I'll wait until I hear from them.

Without Julie here, I'm on the loose as far as restraints go. So… I will have dessert, Toffee and Honeycomb Cheesecake, although I probably shouldn't. I'll even add a glass of port. The cheesecake is very good, a solid 7.35. It would have been an eight if only the foundation had been made of graham crackers and served with raspberries. As I'm thinking about this and cheesecakes in general, I conclude that it's been a good day. So, I'm quite content when I go to bed and continue reading a David Rosenfelt book.

CHAPTER 12

Summer 2024. The blog. The lead gets warm. Ashton under the Hill. Gilbert O'Sullivan.

It's Saturday, so there were no piano scones for me with the morning coffee at today's breakfast. The real estate pitch ended yesterday. But life goes on. In this case, with blueberry scones from the counter, which I was glad to find out tasted better than they did the other day. I've been working on the balcony. Every now and then, I take a pause and listen to the ducks talking politics again. I'm just about to get up and stretch my legs when Linnea calls me.

"Hej morfar," she says. I usually speak Swedish with our kids and grandkids. Julie, who was born and raised in the U.S. but lived with me in Sweden for twenty years, most often communicates with them in English. At home, Kristina and Linnea typically speak Swedish with Jessica and English with Lars.

Anyhow, Linnea is calling to ask me if she and Kristina can invite their friends to participate in the "Finding-Derek" project and—most importantly—if the ice cream reward applies to them as well. Sure! Everyone under the age of twenty who helps out on the project is eligible for the Udderdelicious treat.

I have a delightful pasta with smoked salmon for lunch at Quattro on Prospect Street, not far from the hotel. I see on the beer list that they have Beck's Blue, a close-to-zero-alcohol pilsner-style beer, which I choose and find to be a refreshing compliment to the pasta. I scan the street outside the window, busy with humanity taking gulps of the lovely summer weather. I study pedestrians walking by, going about their early weekend lives. I think about my own life. I decide it's good. I'm also thinking about whether I should stay here in Reading or drive back to London and stay with Jessica and Lars. If Derek has indeed set up a heritage cidery somewhere in the U.K., I have no idea where that might be. I need to go back to Jessica and Lars' restaurant anyhow to pick up some baked goods for Julius and Molly as a token of my appreciation for all their help. I know from chatting with Rufus on the R Farm that his mom is partial to cakes. I've decided to ask Kringlan to make a Swedish Princess Cake that I will take along together with a package of sourdough crackers. By the end of the lunch, I'd made up my mind. I'll leave tomorrow morning.

———

Except I won't!

Last night, while having dinner at the hotel—Greek salad (good but not remarkable), sourdough bread dipped in garlic-infused olive oil (very good), and the House Zinfandel (excellent)—I got a call from Kristina. She was very excited. She said she and Linnea had found a potential lead. She texted me a link to a blog and directed me to the right posts.

This is what I'm studying now during breakfast. I started to look at it briefly last night, but because of a developing migraine, I decided to wait until the morning. What I look at is an excerpt from a post in a curated blog called *The Gardening England*.

Tue September 24th. *I'm new to this Blog, so apologies beforehand if my question is out of bounds. However, I'm wondering if any of you know where to get hold of the "Mother of Kent" apple cuttings. Especially, I'm looking for cuttings that can be traced to the very clone in Newton's Woolsthorpe Manor. —Dorothy L.*

—//—

Tue October 1st. Dear Dorothy. Welcome to the Blog (and your question fits very well with the wide array of gardening topics being discussed on this portal). I'm not sure this is helpful, but I remember our neighbor (who has since moved away) once mentioned a small cider mill somewhere in the West Midlands that proclaimed their cider was from authenticated English vintage apples. She—the neighbor—mentioned the Mother of Kent as well as the Pearmain and Decio varieties—Marjory S.

Wed October 2nd. Dear Dorothy and Marjory. Our daughter was on a school trip to Worcestershire last spring. She brought home a bottle of cider that she got at a farm shop in Ashton under the Hill. She doesn't remember the name of the shop. The cider was called "Gravity," and the label claimed that it was made from Flower of Kent apples originating from "Newton's Tree" in Woolsthorpe Manor, Lincolnshire. There was no mention of the name of the cidery other than "A certified Heritage Farm." BTW, it was a very good cider! Hope this might be useful—Steve A.

There are no more posts on that thread, at least not that I can find. However, this looks promising. It's not conclusive, but definitely promising. I google "Ashton under the Hill" and "cider" and get a few hits. None mentions "Gravity" or the Flower of Kent apples. I look on Google Maps and see that Ashton under the Hill should be less than two hours away on seemingly good roads. I finish off breakfast with coffee and two acceptable blueberry scones, pack and jump in the car. Well, you know…

———

Two hours and eight roundabouts later, I set foot in Ashton under the Hill, a quaint village situated on the slope of a prominent hill. I look for a street sign and find that I've parked the car on the

Beckford-Elmley Castle Road, which seems to be the main artery in town, running in a south-northerly direction. At least, I think I've parked on the road; the houses are built so close to the street I might actually be occupying someone's driveway.

It's in the middle of a Sunday, so there are plenty of people moving about. I start asking for the location of farm shops in the neighborhood and writing down names and directions on my phone. It's slow going, but after an hour, I have six candidates. They are fairly close, so I should be able to reach all of them today. But first I need to have lunch. I should also book a hotel for the night. I do a google search and decide on Beckford Inn in Tewkesbury, a couple of miles away. They have a restaurant, so I go there right away.

I sit in the terraced beer garden enjoying Cornish Stone Bass with supplements and a pint of Butcombe Brewery Summer Ale while studying a move from Bryce in the d4c4 app: *Ng5*. This is a completely unexpected move. I'll set up my traveling chessboard when I get to my room and try to figure out what he's up to. By the way, I got more farm shop names when I checked in, so I now have nine places to visit. However, I was also informed that the only farm shop open on Sundays is the Overbury Farms Estate. On the other hand, this farm is less than a ten-minute drive from the hotel.

Back in my room, I unpack the chessboard and arrange the pieces to reflect Bryce's last move. I study the board for a while, but I'm too anxious to get over to the Farm Shop and can't concentrate on the game. I get in the car and head off for the Overbury Estate, which takes me just seven minutes. On the way over, I go by a pub with a sign saying THE YEW TREE. It looks so inviting I decide to go there for dinner tonight. When I get to the Overbury Estate, I park in a designated visitor area and get out to look around. I see no obvious shop. I spot a girl, maybe six or seven years old, walking away from what I assume to be the Manor House, with a beautiful Samoyed by her side, a female from the look of her. "Hey," I call out to her. "Do you know where the Farm Shop is?"

"You can ask my dad," she says in her cute little voice and trails off. Dog in tow.

Well, that could have been useful information, I think, had I only known where her dad was. I walk up to what seems to be the main entrance of the Manor House. I knock on the door using a large brass door knocker in the shape of a fox. It takes a while, but eventually, a man opens the door. He looks at me and shakes his head. "Sorry, chap," he says, "the lamb sausages are all gone. The demand was so high we ran out already yesterday."

"Well, that's a good testament to your produce," I say—witty as ever. "However, I'm not in the business of sausages. I'm looking for someone who might be able to tell me about a cidermaker around here that makes a cider called Gravity. I'm staying at the Mulberry Cottage, and someone suggested I'd check at the Overbury Farms."

"Ah, sorry about that. By the way, I'm Jake Chapman." I shake his hand. "Ludvig Thovén," I reciprocate.

"Yes, Gravity. It's from the Heritage Farm over by Redmarley d'Abitôt." They also produce the Mediaeval and the Ancient. Excellent ciders, all three. You can get them at Farm Shops and Farmers Markets here in Worcestershire. Here as well, but the supply usually lasts only to mid-June. Then you'll have to wait until the next batch in the fall."

"Do you happen to know who runs the Heritage Farm cider mill?" I ask, starting to feel the excitement building up in me. "I'd like to talk to him about some of his apples."

"That would be John Smith. He's the proprietor of the Heritage Farm. But I'm not sure how much information you'll get out of him. He's a nice enough guy but kind of a recluse." Jake laughs and shakes his head. "He's over here regularly with his cider and jelly, but I don't think I've ever heard him articulate a full sentence; he mainly grunts and shrugs. To be honest, for a while there, I wasn't sure he even could talk. I understand his dog better than him. But, like I said, otherwise, a nice guy."

"Well, I can at least try," I say. "Do you know how to get to his place?"

"Can't say I do. My foreman, Gilbert O'Sullivan, will know." Jake noticed my raised eyebrows. Before I could ask, he added, "No, no relationship to the Irish singer, other than that Gilbert's mom was—or is, rather—a huge fan, and since she married an O'Sullivan, there was no question what name to give their first son. Gilbert has had to live with it, but he's handling it well. Anyhow, Gilbert's been down to the Heritage Farm a couple of times when John's truck needed some attention. He'll be back tomorrow morning. But, if you want to talk to him today, I'm sure you'll find him at the Yew Tree, it's a pub down the road—you must have passed it coming here—watching the cricket match between Lancashire and Somerset. He's from Bath and a staunch Somerset fan. So, depending on the outcome, he might be either approachable or dismissive." Jake smiles. "No, just kidding, he'll be happy to talk to you."

"Yes, I saw the Yew Tree on my way over here. It looked so inviting I decided to go there for dinner tonight."

"Well then, Gilbert will probably be there for at least the third and fourth innings, so you might be able to catch him for dinner." Jake smiles again. "Just don't ask him to sing!"

As I'm folding myself back into the car, I see the Samoyed trotting towards the house with the little girl. I wave at them, but the girl just looks at me. —Okay, Fine.

————

The Yew Tree is packed and noisy, with a warm and vibrant ambiance. Most of the patrons are keeping their eyes glued on the ongoing cricket match that is playing out on three big screens around the pub. I realize I forgot to get a description of Gilbert from Jake Chapman. I ask one of the bartenders if she knows if Gilbert O'Sullivan is around. From the lack of attempted puns, I deduce that Gilbert is a well-known guest.

"See the chap over there?" She points to a crowd by one of the screens. "The one with a back-flipped Nike cap, that's your guy."

I thank her and head over to the crowd. Gilbert is leaning with his elbows on the bar desk, eyes on the screen. I tap him on his shoulder. I don't really know what I had expected from a farm foreman—maybe someone in his late forties with a muscular build? The guy that straightens up and turns around and looks at me is probably in his mid-twenties. He's a lanky guy with red hair reaching out from under his Nike cap. He has a frank face with freckles and noticeably beautiful blue eyes, piercing and soulful at the same time—right up there with Paul Newman, Frankie Boy, and Ed Harris.

"I got your name from Jake Chapman." I have to shout to get through the brouhaha. I start to speak again, but Gilbert gestures to an area in the back of the pub, and we walk over there.

"So, what did old Jake tell you?" Gilbert has a strong and clipped accent. The way he says "Jake" comes out as *"Jaker."*

"He told me you could give me directions to John Smith and the Heritage Farm. But I don't want to steal you away from the cricket match, so just let me know when is a good time. I can wait."

"Well, Lancashire is ahead with ten wickets already (*"alreader"*), so I'm not exactly anxious to watch the rest." He leads the way to a table. On the way over, he has to fend off some friendly slurs from Lancashire fans. When we sit down, I realize it's after six p.m., and I'm getting hungry.

"How about I offer you dinner in exchange for information?" I say, feeling like I'm cast in a Frederick Forsyth spy drama.

"Well, that'll be grand. Thank you."

"John Smith, huh, that old geezer," Gilbert continues and chuckles. "If you want something from him, you need to bring an interpreter; he only speaks in monosyllables."

"Yeah, Jake mentioned something to that effect. But I'll try." I give Gilbert a brief story about being here for a meeting and wanting to bring some specific apple varieties back home to the U.S.

Gilbert brings up his phone. "Heritage Farm doesn't show up in Google Maps, but if you give me your phone number, I'll send you a Google link with the GPS coordinates."

As he does, a waiter comes over with menus. He mentions that today's special is the Sunday Roast. "It's roasted lamb, roasted potatoes, gravy, red current sauce, and accompanied with Yorkshire pudding. If I may suggest a pairing," says the waiter-turned-sommelier, "it would be a porter or dark ale."

Lamb again! I look hesitant. Gilbert takes notice. "If you're worried about the taste (*"taster"*), there's no need to, he says. "This is lamb, not mutton or hogget." He looks at the waiter for confirmation.

"Absolutely, this is spring lamb of the highest quality," the waiter chips in.

This is information I don't need. It's the notion of a lamb I'm wrestling with. But I'm not a stickler about it. After all, I had lamb as recently as last Wednesday. I can go with the flow as well as anyone. So, I follow Gilbert's lead and order the Sunday roast and a pint of Redhog porter from a local brewery. It is an excellent and tasty meal.

As we eat, I inquire some more about John Smith. Turns out he is a real martinet about his cider. He only sells his produce to Farmers Markets, farm shops, and some pubs—The Yew Tree included—but never to grocery stores. I ask why.

"Apparently, John claims that mainstream stores don't honor the expiration date but keep the ciders on their shelves too long. He's not only concerned about the soft apple ciders but also about the hard ciders. The alcohol doesn't go bad, of course, but what I could extract from John's grunts was that there's a deterioration in taste and flavor if the bottles are stored for more than a year. He would get more money if he sold to Sainsbury's or Tesco, but he's stubborn."

We chat some more. I learned that Gilbert is starting Vet School at the University of Edinburgh in the fall, and he will be coming back to Overbury Farm for practice in the summers. I mention that Julie is a veterinarian, although her clientele is probably a little different from what Gilbert is aiming for.

It's close to eight p.m. Gilbert is looking at his watch. "Sorry mate, I have some errands to take care of for the working week. Thanks for dinner, and good luck with John!"

"Well, thank you for the helpful information. And good luck with Vet School."

We part, and Gilbert heads out the door, waving to some friends on the way. After he left, I sat by myself for a while, finishing the pint. Alone again… naturally. (Sorry, couldn't help it).

CHAPTER 13

*Summer 2024. Redmarley d'Abitôt. The Heritage Farm.
John Smith.*

The drive to the Heritage Farm, and John Smith the next morning takes me to Redmarley d'Abitôt, a rural parish in Gloucestershire. Gilbert's GPS coordinates direct me to the village of Redmarley, which I read has an astonishing history dating back to the pre-Norman era. I pass through several orchards and gentle fields. The skyline is dominated by mountainous peaks. I later learned these are the Malvern Hills. I cross a medieval-looking bridge over the river Avon when I realize I'm lost, despite Gilbert's excellent directions. However, I'm close enough that locals at a wayside pub put me back on the right track.

When I arrive at my destination, I look at what I would best describe as a cottage. It's a beautiful house that seems to emerge from the surrounding greenery. There are plants everywhere: trees, bushes, and creeping vines that climb on the walls. There's a detached area with small trees covered with pink flowers that are planted in rows. The vegetation is so thick I can't make out the backyard. However, I assume there must be an apple orchard somewhere. In fact, when I look around, I see a clearing to the right with a gravel road curving around the house. The house itself is rather large, with a thatched roof. The front door is bright red. I park the car in the clearing and walk up towards the house.

When I stand here after knocking at the door, it's with a great amount of jitteriness I'm awaiting the next few moments.

When the door opens, I see right away that this is not Derek Tyne-Callaghan. This is a very different person. Most notably, what I see in front of me is a woman. She could be in her mid-eighties, medium-sized and slightly stooped, with wavy, thick, silver-grey hair. She wipes her hands on an apron, sending off dancing clouds of flour. She gazes at me with warm, brown eyes over thin reading glasses perching on the tip of her nose.

I'm taken aback. For some reason, it never occurred to me that John Smith (or Derek Tyne-Callaghan) might be married. I'm momentarily flustered, but then my powerful brain gets to work and manages to formulate a coherent sentence. "Good morning," I say. Okay, it's short, but it is coherent. "I'm looking for John Smith," I continue.

"That makes two of us," she says. She has a rich voice that reminds me of Anne Murray, the Canadian singer. "He was supposed to be in here for tea at ten, but he's still out meddling in the orchard."

The aroma of baking seeps out through the open door into the chilly morning air and hits my ORs. The signaling transduction cascade instantly reaches my hypothalamus. It's a wonderful smell, and I get a strong craving for bread.

"You might as well come inside, and we can wait for him together. If you're a good boy, you may even get a scone. And watch when you enter; you're taller than most," she says while holding open the door.

We enter right into the kitchen. Here, the smell is so delightful I almost have to sit down.

"Sorry, I forgot my manners," I say. "My name is Ludvig Thovén." I put out my hand, but she just touches it with her elbow. "My hands are too floury. Name's Valerie."

"Nice to meet you, Valerie. What kind of scones are you making?"

"These are quince-jelly scones." She holds up a jar. "You saw those trees or bushes out front with small pink flowers? Those are quince. This jelly is from last year's harvest."

"I've had many kinds of scones," I say proudly, "but never with quince jelly."

"Well, let's see what you think of them then." She puts another couple of baking dishes in the large wall oven. "Where are you from, by the way? You don't sound like a British gentleman—no offense."

"I'm from the U.S., but I'm Swedish by origin." By now, I have my cover story well-developed. "I'd like to talk to John about the possibility of getting some of his apple varieties over to the U.S., specifically Washington State, where I'm from. Washington is the leading supplier of apples in the U.S., producing more than sixty percent of the national supply. I'm here for a meeting that has nothing to do with apples, but when I heard about a cidery that uses old English heritage apples, I got interested. I wonder if there's a chance I could get some seeds to bring to Washington, not for commercial purposes but just for our garden and maybe in the courtyard at work."

"Well, I'm sure Johnny can help you with that. It wouldn't be seeds, though, but stickings. But Johnny can tell you more. Come to think of it…" She opens the door to the backyard and calls out, "Johnny, you have a visitor!"

Valerie goes back to her baking. In a break, she puts another cup and saucer on the table. There are two sets there already. I see that one of them has some pills next to the saucer, one blue and two white. Johnny's or Valerie's medicine, I surmise.

"Visitor?" It's a man's voice coming from the backyard. It's muffled by the closed door, but it's definitely an angry sound. "Visitor?" I hear again, louder. When the voice comes inside, I immediately know that I've found Derek Tyne-Callaghan. He has shrunken, but for a man in his mid-to-upper eighties, he seems structurally fit. The Derek I knew back in the day was heavyset and a little overweight. This version of Derek is lean and almost wiry. When he takes off his cap, I see a full head of short-cut salt and pepper hair.

I rise and offer my hand. "Ludvig Thovén," I say. "It's very nice to meet you, John."

He looks at my outstretched hand as if I were holding up a pile of manure. After an almost uncomfortable wait, he takes it. "Uhrm," he says. It's a firm, albeit reluctant, handshake.

"He says, my name is John Smith, and it's very nice to meet you, too," Valerie explains. She takes out dishes from the oven and starts loading scones into various containers. She puts several on a plate that she brings to the table.

"Now, you two sit down, and we can have tea and scones and a nice chat," she says while she pours the tea.

"Johnny, Ludvig here is interested in some of your apple trees," Valerie says, tapping John on the hand.

"Uhrm," John responds.

"He says, how fun; what exactly is it you want?" Valerie interprets again. I think I see a twitch in the corner of John's mouth as if he's suppressing a smile. I repeat my spiel for him. I add that I fully understand if he's unwilling to share his heritage apple varieties but that I, at any rate, would be very interested in just seeing the trees.

There's no response from John. He sips his tea. Meanwhile, I bite into a quince jelly scone. "This is the best scone I've ever had," I say. And I mean it; the combination of tart and sweet is married to intense floral tones. "What do you do with all the scones?" I nod toward the large piles that have accumulated on the counter. "Do you sell them?"

"We sell the jelly and scones at the Farmers Markets around here. Scones also freeze well, so a fair amount I freeze for our own consumption. Johnny here devours them. Don't you, Johnny?"

"Uhm," John says and nods.

Julie isn't here, of course, so I take a second scone.

"Johnny, take your pills," Valerie taps his hand again. "They're good for your heart."

"Heart's good," John responds.

"Yes, your heart is good because you take the pills!" Valerie says. "Now, take your pills, or I'll take away your scone!"

I'm fascinated by the dynamics and interactions in this couple. I also started to wonder how I should go about beeing alone with John. I don't know if Valerie is privy to all the details of Derek's past. For that matter, I don't even know Valerie's role in Derek's life, but I assume she is his wife.

There's a scratching sound on the backyard door, and John gets up and opens it for a cream-colored poodle who trots inside. Looks like a female, and she's a cutie pie.

"This is Semi-Precious," says Valerie as she pets the dog behind the ears. "Her name used to be Precious," she tells me, "until she chased a rabbit through a fence and wreaked havoc in our nursery. Since then, we call her Semi-Precious. Don't we?" she asks the dog.

I laugh, and Semi-Precious comes up and licks my hand. She tells me that Valerie is exaggerating; most of the nursery was spared. *"And it was a rabbit, for crying out loud. What should I do, just keep looking at it?"*

I give Semi-Precious a supporting nod, hoping that Valerie doesn't notice. Then I turn to John. "Would it be possible for me to take a look at the orchard?" I say.

John fidgets in his chair. "Uhrm."

"Johnny says he'll be happy to show you around in the orchard," Valerie translates again. "And bring another scone for the trip, won't you?" She turns to me. "Don't you worry; he's not nearly as grumpy as he seems. He'll eventually warm up. Most people don't hang around him long enough, so they only know him as a grumpy old man. He's a slow starter when it comes to company; Johnny is."

Again, I think John is trying hard not to smile. I get up and carry my dishes to the sink. I look at the scones. I'm thinking about what Julie would say and resist the temptation. Then I change my mind, take a third scone, head to the backyard door, and look out. Valerie pushes John to the door. She puts the cap on his head and a scone in his hand.

…And out we go.

———

Well, this ought to be interesting. We're walking slowly toward the orchard. Semi-Precious is with us. It's quite an extensive orchard; I count around fifty trees. They're all in full bloom. A wonderful sight of white and pink flowers. Bees are hustling around all over the canopies. A faint, sweet aroma is discernible in the air. A barn-looking building with large doors is set off to the side. I assume that's the cider mill. There are a couple of fenced-in areas farther away. The backyard and its extension look like a big park. I see no workers, but I guess it's because it's off-season.

I brace myself. "John," I say. "I know your name used to be Derek Tyne-Callaghan."

John stops and slowly turns around. Before he has a chance to say anything, I quickly continue. "The only reason I'm here is that you once—a long time ago at a meeting in Greece—told me about your hypothesis for a novel kind of olfactory receptors that you predicted would be found in early hominins. And, this is exactly what we have now found." I go on to tell him about OMICS and the Crassus Project.

Something happens to John as I speak. He at once appears more spirited. His eyes seem to get new life. And—lo and behold—he actually smiles, a big *bona fide* smile. He shakes his head and beckons me to a bench set back in a lilac groove.

"Lilacs attract bees and help with the apple pollination," he explains out of context and makes a sweeping movement with his hands, indicating the orchard. He recedes to his old self and looks lost for a while. But then he snaps back. "How the hell did you find me in the first place?"

So, I tell him. When I'm finished, he shakes his head and seems forlorn again.

"You damned sleuth," he says finally. Then he laughs bitterly. "Well, I have to give you an A for effort and tenacity."

"Thank you. I'm quite proud of my investigative strategy," I joke, trying to take the edge off the conversation.

"The problem is, if you could find me, others might as well," he says.

"I'm not sure about that," I argue, a little hurt. "Finding you was quite an involved process. Why would you care anyhow?" I ask. "I know about the incident at University of Michigan. But that was ages ago, and you've paid your dues. You really think someone would come after you now?"

"Oh, the girls, you mean?" He snorts. "You think that's why I changed my name? Hell no, I couldn't care less. Of course, I know what I did was wrong and reprehensible, but… changing my name? No, I wouldn't have done that." He seems to reflect on this for a bit. Then he shrugs his shoulders. "Although, of course, that's what I've been telling people," he allows. "The few that know about it."

I'm confused. "So, why did you change your name then? And not just to any name, with 'John Smith,' you really went under the radar."

John takes a deep breath. "Oh my, oh my. This is a long story." He stands up and stretches. He looks rejuvenated again like he did when I first broke the news about my visit. "Can you stay for lunch?" he asks, to my surprise.

"Oh, sure, thank you," I say. "I have to ask, does Valerie know about your story? Is she your wife, by the way?"

"No, she's not my wife." Derek sits down again. "But she might as well be; we've been together for over thirty years. And, yes, she knows about Michigan. We actually met at the penitentiary in Ashfield when I did a stint there from 1984 to 1985. She wasn't locked up, but her husband, Lou, was. He'd been a teacher at the Redmarley Academy and apparently had an affair with a student, a boy. Or young man, rather; he was nineteen at the time, I believe. Consensual, as it seemed. However, Lou had AIDS and gave it to the student. Or, so the story went. Lou claimed that it was the other way around. Turns out Lou was right, but they didn't find that out until he was dead. The student came around and confessed that he'd had AIDS for some time before he got involved with Lou. I'm not sure what happened to him—the student. Lou got really sick, though, and I kind of took care of him, helped him with this and that, and looked after him. That's how I befriended Valerie when she came to visit him."

He gets up again and stretches. Then sits back down. "Valerie and I got to talking, and we continued to meet after I was out. I mentioned my idea of setting up a cidery, and she told me about a beautiful parcel of land called Berkeley Park that was for sale. Berkeley Park had been erroneously considered to be the original founding place for Berkeley Castle and was owned by the Berkeley Castle Charitable Trust. However, discoveries of new medieval documents showed that Berkeley Park had no association whatsoever with Berkeley Castle, which is located around fifty kilometers south of here. So, the trust sold the land to the parish. They, in turn, put it on the market." John pauses and looks up. "It was still listed when I got out from Ashfield, probably because of the high price. I had quite a bit of money in assets and accounts from my parents, so I bought the place unseen." He pauses again. "Wow, I haven't talked as much as this for many years, not even to Valerie. My jaw is getting sore."

He stands up. "At any rate, this used to be Berkeley Park, and now we call it the Heritage Farm. But let's continue after lunch. Valerie's going to church at one o'clock to help out with a charity, so we'll have some time for ourselves. Let's go inside and see what Valerie's cooked up."

———

What Valerie had cooked up was sausage and chestnut pasta. Since I am who I am, I asked for details. She had made a ragu with Lincolnshire sausage meat, chopped chestnuts, garlic, rosemary, quite a bit of full-bodied red wine, fennel seeds, and passata. She added that to pasta shells together with a little of the saved pasta water and topped with parsley and grated Old Winchester cheese. I enjoyed every bit of it, and I told her so. We drank water with lemon and cucumber slices. Passata, if you wonder, is strained tomato puree.

The conversation flows effortlessly. We talk about apples, the Heritage Farm, and the town of Redmarley and its neighborhood. I learn that the Heritage Farm extends way beyond the actual farm and cidery. John and Valerie maintain it like a wildlife refuge. The orchard itself is designed and maintained for organic production. John and I keep up the front about the Apple storyline. "You'll need USDA approval," comments John. I say I will arrange for proper APHIS permits. USDA is the United States Department of Agriculture, and APHIS stands for Animal and Plant Health Inspection Service. As we talk, I realize that this is not only a façade on my part; I'm genuinely interested in getting some of John's heritage apple varieties, particularly the Flower of Kent. It would be really cool to have a clone of Newton's original tree in our garden at home.

"Well, you two seem to get along without problems," Valerie says and gets up. She turns to me. "See what happens when Johnny warms up. He turns downright chatty." She continues, "Now, I'm off to church, and I entrust you with afternoon tea and dinner." She pokes John in the stomach. As we pop plates and utensils in the dishwasher, Valerie turns to me again. She stretches out her hand. "It's less floury now," she chuckles. "In case you're not around here when I get back, it was nice meeting you. And good luck with your apple quest."

"Thank you, Valerie, for your hospitality and for the wonderful quince scones."

"Oh, I forgot." Valerie goes and gets a jar of quince jam from a cupboard. "Here, enjoy. It's not only for baking scones. It's also an excellent condiment."

On her way out, Valerie pats Semi-Precious. "Now, you look after these two," she says to the dog. And then to John, "Don't forget to thaw out the lamb chops. I'll be home at six."

When we clear out the kitchen table, John tells me, "Come with me," and we walk into what seems to be a combined living room and library. I see a couple of books on a table that are written in Hebrew or a similar language.

John takes a seat. Semi-Precious immediately jumps up and settles down on his lap. "All right, sit down," he says, "and I'll let you in on something that no one else, including Valerie, knows about. And, I really hate keeping things away from her, but, as you'll see, it's a delicate situation."

"So…" And John tells me his story.

CHAPTER 14

Summer 2024. John Smith's story. The Qumran parchments.

S ince a young age, I knew I had a flair for languages," John begins. He speaks slowly and takes frequent and long breaks. "In secondary school, I had a crush on a girl from France. So, I decided to learn French. Within a month, I had learned enough to write letters to her in French, which I hoped would impress her. It did not. Learning how to speak French was more challenging, and I realized that my real interest was in being able to read books and documents in the original languages. It wasn't long before I was more or less fluent in reading French, Spanish, Italian, and Greek."

John shifts in his chair. "I discovered my real passion at Uni, where I enrolled in Languages and Cultures. I started to learn Hebrew, old Greek, and Aramaic and got involved in analyzing old biblical and Assyrian texts. After Uni, I spent over six years—from late 1973 to early 1980—traveling around the Middle East, looking for opportunities to study old Hebrew and Aramaic documents and inscriptions. Word got around, and I soon found myself being engaged by museums and other institutions to interpret texts that remained ambiguous or difficult to understand, even for scholars. I still don't understand why it came so easy to me to delve into these texts when professionals stumbled. It just felt natural to me."

"Those were happy times," John continues after a contemplative pause. "From 1978, I lived in Givat Ram in Jerusalem and spent almost every day at the Israel Museum studying the Qumran scrolls. I was offered a five-year position as a curator and tour guide at the Museum. I teamed up with a Bedouin, Jamal Mufti, and the two of us served as registered guides for tourists in the Judaean desert. Jamal knew about the Qumran Park grounds and the caves, and I informed about the discovered scrolls and their writings. My role was also to encourage people to visit the Museum campus and the Shrine of the Books Complex, where the first Dead Sea scrolls were on exhibit."

John clinches his fists, and his face turns sinister. "Then came April twenty-third, 1979."

It's now two-thirty in the afternoon, and it's getting warm inside. John motions Semi-Precious down, gets up, and opens a window to let in some air. He stares out the window and continues to talk with his back to me. "That day, the Visitor Center asked Jamal and me to take on a new Israeli security guard… Greenblatt, or something… No, Greenberg, Tobias Greenberg was his name. Anyhow, we were asked to bring him with us and show him around in the park. And so we did. Jamal and I were guiding tourists most of the morning around Caves 1, 2, and 3, and Tobias came along. A nice guy and a little shy. Didn't look at all like no security officer to me. I had my Hasselblad and took pictures of the tourists as usual that people could buy at the Visitor Center the following day."

John comes back and sits down again. Semi-Precious opts to stay by the window and scout the terrains for rabbits. "Later in the afternoon, it was just the three of us, Jamal, Tobias, and me. Jamal and I decided to walk the hiking trail and show Tobias the Archeological Site, the caves along the trail, and the Qumran Canyon. We usually ate lunch—Jamal and I—around three p.m. on most days that we worked. All three of us had sandwiches prepared by the Visitor Center, and it was now close to three o'clock. Jamal and I knew of a bench a hundred meters or so off the trail close to Cave 11. So, we set off toward the bench."

John pauses and throws up his hands in the air. "Then, suddenly, all hell broke loose; the ground shook violently, and we fell right down into a deep, maybe two meters, hole. A forceful sandblast blew by, and we heard a clinking and crashing sound. Then, just like that, everything got still and quiet. We could see the sky at the top of the hole. When I looked around—we had ended up in some kind of cavern—I noticed shelves full of square clay pots or boxes. Several boxes were shattered on the ground next to parchments that had spilled out. Several of the parchments were intact, but others were in fragments and a few of them were being disintegrated right before my eyes. The parchments were not rolled up but were packed as sheets with some straws in between. We were all in shock, but by pure instinct, I got my camera up and took as many pictures as I could, some with the flash, but there was enough light I didn't really need it."

John looks around as if he were talking to a big audience. "I think all three of us recognized that we had fallen into an archeological site of enormous importance. Our reactions were different, though. I continued to take photos as I deliberated with Tobias about notifying the Israel Museum right away once we got out of there. Jamal, on the other hand, wanted to smuggle pots out of the park and sell them on the black market to antiquities dealers. He said we could do whatever we wanted, but he was going to take four pots to his car. Tobias and I started to talk him out of his plan. Then Jamal got agitated and red-faced, and his whole demeanor changed. He drew his knife and threatened us. A totally stupid thing to do since we had an armed guard with us. Tobias pulled out his gun and told Jamal to put the knife away. I had my own knife—mostly for poking in stone walls and such—

and I took that out as a reflex, without much thinking of what I would do with it."

I have no idea where this is going, but I am mesmerized by John's story. He takes another long pause. Semi-Precious comes back and jumps up in his lap. John pets the dog distractedly and sighs deeply. He looks at me and then continues.

"Jamal had turned completely mad, and I didn't recognize him anymore. He lunged forward and tried to stab Tobias. Tobias fired his gun and shot Jamal in the stomach. At that very moment, another series of shock waves hit us. The first quake threw Tobias towards me and right on my knife. I don't know how badly he was hurt, but the knife definitely got in somewhere on his body, and blood gushed out through his uniform. The second and third quakes threw us in the opposite direction and further down through the floor of the cave that had now opened up. Tobias grabbed onto my neck chain—a chain with my name and museum credentials—and tried to stop his fall, but the chain broke, and Tobias fell down into the deeper hole that had now formed. If he instead had tried to grab my camera strap, I might have fallen down with him, or... I might have been able to help him from falling; I don't know. Anyhow, I must have let go of the knife and managed to dig myself upwards. I didn't see Jamal, but I assumed he had fallen as well. I don't know how I got away from being dragged down myself—the hole must now have been at least four meters deep—but somehow, when the quakes stopped and everything got quiet, I found myself lying above ground on top of the now-covered cavern. When I came to, I realized that the whole episode couldn't have taken more than ten minutes, although it seemed much longer. The camera was still hanging around my neck."

John holds out his palms and looks at me. "So, we have one Israeli security guard buried with my knife in him—a knife with my initials and fingerprints—and holding on to a neck chain that can be clearly identified as belonging to me. He was most likely dead, either from being buried by sand and gravel, or from the knife wound, or both."

He gets up again, gently pushing Semi-Precious to the floor. "So, what would have been the right thing to do?" he asks me rhetorically. "Obviously, I should have run back to the Visitor Center and notified people to start a rescue operation. I didn't do that. Why?"—and he starts to sound defensive—"because I was terrified. For the fleeting moment I was considering telling people what had happened, I quickly realized the dire consequences. I would be hard-pressed to convince anyone that I hadn't killed an Israeli security guard. If I decided to go down that route, I would have to come to terms with the prospects of being imprisoned in Israel for years, or maybe life."

John sits down, and Semi-Precious jumps up. John goes on, "There was an earthquake recorded in the area at that very time; one minute after three p.m. on April twenty-third, 1979, a 5.1 magnitude earthquake hit close to En Boqeq in the Dead Sea region. There was seismic activity noticed west of the park, and it must have been those tremors that propagated to where we were headed for our lunch. I could have referred to the En Boqeq earthquake when I told my story. But ... explaining the dead security guard with my signatures all over him... Well, I wasn't exactly looking forward to that. So, what should I do?"

There's a pregnant pause here, and I take the opportunity to take stock of my situation. It's now after four in the afternoon, and I don't know how long I should stay. When is Valerie coming back? Will they invite me for dinner, and if so, should I accept?

Speaking of dinner, "John," I say, "before you go on, I don't want you to get in trouble with Valerie. She told you to get the lamb out for dinner. And it's now after four."

"Oh, shit!" John motions Semi-Precious down and gets up. He moves quickly, and I'm struck by how agile he seems for his age. "And, I guess we never had afternoon tea, did we? I'll put the lamb chops in some cold water. I'll be right back. You're staying for dinner?"

Hm… that's the question, isn't it? I definitely want to hear the rest of John's adventure. But I'm not looking forward to chatting with Valerie at the dinner table, knowing that she's unaware of what John and I have discussed. That's too much of a charade for me. And, really, how much lamb can a man eat, let alone a preferred vegan? If I'm not mistaken, I had it for dinner last night too, and then again not long before that. I decide that the best strategy for me is to politely decline the dinner invitation, let John finish his story, and then take off before Valerie is back.

"Thanks, yes, I'll be happy to stay for dinner," I hear myself say …*Oh well.*

John comes back. Semi-Precious has taken his chair, and John politely pulls out another one and sits down opposite me. "Where were we? Oh, yes. Well, what I did was play ignorant. I went back to the Visitor Center and told them I didn't know where Tobias and Jamal were. A few days later, I resigned from the Museum. In the meantime, I looked for postdoc positions, and I found the one at UM," (he refers to the University of Michigan), "so that's how I ended up in Ann Arbor. What happened there, with my, ehr… dishonorable exit, you already know about."

He gets up again to grab his phone from a desk. "Okay, now, I'll first show you some of the photos I took of the parchments that spilled out on the ground from the shattered clay boxes when we fell down in the cave after the initial shockwave." He gives me the phone, and I look at what I assume to be parchments strewn around the floor of the cave, most more or less intact but some in fragments. The parchments have letters and words in a language

I take to be Aramaic or Hebrew. "Scroll down," John tells me, "there are several photos." I do, and I see around thirty photos with the same patterns: parchments and parchment fragments distributed among pebbles and other debris.

John takes the phone back. "I spent a great deal of my time at UM organizing parchments and piecing parchment fragments together, aligning and pasting—this was before Photoshop." He hands me the phone back. I now look at eleven parchment pages and some loose, non-adjoined fragments.

"Now," John continues, "the text you see here is Standard Aramaic, or Imperial Aramaic as it's also called. With my background, it was not too much of a feat to translate the text. One of the parchments seemed to be a version of the Book of Esther in the Hebrew Bible or the Old Testament. This is noteworthy because the Book of Esther has not yet been found among the Dead Sea scrolls. I'm not showing you this, however, but instead, some other texts. This is an excerpt of the texts; there's a whole lot more. But this is a selection of—I would say—the most stunning parts. There are still some gaps, some Aramaic words that I just couldn't interpret because they were faded." He gives me the phone back. "Now, just study this for a while, and we can discuss it later. I'm going to mess around in the kitchen."

I look at a list of four bulleted paragraphs with full and partial sentences in English. I read them over and over again. As I do, I sense a strange feeling emerge in my head, something between eerie and unreal. If John's account for what happened in Qumran is accurate, and I've come to accept that, and if his translation of the text is correct, which I have no reason to doubt, then the implications of these Qumran manuscripts are astonishing.

John's back, holding two small glasses. "Whiskey," he says. "I thought you might need some balsam for your brain. I would offer you hard cider, but out of principle, I don't serve it unless it's the highest quality, and it's too late now for last year's harvest to be top-notch." I gulp down the whiskey in one swallow. As it burns its way down my throat, it helps me shake off the almost unnatural feeling that still lingers in my head. "Thanks," I say. "That's what I needed."

John sits down, and we look at each other for half a minute or so, not saying a word. I finally break the silence. "Well, there's a lot to unpack here, wouldn't you say?"

John produces a horse chortle. "Yes, I would say so."

"At different levels," I add. I think there are, first and foremost, the overall religious viewpoints of the texts. Second, there's the reason I'm here at all: to figure out what John—or Derek, as it were—meant by his hypothesized discovery of novel ORs (olfactory receptors, for you who have forgotten). At first readthroughs, I didn't make any connection, but then I gradually started to understand what this whole narrative is leading up to.

"Well, where do you want to start?" John asks. And, I should add, I've used my own words, so the texts are less archaic than you might expect. But the translations are correct.

I look at the list again.

• *My brothers and friends, I write these accounts of the year of Pharaoh Ptolemy's reign...*

• *In six days, the formed Earth and its beings were defined.*

• *...the formed Earth where the progression of beings, from simple to complex, was set forth... defined it in six days... the progression of beings on the formed Earth was good and proceeded similarly to what... had set forth in other places.*

• *The progression of mankind was intervened long after the words of the mouth succeeded the images of the mind... made a covenant with all of mankind... allowed... being stewards of Earth... representing Earth.*

"So, this might not be where I would want to start, but I think this is where we ought to start, given the reason I'm here talking to you in the first place. It took me a while to figure out, but I'm assuming that it's the 'views of the mind' that serve as the cornerstone in your prediction of a different kind of olfactory receptors."

"Well," John says, "I wouldn't say it's the cornerstone. So, let me give you some background. Already way back in grad school in Reading, which is, what… early seventies… I was at DLC—Department of Languages and Cultures, that is—and already then, I entertained the idea that early hominids might have possessed the faculty to communicate via some kind of mind perception. Full disclosure here; I'm pretty sure, although not one hundred percent certain, that I had this idea before reading William Golding's The Inheritors—have you read that book, by the way?" I shake my head. "Well, anyhow, in The Inheritors, Golding describes the Neanderthals as being able to communicate via telepathic abilities. Well, we now know that Neanderthals most likely had a pretty good vocabulary, but that's beside the point. So, anyhow, either Golding inspired me to consider mind perception, or—which I believe is the case—he put fuel on my idea. I think it makes good sense that prior to the development of speech, hominids used mind viewing to communicate with each other, in addition to body language. They most likely also had a different olfactory system than ours to better sense their environment. When the speech was advanced enough to serve as a more or less fluent means of communication, mind viewing, which I took to be a sensory system mediated via G-coupled, olfactory-like receptors, was gradually lost, together with a reduction and rearrangement of the entire olfactory system to better fit a new lifestyle and new environments."

John's voice dries up. "Another whiskey?" he croaks and holds up the bottle. Why not. "Yes, please." I take the whiskey in one gulp again. I feel a little light-headed. I don't know if that's because of the whiskey on an empty stomach or from John's Qumran texts. Probably both.

"But why do you think mind viewing would have anything to do with olfactory receptors?" I ask. As I say this, it dawns on me that I have come to a juncture where I think of the mind-viewing concept as a fact.

"I never said olfactory receptors; I said olfactory-*like* receptors," John argues and takes his whiskey. "Ahh," he smacks his lips. "Just so you know, this is an excellent rye malt whiskey you're drinking. At any rate, I think it's logical to assume that G-coupled receptors should be involved in one way or another, given their roles in sensory systems. In olfaction—as you might know— volatiles are processed in a combinatorial fashion in the olfactory bulb, allowing the detection of millions of odorants. We don't know how mind viewing works—or worked, rather— but say that if you're looking at something, for example, a tiger, then signals such as energy particles and/or chemical moieties—I was going to call them olphons in the manuscript— might be emitted from your brain. Conceivably, when olphons are perceived by someone else not too far away, they are processed by a specific sensory bulb similar to olfactory bulbs for odorants, resulting in a mental image—in this case, of a tiger. Also, when I planned the manuscript at UM, I discussed it with neuroscientists and learned that because of the location of the olfactory bulb in the brain, odorants are directly routed to the amygdala and hippocampus in the limbic system, which constitutes the center of emotions and memory, and that there exists an association between visual images and olfaction. Olfaction is different from other senses in this respect. So, altogether, I thought it plausible that however mind viewing operated in these early hominids, olfactory-like receptors were involved.

I look at John. "Still sounds like science fiction to me," I say. "And, no offense, but if it hadn't been for your Qumran texts and the fact that we now have evidence for olfactory-like receptors in Fat Man, I would be skeptical. By the way, when do you reckon these texts were written?"

"Well, that's interesting, isn't it? If you look at the texts, it says Pharaoh Ptolemy's reign—just Ptolemy, not Ptolemy I, or Ptolemy II or III or IV. This suggests to me that the writer was living at the time of Ptolemy the I's reign, and he was the Pharaoh of Egypt from the beginning of 300 to around 280 BC."

John gets up. "We better start moving to the kitchen and rig up some dinner. We can continue chatting while we're cooking. Can you peel potatoes?"

"You mean 'can I' as in, do I have the skill set, or 'can I' as in, am I willing to?" I say. I joke, of course, since I'm such a funny guy. John turns around. "Just do it, you blockhead!" he says.

CHAPTER 15

Summer 2024. Derek's hypothesis. An exegetical headache.

I'm peeling potatoes—Jersey Royal, he tells me—and I'm good at it. Although, at home, we usually keep the skin on the potatoes. I ask John, "How do we know these parchments you and your colleagues found are not forgeries? You haven't been able to carbon-fourteen-date them or authenticate them in any other way, right?"

"No, I don't know for sure that they're not forgeries. But if they were, it would have been a very elaborate and major undertaking. Also, if they were, I tend to believe that the Israeli authorities would have reported it."

I'm confused. "What do you mean? I didn't think they knew about it."

"Oh, but they do! You see, they continued to survey the Qumran and nearby areas with GPR and Lidar." He's talking about Ground-Penetrating Radar and Light Detection and Ranging techniques to detect structures underground. "In 1989, after I left Reading…" He stops and looks out the window. "The second bright academic exit in my life," he says sarcastically and chuckles. "Oh my, I was in bad shape from all the drinking. But, anyhow, right about the time after I left, I found out that the Israeli Museum in Jerusalem reported about our cave."

John turns around from the window. "I shouldn't really know about this, but by a fluke of nature and the quirk of a Museum staff member, I do."

He looks at me and explains. "When I was working at the Museum in the seventies, I was a temporary staff, and I didn't have immediate access to all material. There was a temperature-controlled room in the basement with particularly valuable papyrus and parchment collections. To get access, you needed the code for a padlock to open the door. Now, the Head Curator at the time, Alan Gurewitz, was the one who was overseeing this collection. If I wanted in, I first needed to talk to his assistant, Barbara Hirschberg, who would go down and unlock the door for me and then reset the padlock."

John takes a break and attends to the lamb chops. He spice-rubs them with rosemary, pepper, and salt and sears them in a big cast-iron pan. Then he puts them, still on the pan, in the oven. John was going to have me just boil the potatoes, but I suggest making Hasselback Potatoes instead, an old Swedish recipe. John is on board. They've had it before and like it. I cut the potatoes in thin slices, just not all the way through (you can put the potatoes on two chopsticks when you slice to make it easier), then put them in a baking dish lined with parchment paper and brush them with a mix of olive oil, salt, and pepper, and sprinkle with bread crumbs. I put the dish in the oven with the lamb chops.

I prompt John, "So, the room with the padlock?"

"Right, I was down in the Gurewitz room, as it was called, so often, it became almost ridiculous for me to have to find Barbara all the time I needed access. Now, Barbara had a crush on me—I was a good-looking lad if you can believe it. Plus, I was in very high regard for my linguistic skills. So, when I asked her if she could simply give me the combination to the padlock, she squirmed a bit but finally gave in. She also let me in on a little secret. Turned out that Alan was heavily into Gematria—assigning numbers to words or phrases—and he was also very superstitious. He had the number 5821 for everything that needed a code or a password—and that was the code for the padlock. If more than four digits were needed, he started from the beginning again. If it were letters rather than numbers, he converted them to numbers. According to Barbara the number 5821 can be translated as 'very strong' and appears in the old Hebrew Bible. Alan was convinced that it was bad luck to ever change his code or password, so, apparently, he never did. Supposedly, he also had to scrape his shoes three times before going through a door. Strange but a nice enough guy to be around."

While he's talking, John is whisking up a mustard dressing. I opted to make a salad. I cut cucumber, tomatoes, and avocado into small chunks. I put them in a bowl and add olive oil—I did find extra virgin, first cold press in their pantry—a little salt, and quite a bit of granulated dried garlic.

John continues, "So, that was the seventies. Move forward a decade and a half, and I'm on my way to planning my life after Reading—Reading two, you could say. I was in the habit of checking out the Jerusalem Israel Museum website every so often just to get some general info about what was transpiring. There were sites for public access, and there were sites for internal use that were not public, and they were only in Hebrew. I know that Alan Gurewitz was still there because I saw his email address listed in the contact info—he must have been in his eighties by that time. One day I noticed a new internal link dedicated to the Excavation Committee, also only in Hebrew. The committee consisted of Alan and five other people I didn't recognize, all listed with their email addresses. About one week later—I was in the car, transporting apple tree cuttings from a nursery outside of Reading—it suddenly occurred to me that maybe I should try to log in to the site using Alan's email address as ID and his 5821 password. I first tried just 5821, but that didn't work. I was informed I would be locked out if I failed two more times. I then tried 58215821, but that also was wrong. I finally converted 5821 to Hebrew letters and entered those followed by 5821." John looks at me with a conspiratorial smile—well, he smiles, and I interpret that as a conspiratorial smile, given the circumstances—and fist bumps himself. "Lo and behold," he says, "I was in!"

John continues as we're setting the table. "So, that's how I found out that they had discovered and excavated our cave. It was named 13QT. The T might be after Tobias, but I'm not sure. I assume his remnants, together with those of Jamal, were found in the cave, but there is no mention of them. All in all, they collected sixty-four clay boxes with parchments, plus other artifacts that suggested that the cave had once been inhabited. I got in and poked around on that website a few more times. Alan has since passed, so I haven't been able to visit the site for the last twenty-five years. I know the parchments from 13QT were deposited in the Gurewitz room. Nothing was ever reported, though. Not even until this day, and this is now, what… more than thirty years ago. There's a possibility that the 13QT material is still being evaluated or has been forgotten. The Museum was heavily understaffed when I was there, and this could still be the case."

John looks at me quizzically. "There is, of course, another possible reason why nothing has yet been reported, and I assume that hasn't escaped your attention."

"No, it hasn't. The bullets on your list are more than enough to cause an exegetical headache in many religious headquarters. And who knows what other texts or artifacts they might have discovered in the cave. I can understand if the Museum spends years of investigative efforts to get as complete a story as possible rather than piecemeal it out. Also, it might take a long time to rule out forgery. But I agree, if there had been an obvious form of counterfeit, we would probably have known by now. It's a sensitive topic. And I'm sure the last thing they want is for some outsider to find out about it prematurely. Especially a foreigner, which could lead to political consequences."

John looks at me again, more intently this time. "So, Ludvig, what are you going to do with all this information, and, more to the point, what are you going to tell your colleagues at the Lab?"

John's question strikes a chord that has been vibrating in my brain for some time during our discussion; the dissemination of what I've learned this afternoon. This is an integrated, two-faceted issue. One aspect relates to John's mind-viewing hypothesis and the potential function of the Crex-ORs. The other concerns the content of the Qumran parchments and their apparent support of John's postulation. The parchments present the biggest problem. I don't feel mentally prepared to deal with either the religious or the political implications of the documents. Although, as a Christian, I'm very excited about the former. There's a reason why nothing has been reported on the 13TQ cave, and I'm not about to offer myself as the centerpiece in what might end up in a religious and/or political conflict by going public. Not to mention whatever consequences that would have for John and Valerie. Strangely enough, John never put any conditions in place for telling me his story. You should know me well enough by now to realize that I'm a very decent guy. Obviously, I wouldn't want to do anything that could harm John or Valerie. I've pretty much decided that—at least for now— the only people I would tell about the 13QT parchments are Julie and Bryce (Bryce Vogel, my friend and colleague in DC).

A potential mind-viewing faculty in early hominins is easier to handle, although also not exactly a walk in the park. At an academic level, it's merely a hypothesis based on scientific reasoning that was meant for publication. So, no real reason to treat it as a secret. However, DHS will probably insist that I do. That is if they believe it in the first place. And that touches on a second point, the credibility issue. I've now gotten used to the idea of an extant mind-viewing sensory system. That doesn't mean my colleagues will accept it. They likely will think of it as pseudo-science or a science fiction dream by a disgruntled and failed researcher. Of course, they might feel differently if I showed them the 13QT texts. But I won't.

And I suddenly realize I don't have to. It occurs to me there's a way to test the mind-viewing hypothesis. It's rather crude but should be conclusive.

So, I answer John, "I'll tell them that I found 'Derek' and that he's changed his name but prefer not to have that revealed. I'll tell them that your hypothesis is that early hominins used mind viewing as a means of communication and that this sensory system was mediated through some kind of G-protein coupled receptors, most likely similar to olfactory receptors, which could perceive molecular moieties or energy particles—olphons— through the nose. And, erh… I'll tell them that the 'supporting evidence' you mentioned to me in Greece was just bragging, fueled by a high alcohol titer."

"Ha, ha… yeah, that's okay. Small correction: I never said that I think the olphons are necessarily taken up through the nose. I mean… I think they are processed in the nasal cavity, but they might as easily enter there through the skull, depending on what olphons really are and their properties."

The timer for the lamb chops goes off. I leave the potatoes in the oven for maybe twenty more minutes. What some people do is put cheese between the potato slices and then bake in the oven until the cheese melts. I opt not to do that.

It's almost five-thirty p.m., and I'm getting anxious to wrap up this discussion with John before Valerie comes home. "So, why didn't you tell Valerie about this?" I ask.

"Well, would you have? It's not exactly a heroic escapade, is it? Running away! Instead of getting help and maybe saving Tobias and Jamal? Also, if they came after me—Israeli authorities, I mean—I didn't want her to be complicit in the cover-up. Today? Well, the statute of limitation for the most serious crimes in Israel is twenty years, so if they were to get to me now, I might still be found culpable of a crime and get questioned, but that's about it. That was not the situation back in the eighties when I left Reading. If I'd been found then, I could easily have been charged with murder and asked to be extradited. I wanted Valerie to be able to claim plausible deniability. Of course, I could explain it to her now, as I've done to you. She knows about my work at the Jerusalem Museum and the Judaean Desert and my interest in ancient Mid-Eastern languages and history. I'm even teaching her to read the Old Testament in Hebrew. There've been occasions when I've been tempted to tell her the whole story. But I would feel silly and embarrassed to come out now, after all these years."

"At any rate," John continues, "Thinking about all this, I just made a decision. Give me your phone number, and I'll send over all the documents and photos relating to 13QT. When I'm gone, or if something happens to me, I want someone around who can bear witness to these parchments. I'll also give you the manuscript draft I was working on back at UM. At least that you can show your colleagues."

We chat for another half an hour until we hear a car coming up the gravel driveway. We rush to set the table. I pour Irish stout into our glasses, leaving a soft and creamy head. As I finish, Valerie opens the door.

———

In the car back to the hotel, I try to sum up the afternoon and what could easily be the most memorable encounter in my life. By the way, the dinner was first-rate. Preferred vegan as I am, I must admit that the lamb chops, with the fragrance of rosemary hitting my ORs, were delicious. As I left, I told John I would apply for APHIS permits for the Flower of Kent sticklings, which I plan to do. Having a clone of Newton's apple tree and our backyard, as well as in OMICS' courtyard, would be very nice indeed. Not only for the fruit but also as a foray into discussions on science and history, not to mention pomology.

Of course, what primarily occupies my brain is John's Qumran parchments. There is so much more I wanted to unpack and discuss with him. Not least of which is the inference to evolution in places other than Earth. But I also realize I should focus on the business at hand, that is, what I've learned about the potential function of the Crex-ORs and how to sell that to my colleagues at the Lab.

When I got to my room, I first looked through the files John sent me. There are several more photos of parchments and lists of translations. I recognize some of the translations from the Book of Esther. Others are slight variations of what I saw before. For example,

- *…the time to intervene with the progression of humankind on Earth after they started using their tongue and viewing of the mind was recessed to the background.*

- *…the progression of life on Earth and left it to have its course, the way… before … elsewhere.*

I start thinking about C. S. Lewis and the *Chronicles of Narnia*. In Narnia, God appears in the form of a lion, Aslan. In "The Last Battle," at the end of the *Chronicles of Narnia*, Aslan acknowledges that there are many worlds and that the incarnation of God differs between the worlds.

There are other, less jaw-dropping, excerpts in John's files, most of which align with texts from the Old Testament. I stash the 13QT parchments away in some corner of my brain and force myself to focus on the Crex-ORs and their presumptive role as receptors for olphons. I look at my emails. There's one from Noa. They've now concluded that the spurious signals from the chips correlate with the presence of people milling around the equipment. I realize that even before I met John Smith, I had the sense that the signals from the chips were due to some kind of body emissions. Why did I think that? I'm not sure. I'm brighter than most, so it could be that…yes, I'm pretty sure that's it. And, of course, being the fantastic mentor I am, I wanted Noa and her team to propose the idea first.

I look at the unfinished manuscript John gave me. There's nothing in there that I don't know now. He has also integrated substantial parts from his two postdoc papers. No reason to show this around, I figure.

I decided to call a two-day meeting with a select few, including folks from DHS, when I'm back home to discuss the mind-viewing hypothesis. I send an email to Hanne, asking her to book the meeting at the Gaylord in National Harbor. It's in DC, overlooking the Potomac. Well, I guess it's technically in Maryland, but close to DC. I've been to the Gaylord several times for conferences, and I like the location. I particularly like the excellent seafood restaurants within walking distance from the hotel. My favorite is McCormick & Schmick's Seafood & Steaks, a facility I've frequented on many occasions. I ask Hanne to try to get the meeting on Thursday, August first, starting after lunch. I ask her to contact the office of Vanessa Ashby, the DHS Secretary, and alert her to the meeting. I also ask Hanne to invite Bryce Vogel, Brad Johansen, Scott Krasinski, Steve Bayley, Joe Buchanan, and the Crassus Team: Noa Malka, Mike Baker, Ron

Chakraborty, and Laxmi Singh. I plan to spend close to a week at home after I return from the U.K. and then head directly to the meeting in DC before going back to my office at OMICS. —Okay, it's Maryland, I know.

CHAPTER 16

Summer 2024. The ice cream reward.

I'm dispensing ice cream. Or, rather, I'm dispensing money for ice cream. We're at Udderdelicious in Covent Garden. As promised, Linnea, Kristina, and their co-investigators—a full eight of them, as it turned out—can choose their favorite ice cream. Per Jessica's instructions, each kid is limited to two scoops. I don't report to Jessica—and Julie isn't here—so I'll have three scoops. I have a hard time choosing between Raspberry Cheesecake, Glenfiddich Whiskey and Chocolate, Liquorice, and Chocolate Orange, so I take one scoop of each. —Okay, I know, I know… and who is counting, anyhow?

Yesterday, which was Tuesday, I'd been in the U.K. for a full week. And, as you've noticed, I've accomplished what I came here for. I left the hotel in Tewkesbury early yesterday morning to go back to London and Kringlan to pick up a Swedish Princess cake and sourdough crackers that Jessica had prepared for me. A Swedish Princess cake is a traditional Swedish torte with alternating layers of airy sponge cake, pastry cream, raspberry jam, and a thick-domed layer of whipped cream covered by a layer of green marzipan. I then drove to Julius and Molly McIntosh's home in Reading, delivered the baked goods, and thanked them for all their help. I'd been contemplating waiting until today so I could again join them at the Park House for their weekly beers day wedding anniversary. But, mindful of the time and my pending trip back home, I decided against it. I stayed with Julius and Molly for a couple of hours. I told them about John Smith's mind-viewing receptor hypothesis. They were more amused than anything, although Julius—the true scientist—admitted that one should be humble enough to at least consider the possibility of mind viewing as an extinct evolutionary trait. I left the McIntoshes with the same feeling as last time; that we've become great friends. I'm looking forward to meeting them again.

Last night, Jessica, Lars, and the girls went to Linnea's and Kristina's piano recital with a follow-up dinner. I came too late to join, so instead, I walked over to The Faltering Fullback by Finsbury Park. I've been to quite a few pubs in London, and in Oxford and Cambridge, as well as in the U.S. If you were to ask for my—not-so-humble—opinion about which is the best pub in the entire universe as we know it, I would answer The Faltering Fullback. For sure, I would say it's the best pub in the U.K. Or, at least, the best in London. Without any doubt, I can say it's the best pub within walking distance from Jessica and Lars in Highgate. To be clear, The Faltering Fullback is a wonderful pub. I've been there several times before, mostly with Julie. Since it is my favorite pub, I'll give you a rundown of the premises to entice you to pay a visit next time you're in London. The pub consists of three sections, each presenting a different environment more unique than the next. When you first enter The Faltering Fullback, it looks small and dark. There is a half-moon-shaped bar serving all the classics, but their best, if you ask me, is a pint of Blue Moon served with a fresh slice of orange. In the wintertime (we've been there twice over the Christmas holidays), the front room is at its best as it consists of tall round tables with candles, giving you that cozy, classic English pub ambiance. If you look up at the ceiling, you'll be met by many random dangling objects, such as a guitar and a mini plane. The second room looks like a big beer hall. This is the main dining room where they serve lovely Thai dishes. The chef himself is Thai, so you know it'll be good. This room is also amazing to sit in when they play live music, do trivia nights, or watch big sports games. Once you leave the second room, you head outdoors to the "Secret Garden." The first time I entered this third section, I was taken by the atmosphere. It can most easily be described as a lush beer garden, where the garden stretches into three to four different levels. Each level is covered with greenery everywhere, ivy stretching along the tall walls, making it perfectly hidden from the outside world. Tables are spread out from each corner, some perfectly positioned under the daylight and some hidden in little nooks. You'll find random objects splattered around the garden, from fake chickens to little faces in the wooden structures. In the summertime, people will queue from eleven a.m. to get the best sunny spot once they open at noon. It's one of those rare locations worth queuing for. —Wow, I almost went poetic there, but it is a lovely place.

Anyhow, The Faltering Fullback, that's where I went last night. I had a couple of pints of the Blue Moon that paired well with Pla Lard Prig, which was pan-fried sea bass in spicy sauce. As I was sitting there, revisiting the meeting with John Smith in my mind, I got a ding on my d4c4 app. I checked it out: *Qxg4*. So, Bryce accepted my bishop gambit after all. My strategy worked! But, if you remember, I now have advice from the girls at the Crown Caversham in Reading a few days back to offer up also my second bishop. Am I going to follow their recommendation? I remain indecisive. But just for a few minutes. I may be devious at times, for example, when trying to coerce Bryce into making a rush move before leaving for San Francisco last week. What I'm not, though, is dishonest. Bryce and I have promised each other not to act on external strategy suggestions. There's no way I would have been able to analyze the chess board the way the Checker girls did, and I'm pretty sure Bryce won't either. So, I stood by my original thinking. Before any deep recesses in my brain got a chance to talk me out of it, I entered *Qa5* in the app and added the move. I leaned back and relaxed. I was proud of my decision. So proud, in fact, that I felt a dessert was in order. But... problem! There's no dessert on the menu. I asked my waiter, and she said that, unfortunately, they don't serve desserts. When she saw how disappointed I looked, she took pity on me and directed me to the White Lion three blocks up. I paid, left a good tip, and wandered up to White Lion. Less than ten minutes later, you'd find me at a table with a super-sweet and succulent Sticky Toffee Pudding and a glass of port. —2016 Dow's Vintage Port, since you're asking. Life is good!

I walked back to Jessica and Lars' place. It took me forty-five minutes, a pleasant evening stroll. I went by Kristina and Linnea's school, Whitehall Park School. Or, at least it's Kristina's school; Linnea will transfer from Whitehall Park to a secondary school now in the fall. Kids grow up so fast!

———

Well, today is Wednesday, as you may have surmised from the foregoing testimony, and my time in the U.K. is soon up. I spent the afternoon with Jessica, Lars, and the girls, and now we're at Western Laundry for dinner—my treat. Westerns Laundry is also within convenient walking distance from their home, so Jessica and her family come here every so often for Sunday brunch after church. We're sitting outside. It's a bit chilly tonight, but the heating lamps provide enough warmth. If you come here, I recommend you try their grilled scallops in garlic butter for an appetizer. That's not what we had, but I've heard they're excellent. No, our appetizer was roasted onion in Romanesco sauce. That was delicious, and I can recommend that as well. As an entree, we shared—per Jessica's suggestion—a family-size ricotta, peas, and mint gnocchi dish. Very good. Lars and I had a couple of glasses of Zinfandel, and Jessica and the girls had Pellegrino.

Our walk home is slow going, given that Jessica is in her third trimester. But it's a very relaxing and joyful stride despite the cold evening breeze. Blackbirds treat us by performing their evening serenade. We discuss my pending trip home tomorrow. Although I now consider myself a seasoned driver on U.K. roads, I take Lars up on his offer to return the Toyota to a nearby Hertz in Tottenham and hail a FREENOW to Heathrow tomorrow morning. Lars says he has an errand in that area of Tottenham anyhow. Not sure I believe him.

I want a good buffer for my nine fifty-five a.m. flight out of Heathrow, so I plan to leave around six a.m. tomorrow morning. When we're back, I finish packing. I say goodbye to the girls and thank them once again for their support in helping their hotshot scientist grandpa. I'll see Jessica and Lars at breakfast tomorrow before I take off. I'm slightly melancholic, as often, when saying goodbye to the kids and grandkids. But, with FaceTime and whatnot, farewells are not that dramatic.

I text Julie and tell her I'll be home around wine time tomorrow. I send another text to Hanne to let her know I'll be taking a week off before returning to my office and to ask her to send out reminders for the meeting in DC next Thursday. —Or Maryland, then, since you're so picky.

As I'm drifting off to sleep, my brain jumbles up inputs from the last couple of days. I find myself eating ice cream with John Smith with sugar cones made of repurposed Dead Sea scrolls. I try to collect all the cones from the shoppers and argue that they should be handed over to a museum. There was more in the storyline, but, as usual, most of the details evaporated when I woke up.

CHAPTER 17

Summer 2024. Back home.

Well, I'm back in our *Rio Casa*, our house by the river. It's Saturday morning, and Julie and I are having coffee on our Amish swing in the backyard. I've just returned from one of our local coffee shops with a medium Americano for Julie and a large Amethyst (coffee with dark chocolate and lavender—you should try it) for me. They advertised freshly baked cherry scones, so I bought two for each of us, knowing full well that Julie would pass on her second scone. So, here we are. I'm dipping my third scone in the Amethyst while Julie, with an admonishing look at the scone, fills me in on some discussions she's had with neighbors about arranging a Swedish crayfish party in August.

I came home the day before yesterday, just on the clock for wine time. Julie welcomed me with a glass of 2018 Alma Rosa Grenache set out on a table on the front lawn. She got the bottle as a gift from a grateful dog owner whose lab Julie had successfully operated on. The dog owner claimed to be a wine connoisseur and said that it's the best wine he's ever tasted. He said it had an aroma of oregano and notes of cracked peppercorn and minerals. That sounded very interesting. I might have very well agreed with his assessment of the wine had I only had a chance to enjoy it. But Jupiter, with pent-up anxiety from my absence and sudden exhilaration of seeing me again, channeled her emotions with a five-minute zooming on the lawn. In the process, she tipped over the table with wine glasses, bottles, and cubes of goat cheese. Julie, who was drinking a Barnard Griffin Alberiño, managed to salvage most of the content in her bottle. The Grenache, however, was history. Oh well, it could have been worse. Or… actually, maybe not. But I could handle it. And, at the end of the day, what is a bottle of wine, never mind one that promises a bouquet of oregano and a taste of peppercorn, compared to a dog's display of unadulterated joy? Not much is my answer. Jupiter, true to her personality, blamed the accident on me: *"If you can't hold your fucking wine, don't drink it!"*

Luckily, our small stash of wine also harbored some other red wines. I selected a local Pinot Noir and added cracked peppercorns and dried oregano. No, I didn't. Of course, I didn't. While sipping our wine, I informed Julie about my encounter with John Smith. I showed her the photos of the Qumran parchments. Although she was intrigued about the idea of a mind-viewing faculty, she was even more excited about the propositions brought forth by the parchments. Naturally, she wondered to what extent John Smith and his alleged finding of the parchments could be trusted. I told her that my impression of John Smith was that he was trustworthy. Also, just like me, Julie eventually came to subscribe to the notion that if the parchment photos indeed were a forgery and John's story was just a theatrical performance, it was one hell of a scam. It also begged the question of why he would do it. It made more sense that John was telling the truth.

Yesterday, I spent most of the time planning my upcoming meeting with DHS next Thursday. I talked to Hanne over the phone, and she let me know that the DHS Secretary has accepted the meeting and that she will be present together with a few more DHS-affiliated people. All other invitees will also be there. Hanne has reserved tables for dinner at McCormick & Schmick's on Thursday night. She was also going to arrange for catered breakfast and lunch on both days but was informed that DHS would take care of that. Well, so far so good. Before the Thursday meeting, I want to have a discussion with Bryce. I texted him to see if he was available on Wednesday evening. He is, and we decided to meet at Bond 45, an Italian restaurant close to the hotel.

————

It's Sunday morning, and we decide to skip church. Instead, per Jupiter's suggestion, we pack a picnic with dog chews, egg sandwiches—my own home-baked Finnish one hundred percent rye bread, thank you very much—coffee and water, and take her on a long hike. We're heading for the Badger Mountain Skyline Trail Loop, and we're there before eight a.m.. In the heat of the day, it's still close to forty-five degrees, but the mornings are nice.

We have a grand time. I like hiking, but I must admit that my favorite part is the picnic itself. Coffee and egg sandwiches out in the open, surrounded by lush vegetation—or, as in this case, sage brushes—are hard to beat. Well, of course, if offered, I would add a scone or two to the menu.

————

The next couple of days, I mainly relax. Which, for me, includes baking. I make more Finnish rye bread. With the risk of getting technical, I'll let you know that I keep my rye sourdough starter at one hundred percent hydration for Swedish and Finnish rye bread and one hundred sixty-five percent hydration for Danish rye bread. All my rye bread is made with one hundred percent rye flour, whole grain. For the bread, you first make the levain, which you do the night before baking. On the morning of, you first have breakfast. For today, I'm having a mix of rye, barley, and oat flakes that's been incubated in oat milk and a little goat milk kefir in the fridge overnight. I add berries from our garden, such as red and black currents, gooseberries, strawberries, and raspberries. I also throw in a handful of nuts and a couple of prunes. I pour in some more goat milk kefir. That's it. After breakfast, you sit down in the recliner with a cup of coffee and a piece of dark chocolate. For me, it's chocolate infused with chili pepper. While you're having coffee and chocolate, you relax and maybe read some news outlets on your tablet, check social media, and possibly do crosswords or play some games. In my case, I look through the *New York Times* and *Dagens Nyheter* (a major Swedish newspaper), check my Facebook, and play some puzzles. I got Wordle in two today, so I feel triumphant.

When you're done with the coffee, you take your dog out for a walk. In my situation, of course, I go out with Jupiter. We stroll around the neighborhood and then down to the river. We talk about the stock market and the political polarization in the U.S. Jupiter had some disturbing dreams last night, and we're trying to sort out where they came from.

When you get back, you're ready to bake. Now, you have two choices. You can start the baking right away. Or, you might feel that it would be nice to sit down and relax some more with a second cup of coffee. This is when you wish you had a scone or two to go with the coffee. But you don't, so if it's me, I compromise and have the coffee on the side while baking. Now, at this point, depending on your life's situation, you're either still alone in the kitchen with your dog, or your morning routine gets folded in with those of others. You might even have a cat that comes by to check out what you're doing and lays down right on the floured space you've designated for the baking project. Either way, now is the time when you ask Alexa to play some music. For me, it's usually *70s on 7* on Sirius XM.

Okay, the baking. You add the levain to the rest of the flour and the other ingredients. Mostly, when I bake, I use my trusted clay Dutch oven or bread Cloche. After baking, you let the bread rest on a rack covered with a tea cloth overnight. The next day, you freeze one half and start enjoying the other half.

———

"Pappa will only be gone a few days this time. And mamma will be home. She starts her vacation on Monday. So, it's not that bad, right?"

"What I don't understand is why the fuck you have to leave again. You've only been home less than a week!"

That's Jupiter and I having a conversation. She is upset because I'm leaving again. But, as I told her, Julie goes on vacation starting Monday, so it will be much more pleasant than last week when she was in the kennel most days. To distract her, Julie and I take her on a long walk. As usual, we end up by the river. The Columbia is like a painting. The water is calm with a shimmering blue-green hue, and the tree reflections from the park on the other side make the scene look like oil paint on canvas, something out of a Monet collection. A flock of pelicans is effortlessly floating by downstream, some backward or sideways. They don't care. I look at them. —I've said it many times, and I'll say it again: if I were a bird, I want to be a pelican. Preferably one in the San Francisco Bay area. They seem to know how to enjoy life. No real predators. Hanging out by the harbor, doing Otis Redding, and eating a fish every now and then. Julie has a harder time committing to an avian life. She can consider being a swan or a bald eagle. A swan, I can see. But an eagle… they have such a hectic life, hunting for prey all the time and being attacked by feisty crows. Julie is more and more warming up to the pelican avatar, though. The problem is that if I'm a pelican and Julie is a swan, we won't be a couple. Since this is all hypothetical, I try not to be too bugged down about it. Also, pelicans may be seasonally monogamous, but I don't think they necessarily mate for life. So, even if we're both pelicans, we still have an issue. This is a discussion Julie and I need to have at some point. Maybe over wine time.

CHAPTER 18

Summer 2024. Bryce Vogel. The Stargate and Simul projects.

"Well, this is one hell of a story, Symphony. I don't know what I expected you'd find out from Derek—or John, I guess—but it wasn't this." Bryce leans back and takes a sip of his wine, Copper Mountain Pinot Gris from Oregon. Which pairs well with the Diver scallops we're both eating. We're at Bond 45 in National Harbor. Trend-breaker as I am, I drink a full-bodied Italian Barolo. The sommelier informed me that the wine has a classic "tar-and-rose" aroma with added tasting notes of truffles, chocolate, eucalyptus, dried fruit, and leather. I pick up a delayed, floral scent and a licorice flavor. It's a complex wine, and I've encountered similar characteristics in other Barolos. I know it's a combination I like, and this is no exception.

I've just told Bryce about my discussion with John Smith. He's intrigued about the prospective function of the Crex-ORs and their potential applications. But we spend most of the time musing over the Qumran parchments and what conclusions to make. If we assume that John Smith's story is accurate and that the 13QT parchments are authentic—granted, two significant assumptions—then, it seems as if: 1) Evolution was kick-started not only on Earth but also in other locations in the universe; and 2) Mind viewing was a means of communication in early hominins, predating the development of speech. We're at the stage of the last scallops when we finally start to wrap our heads around tomorrow's meeting and how to go about setting the stage for the disclosure of John Smith's hypothesis.

We've had roasted Brussels sprouts for starters, the scallops with mashed potatoes as the entrée, and plenty of olive ciabatta. So, when the waiter hits us with the dessert menu, I've decided against ordering anything more. I feel proud and very strong when I tell him that I'm good. Such is the resolve and willpower of Ludvig Bertil Thovén! I wish Julie were here to witness this achievement.

Of course, when Bryce points out that they have New York-style cheesecake, we're in a different jurisdiction, and previous declarations are null and void. We ask for Ruby Port to go with the cheesecakes. I'm glad Julie isn't here. The cheesecake, by the way, is very satisfying. Dense cream cheese layer and a firm graham cracker bottom. An 8.6 on my scale.

We've paid and are getting ready to leave. "So," Bryce pushes back the chair to give his round midsection—which likely has expanded from the meal—some air, "you're saying that Derek… I'll just call him Derek since that's how I'm thinking about him. You're saying he had the idea of the mind-viewing capability even before he found the Qumran texts?"

"That's what he states. He said he thinks it's logical to assume that early hominins, at this stage in evolution, had a primitive, non-verbal language based on images. He also considered the possibility of a cloud mind or hive mind, that tight-knit bands of people shared images. This, in a way, makes sense since it would be difficult anyhow to know from whom in a group an image emanates. But they might have developed that skill as part of growing up. Of course, when he started on his manuscript, he was emboldened by the fact that he had the Qumran texts. Also, you know… because of what happened and his rather poor track record, it's easy to think of Derek as a smeared and marginal figure in science. But, in fact, my understanding from talking to him and from what I learned about him from his colleagues,

Derek had acquired a deep knowledge and an intuitive feeling for hominin evolution and the evolution of communication in particular. This is in addition to his astonishing linguistic skills."

"Okay, but why would this mind viewing, if it existed, have anything to do with olfactory receptors?"

"Well, first off, he didn't say olfactory receptors, but olfactory-like receptors. Second, he thinks, and I concur, that there is very likely more to chemosensory communication in humans than we're currently aware of. For example, there are lots of olfactory receptors outside of the nasal epithelium, such as in the brain, on the skin, in the kidneys, the liver, and the testis. The activating ligands for these receptors are to the most extent unknown. There's also the vomeronasal, or Jacobson's organ, which is part of the auxiliary olfactory system. It might be involved in pheromone signaling in humans, but its role in humans is poorly understood. So, I—"

Bryce holds up a finger and interrupts me. "Hm… wait a minute, this gets me thinking. You remember I told you about the Star Gate Project? Just for reference, that was at the OMICS all-hands meeting you held two years back, and the same evening, I won in chess, even though you had captured my queen." He gives me one of his jaunty smiles. I give him a sideways look in return. You can't get mad at Bryce. You can throw things at him, though, which I do. A crumbled-up receipt hits him right in the forehead. Small pleasures.

But, yes, the Star Gate Project that Bryce mentioned. Stargate serves as an umbrella name for a top-secret operation carried out by the U.S. federal government, mainly through the Defense Intelligence Agency (DIA) and the Central Intelligence Agency (CIA), from the beginning of the 1970s to 1995. Throughout this time, the project went by different code names, such as Sun Streak, Center Lane, Grill Flame, Gondola Wish, INSCOM, SCANATE, and, from 1991, Star Gate. The purpose of Star Gate was to explore the psychic abilities of certain individuals to perform remote viewing. In other words, to see things (people, objects, or places) in an out-of-body experience, preferably at a great distance. Individuals deemed promising were trained to use their talents for "psychic warfare." Star Gate was initiated by the CIA in 1970 in response to purported successful investigations of psychic powers for intelligence and military purposes in the Soviet Union. An estimated twenty million dollars was spent on Star Gate, most of which was allocated in the 1980s to 1990s. The funding was used to support operational activities, as well as basic research in remote viewing. By the end of 1995, Star Gate had conducted thousands of review-viewing sessions, which resulted in several hundred intelligence gatherings.

The Star Gate project was evaluated in 1995 by the American Institutes for Research (AIR) at the bequest of the CIA. Based on the recommendation by AIR, the CIA concluded that remote viewing had not aided in providing valuable data in intelligence operations, and they closed down the project. The AIR report and a number of intelligence collection projects performed as part of Star Gate have since been published.

"As I told you," says Bryce while we're walking back to Gaylord, where we checked in earlier today, "CIA declassified Star Gate in the mid-90s, and the information was released to the public. Most of the information, I should say. What I've learned more recently is that one of the intelligence explorations under Star Gate was not released to AIR and was not included in the publicized documents."

I should add here that Bryce's focus on national terrorism, with a position at the upper echelons in the DHS, and with a close connection to several senators in the Homeland Security Committee and Governmental Affairs (HSGAC), to DARPA, DIA, and the National Security Agency (NSA), is privy to many revelations and rumors regarding classified operations in the intelligence and military communities. And, just to let you know, Bryce is slated to take over as the DHS Secretary when Vanessa Ashby retires next year. It's contingent on Senate consent, but it's considered a foregone conclusion that Bryce will be appointed.

Bryce continues, "This project was called Simul and was performed at Fort Mead, like several other investigations in Star Gate, from the late 1980s until 1995." (Bryce is referring to the U.S. Army installation in Maryland that houses, among other entities, the headquarters for the NSA). "Simul was initiated and led by James MacLester, a psychologist from Towson University. The inception of Simul was the observation that close relationship often results in synchronized minds, or 'mind melding,' where two people simultaneously say the same thing, think about the same thing, or finish each other's sentences. By the way, 'simul' is Latin for 'simultaneous.' This phenomenon apparently happens in different longstanding relationships but is particularly common in couples that have been married for a long time, as I'm sure you've noticed." I'm nodding. I can definitely contest this. Julie and I often—and seemingly unprovoked—say the same things in chorus.

"So," says Bryce, "MacLester's idea was to examine if this synchronized-mind phenomenon could be exploited in intelligence gathering. For example, could you plant a spy in an organization and have him or her enter into a liaison with a target person and foster a connection that eventually could lead to synchronized minds."

"Wow, seems real far out!" I say. "So, should the spy establish a connection, get married, have a family with two kids, a dog and a cat, and two cars, go to Rotary meetings, and then suddenly, after ten to twenty years, start to siphon information out of his or her spouse? I mean, this is simply stupid!"

"Well, yeah, it certainly didn't lead anywhere, as far as we know. When MacLester passed away in 1994, Simul was soon transferred from the operational unit at Fort Mead, where it was sorted under the NSA, to basic research at the University of California at Berkeley, under the auspices of DARPA—still highly classified. At UC Berkeley, the project was first headed by Seth Andersen, another psychologist. However, under his regime, the project was plagued by divisiveness and poor management, and DARPA was about to pull the plug in 2017 but decided at the last minute to turn it over to Ronda Trueblood, a person I know quite well. We both served on the UC Berkeley Planning and Budget Committee. Ronda turned Simul into a molecular biology project. In 2020, Ronda appealed to DARPA to have Simul declassified, a process that takes a few years."

We are now inside Gaylord, and Bryce directs us to a corner in the foyer. He looks at me. "When I was at the DARPA meeting in San Francisco in mid-July, the declassification evaluation of Simul and a few other projects were on the agenda, and I got to speak in some detail with Ronda about the progress of the project. Under Ronda's tenure, Simul focused on the effect of pheromones on gene expression in humans. A cohort of four hundred thirty-five couples who had been married for ten years or longer was compared with a control group that included couples who had no previous interaction or had been together for less than a year. The results are really fascinating. There was a dramatic and statistically significant increase in pheromone emissions in the marriage group compared to the control. And, here's the kicker, there was a similar statistically significant increase in the expression of olfactory receptor gene clusters in the marriage group, presumably pheromone-mediated. This increase was not observed in the upper nasal cavity but seemed restricted to certain neurons in the brain—primarily in the axons—and to some neurons in the vomeronasal organ. They also confirmed the results by proteomics. Incidentally, she mentioned that most of these analyses were carried out at OMICS."

I'm not surprised. Although single-cell genomics and proteomics can be performed at many places these days, OMICS has by far the most expertise and advanced technologies for these kinds of analyses. This is an example of the competitive OMICS grants I mentioned earlier.

"So," says Bryce, "I think the Simul project—the way it turned out—gives credence to your notion that there's more to olfaction than meets the eye. All this is confidential, as I hope you understand since they haven't yet published the results."

"Intriguing," I say. "So, will the project be declassified and be made public?"

"I recommended declassification, and so did the other two in the panel. This is fascinating basic research, and there's no need to keep it classified. Ronda's group has several manuscripts ready for submission. So, publications should be forthcoming in a few years' time. They will first need to be vetted by DARPA."

We had an early dinner at Bond 45. It's now only seven-thirty p.m., and we decide to play chess. We usually make sure that at least one of us brings a chess set. But this time, Bryce suggested calling ahead and having the reception order one. He gets over to pick it up while I take off my blazer. I usually think better if I'm a little bit on the cold side. When I see Bryce returning with the chessboard, he's laughing and shaking his head.

"Well," he says, "when I called, I asked them to get us a chessboard. And, that's what we got— a chessboard... but no pieces."

We're both Marriott Bonvoy Titanium Elite members, and we can probably have the reception help us out. But that might take half an hour. Instead, we choose to go rough and play *sans voir* or blindfold chess, something neither of us has done before. Just so you know, if you don't already, blindfold chess—to play chess without pieces or even without a board—is a real thing. For example, there are tournaments in blindfold chess.

As you're aware, I have many good qualities; I'm brilliant, good-looking, and a very likable and easy-going guy. However, such attributes just take you so far in blindfold chess. Playing this kind of virtual chess requires extraordinary visuospatial abilities and memory, and you'd be hard-pressed to find anyone who would suggest that those are qualities I possess. Bryce is probably better than I am, but it's a pretty low bar. Anyhow, we thought we would give it a try. We played rock, paper, scissors to decide who would be white. Bryce wins, so he goes first.

Bryce: *d4*

Me: *c5*

Bryce: *d4*

Me: No, I'm not going to be that classic, *Qa5*

Bryce: *Nc3*

The setup is already starting to break up in my head. I try desperately to remember where the pieces are on the virtual board, but...

Me: "I give up."

Bryce: "Me too."

Well, this will not be in the history books. But at least we made an honest effort.

The next day is tomorrow. And that should be interesting

CHAPTER 19

Fall 2024. The Gaylord meeting. A Proustian flashback.

M ost, if not all, of you know Symphony, and he will be leading the discussion." She nods at the agenda displayed on a wall monitor. "I will first go through some safety and housekeeping points. Then, we'll make a short round of introductions before I turn the meeting over to Symphony."

This is Vanessa Ashby, the Secretary of the DHS. It's eight a.m. on Thursday, August first, and we're starting the meeting while having a catered breakfast. As far as breakfasts served on a federal budget, this one is okay. I have a vegetarian omelet with avocado, sundried tomatoes, and potatoes—kind of a Spanish omelet—and coffee. No scones as far as the eyes can see. A major oversight, if you ask me. This is what happens if you let a federal agency take control. Had Hanne been responsible, as was initially planned, I would now be looking at platters with at least two different kinds of scones. Hanne knows me quite well. But I can be strong when needed, so I don't make a scene.

While I'm pondering these essentials in life, Vanessa leads us through a safety routine should anything threatening happen and points out where the restrooms are located. She continues, "I remind you that we still are in a continued moratorium for the Crassus Project. And that includes the discussion here today. Until we know more about the applications of this project in the realm of national security, we'll remain in this indeterminate situation." Vanessa looks at Noa, Mike, Ron, and Laxmi, who she knows are the ones most affected by not being able to publish their research. "And I appreciate your patience here. I trust you continue to use proper judgment when talking to family members, friends, and colleagues about the project."

Vanessa stops and looks around. "Any questions so far? No? Okay, then let's go around the table and briefly present ourselves. I'll start. I'm Vanessa Ashby. I'm the Secretary of the DHS, at least for the remainder of this year. I've announced that I plan to retire after Christmas, and, as I'm sure many of you know, Bryce Vogel—she points to Bryce—will take over after me, starting next year."

We continue clockwise around the table. To the left of Vanessa is first Bryce, and then six DHS folks; her Military Advisor, Randolph Sergione, two staff from the Science and Technology Directorate, Amy Hubb and Stanley Agnew, the Chief Information Officer, Don Gomez, a Program Manager from the Chemical and Biological Defense Division, Lisa Carlson, and one staff from the Office of Intelligence and Analysis, Lisa Polkowski. Then there is Brad Johansen, Joe Buchanan, Scott Krasinski, and the Crassus Team, Mike, Noa, Laxmi, Ron, and there's me.

Vanessa said, "Okay, Symphony, the floor is yours."

"Thanks, Vanessa." I bring up my PowerPoint presentation. None of the DHS people are biologists. I start with a general overview of olfaction and the pathway from odorant binding to sensing a smell. I explain what G-coupled receptors mean, show how ORs work, give a schematic representation of the OR structure, and point out where the odorants bind. I then turn to the Crassus Project.

"Two years ago, we obtained a remarkably well-preserved cranium of a five-hundred-fifty-thousand-year-old hominin fossil from Professor Elke Westhoff at Max Planck Institute for Evolutionary Anthropology in Leipzig, Germany. The fossil was unearthed in Morocco in the 1960s. Due to circumstances surrounding the discovery of the site, it became known as Fat Man's Cave, and the fossil itself was coined Fat Man or Crassus in Latin. So, scientifically, the fossil is known as *Homo crassus*, and that's why we refer to the project as the Crassus Project. Professor Westhoff and her team wanted us to see if we could extract and sequence genetic material from the Crassus cranium. Amazingly enough, we were able to isolate and purify not only DNA but also proteins, several of which were intact. This is all work by Laxmi and Ron here, with Noa and Mike at the forefront."

I turn the PowerPoint presentation to a black slide. I want to keep the next section at a high level. "Most of the proteins we found are olfactory receptors, or ORs, or look like olfactory receptors. But they are distinctly different from any other olfactory receptors we know of. This suggests that whatever they bind or respond to is different from the odorants we're used to. Some of the DNA or DNA fragments we sequenced encode this new kind of olfactory receptors, which we call Crex-ORs, for Crassus extra ORs. We also saw genes for normal ORs, the kind humans have today. Altogether, we count eleven putative, unique Crex-ORs for which we have partial or full-length DNA and/or protein sequences. For whatever reason, the only intact proteins we found were from Crex-ORs. Possibly, they are unusually resistant to degradation, or they might have been embedded in protective tissue during fossilization."

Amy Hubb, the woman from the Science and Technology Directorate, raises her hand. "So, when you say that you have found eleven of these receptors, do you assume that represents the full repertoire in Fat Man"—and here she smiles and lets out a short, amused chuckle—"or do you think he had more?"

"I think he had more," I reply. "Why? Because when we look at the binding sites on the Crex-ORs, they differ according to a specific pattern, structurally as well as chemically—in amino acid composition. When we feed this information into our protein-prediction modeling programs, we repeatedly end up with forty-one potential receptors."

I'm waiting to see if there are more questions. There aren't. I advance to the next slide, showing an OlfactoryChip, or ORChip. "We have discussed the OlfactoryChip technology on many occasions during the last couple of years. Suffice it here to say that we can, in one continuous process, synthesize and immobilize ORs on silicon wafers in such a way that they all have the odorant-binding site on one end of the wafer, and the signaling end on the other side, connected to an electrical sensing device. So, while in the biological system, the chemical interaction between odorant and receptor generates an electrochemical signal, in the ORChip, the interaction instead leads to an electrophysical signal. When an odorant binds, we can decipher the electrical readout to identify the odorant. We have made the same kind of chips with the Crex-ORs and challenged them with all possible volatile organic and inorganic compounds. So far, we haven't had any hits. We have doped the chips with normal ORs so we can tell that they are okay. So, we are at a loss in trying to figure out the function of Fat Man's ORs, or OR-like receptors."

I see Amy Hubb raising her hand again. I pause. "I'll be happy to take questions," I say. "But I suggest we wait until I've told you what I've recently learned and about one hypothesis for these Crex-ORs. That way, we can have a more informed discussion. Let's also take a fifteen-minute break to stretch our legs and get some air. We'll reconvene at ten-thirty."

So far, it's been smooth sailing. Standard science presentation, fairly interesting but nothing remarkable. What follows, I suspect, will be bumpier. I'll push boundaries that challenge my credibility.

I don't want to be cornered in discussions at this stage, so I quickly depart and take aim at the main entrance—which also happens to be the main exit. There's a Starbucks nearby. I know they have scones, so I head over there. It turns out they have a weekly rotation of scone flavors, and the flavor of the week is black currant, a rarity in scone circles. With coffee and two scones on a tray, I park myself at a window table.

As I take the first bite into the scone, I am hit by the grape-like and musky flavor. A fascinating thing happens; I get a Proustian flashback. Has that ever happened to you? My mind suddenly floods with an image of me and my younger brother in our kitchen in Sweden. I was twelve, and he was ten. My parents are there. Theirs was not precisely a happy or harmonious marriage; they almost always argued. My dad was a hard man; he drank too much and was often violent—I later found out that he was not my biological dad, but that's for another day. Most days, there was an air of hostility at home. As a young kid, the situation felt fragile; anytime, an explosion of arguments and violence could erupt. But this day, a Sunday in June was one of these rare moments when my parents were not latching out at each other. They were laughing—and even seemed affectionate. My mom had baked a black currant pie. I felt happy and tense at the same time; I knew that this congenial atmosphere wouldn't last long. But, for the moment, I harbored a sense of joy.

This phenomenon of sensory déjà vu evoked by the scent and taste of my black-currant scone is famously captured by Marcel Proust in one of the most quoted passages in literature, *"À la Recherche du temps Perdu"* ("In Search of Lost Times" or "Remembrance of Things Passed"). It is also referred to as the "Proustian effect" or "Proustian moment," or, by Proust himself, as "Involuntary memories." When Proust wrote these lines in 1913 and described how childhood memories came rushing down on the protagonist, the experience didn't come from eating a scone at Starbucks but from munching on a Madeleine cake dipped in lemon-scented tea at his home.

As John Smith alluded to when we met a few months ago, olfaction is unique among our senses in that it bypasses the thalamus and relays information directly to the hippocampus and amygdala, where emotional memory is processed. That's the neurological explanation for a Proustian flashback or involuntary memories. That's likely also why a system based on olfactory-like receptors lends itself to be involved in a mind-viewing faculty.

My Proustian flashback is short (maybe half a minute) but intensely powerful. When it fades, it leaves me with a feeling of slight melancholy, complex, and challenging to describe in words. I try to shrug it off and text Julie. She is dropping off Jupiter at the kennel and messages back with a selfie of the two of them. I contemplate life as I down the coffee and pick up crumbles from the napkin. I decide it's good. Life is good.

As I leave Starbucks, the remaining tinges of melancholy vanish in the brisk autumn gale. *À la Recherche du temps Perdu.*

———

You say ten-thirty to a bunch of academics, and you know you'll end up meeting at around ten forty-five. You say ten-thirty to folks from the Department of Homeland Security, they're there at ten-thirty. So I'm a little late, as is the Crassus Team, but not by much. We are, after all, national lab people. As I enter the room, I can sense the anticipation. I'm sure everyone is eager to find out about the Crex-OR hypothesis I alluded to, including Laxmi, Ron, Noa, and Mike. I feel bad that I haven't told them yet, but I wanted to have this first discussion about the mind-viewing concept in the presence of DHS in case we receive specific instructions in moving forward. Of course, I've already told Julie and Bryce, but that's different. Come to think of it; I also told the McIntoshes, and Jessica and Lars. But that's also different. —I can rationalize almost anything.

"I will tell you a story" is how I start out when people settle in. "Many years ago, in the 1980s, I met a man at a science convention in Greece. The venue—this was in Halkidiki— hosted two or three different conferences at the same time. He attended a paleozoology symposium, and I was there for a photosynthesis meeting. The man—he wants to stay out of the limelight, so let's just call him John—was an Associate Professor at University of Michigan." (I look at Bryce and see him smiling slightly at the mention of "John.") "At the convention's farewell dinner, I happened to sit in his orbit while he was bragging about a manuscript he was writing. He'd had quite a bit to drink, so most people didn't think too much about what he was saying. Neither did I, really, until a couple of months ago."

I go on to describe how John ended up in Reading in the U.K. and how I tracked him down. I leave out most details in my pursuit— impressive pursuit if you ask me—and just say that I got help from the University of Reading. As I summarize my meeting with John and his theory about mind-viewing mediated by olfactory or olfactory-like receptors in early hominins, I show a PowerPoint slide I've prepared.

I stop momentarily as a door opens, and a catered lunch is being rolled in on three tables.

"So, as you can see," I explain and point when the door has closed again, "Person one sees an object, in this case, an antelope, and when the visual image of the antelope is processed, the brain emits olphons. When Person two, here—who does not necessarily see the antelope—perceives the olphons via olfactory-like receptors, his or her brain generates a mental image of the antelope. Similarly,"—I show another slide—"Person one sits with a few others in a gathering and thinks it's time to start a fire. He brings up a mental image of wood and fire. Again, olphons from Person one are sensed by Person two and others. They get the hint and start gathering wood. John told me he learned from talking to neuroscientists when working on his manuscript that the processing of physical and mental images in the brain is similar. So, he meant—John did—if looking at a physical image sparks off olphons, it stands to reason that the same would hold for a mental image. That, in a nutshell, is John's mind-viewing hypothesis. What these olphons are, we have no idea. Nor do we know how far they can travel or what kinds of materials they can or cannot penetrate. If they even exist, that is."

While talking, I've been trying to gauge peoples' reactions. I see hesitant smiles and inquisitive looks mixed with some degree of excitement. I pause and look around. I expect a lot of questions, but it's uneasily quiet. I break the silence by looking at Amy Hubb. "Amy, you were going to ask a question before. Maybe we can take that now?"

"Uhm… well, I was going to ask if there might have been odorants these early hominins encountered but that we don't have today. Maybe from extinct plants or animals. So, these Crex-ORs could have been specific for such compounds."

"That's a possibility," I agree. I remember that this idea was floated at a meeting we had in the spring of last year. "We can reach out to some paleologists to see if they know of or have suggestions for potential compounds." As I'm saying that, I realize I almost hope that Amy's idea is correct. There would be no obvious NSNH applications—I'm talking about OMIC's National Security-National Health mission—and the moratorium for publications would be removed. Then, the team would have some very interesting papers to write in collaboration with

Westhoff's group. Finding extinct olfactory receptors in early hominins that were specialized for odorants that existed in their environments but have since been lost holds a definite general appeal. We would have an excellent chance to get at least one paper into *Nature*.

Of course, given that I'm aware of Johns Smith's Qumran parchment excerpts, I'm reasonably convinced that the mind-viewing hypothesis is somehow connected to the Crex-ORs. I'm also fairly confident that no matter what, DHS will insist that the moratorium remains in place until we have more information. Vanessa confirms my suspicion. She stands up.

"Symphony, this is absolutely intriguing and interesting, bordering fiction. I haven't made up my mind about what to believe yet. But… I think it's fair to say that if there would be any truth to the mind-imaging or mind-viewing concept, there's a clear national-security angle."

Lisa Carlson, the Program Manager from the Chemical and Biological Defense Division, chimes in, "I agree with Vanessa; it sounds like a fiction novel. I think Amy's suggestion holds more promise. But certainly, we need to find out, one way or another, if there's anything to the mind-viewing hypothesis. By the way, considering what you've told us about this John, how reliable do you think he is?"

Other people had apparently been thinking about this very issue, and there's a buzz of assenting voices from the DHS contingency.

I had, of course, expected this question. I reiterate what I told Bryce yesterday. "So," I conclude, "although his standing in the scientific community is far from stellar, I don't doubt his credibility. But, of course—"

"Sorry, Symphony, but I have to ask," It's Vanessa again, "Even if we were to consider this mind-viewing idea, why on earth would that have anything to do with olfactory receptors? I'm definitely not an olfaction expert, but wouldn't receptors in the eyes be more likely? Or, did these humans—or hominins, I guess—smell images?"

That brings down a chuckle, and I join in. "Well," I say, "eye receptors—opsins—are also G-coupled receptors. And, it's clear that what we have in the Crex-ORs are not classical olfactory receptors. We may think more in terms of olfactory-*like* receptors." Again, I regurgitate the information I gave Bryce. "Then, if we take all that into consideration, we need to accept that our understanding of olfaction in humans, not to mention pre-historic humans, is rather meager. So, it's not that far-fetched to buy into the idea that hominins—present-day as well as extinct humans—have or had chemo-sensory faculties that we are unaware of."

I look around. "I rest my case."

Vanessa smiles. "You make a strong closing argument, Symphony. And, don't get me wrong, I would be thrilled if the mind-viewing hypothesis turns out to have legs." She looks around. "So, then, how do we move forward? Any suggestions?"

"Well," I say, "Before we open the floor, let me point out that I think the mind-viewing hypothesis is testable. It's a simple approach, but I think it could be conclusive."

You know I'm a good mentor, right? I've told you that. So, the good mentor in me wants to let someone in the Crassus Team, such as Noa, describe how to perform the test. This would give her another chance to shine in the presence of DHS dignitaries. I'm sure she could pull it off. It's, after all, a pretty obvious way of going about it. I cast Noa a glance to see if she's on top of it, but I get no connection. Oh, well. I'll do it myself. I just wanted you to know how a good mentor thinks. That's me, by the way, a good mentor. So, anyway…

I've also prepared a slide deck for this, and I start the presentation. "Basically, this is about measuring the correlation between two variables, a visual image and the readout from the receptor array. Person one looks at a blue ball in front of the array, and we record the readout pattern. The same person then looks at a red house, a green field with cows, a green field without cows, just cows, and so forth. For each image, we record the readout. Then, this is repeated with a second, third, and so on person. We do this with a large enough cohort and enough images to make statistics. If there's a statistically significant correlation between images and array readout, we're probably on the right track. We would also expect that different people might not elicit an identical readout for the same image. Just like we have different dialects and pronounce words differently. We also may recognize other patterns. For example, we might pick up elements in the array readout for 'green field' in both the 'green field with cows' and the 'green field without cows' images. Similar for the 'cows' element." I show some graphics for this in the presentation.

Lisa Carlson asks, "Shouldn't you also do the same with people thinking about something, rather than looking at an object, as you showed in your slide? I think that would be informative. I'm thinking of potential intelligence gathering."

"I was going to do that at a later stage. Because I think that's so much harder. If you ask me to think of a blue ball..." and here I close my eyes. "Okay, I can force myself to see a blue ball. But I also see... like, a sheep... and I see the sun and grass." People start laughing. I look at Lisa. "Of course, from a DHS standpoint, I can see how this would be valuable. So, yes, we can add this to the initial test."

"Sounds like a fun game," Amy says. "I wouldn't *mind* participating." Some people got the pun and laughed.

"I'd like to play too," says Vanessa, laughing.

"That could be arranged," I say, looking at them.

"But," I continue, "before we get too excited, there are a couple of caveats here. First, if evolution has gotten rid of the mind-viewing receptors, the ability to emit olphons might also have been lost. If the Crex-OR receptors and olphons constituted the basis for the mind-viewing trait, modern humans might have neither the receptors nor the olphons. John, who clearly thought a lot about this, assumes that olphons are an inherent part of image processing also in today's humans. Second, if I see an antelope, I can choose not to say anything. Similarly, maybe Fat Man and the hominins of his time could choose whether or not to emit olphons. Perhaps the default was off, and they learned as toddlers how to turn it on when they wanted to communicate, the same way we learn to speak. Or, maybe the default was on, and they learned how to turn it off, just like we close our eyes when we want to sleep."

"So…" I continue, "the first thing we need to do is to ascertain that the Crex-ORChip device is triggered by the presence of humans." I have a strong feeling this will be the case, given the results so far and, of course, based on John's Qumran texts. "The next thing to do is to check if the Crex-ORChip device, or analyzer, responds differently—just by assessing the signal strength—to a person looking intently at something, or," I look at Lisa Carlson, "thinking hard on something, as opposed to keeping eyes closed and the mind blank."

"If you were to go ahead and test for the mind-viewing hypothesis, how long do you think that would take?" This is Lisa Carlson again.

"Well," I say. "As I mentioned, it's possible that Fat Man had forty-one different kinds of Crex olfactory receptors. It's a speculative but reasonably logical assumption. So, we would first synthesize the remaining receptors and manufacture arrays with all forty-one receptors. We would aim for at least one hundred thousand copies of each receptor per array, hopefully, more, if that can be arranged. So, I estimate this would take two to three months." I look over at the Crassus Team. "What do you guys think?"

"Yeah, I'd say three months," Ron says, and the others nod in agreement.

"And, do you have funding for that under the current Crassus grant?" asks Lisa Carlson.

Again, I look at Ron. He shakes his head. "If we're going for one hundred thousand copies, we may need additional funding."

"Send us a short write-up with an approximate budget. And if you want to test Amy's hypothesis, I guess you first need to track down some paleontologists," Lisa submits.

"That's correct," I say. "We'll get going on that as well."

Noa raises her hand. "Another, not mutually exclusive idea, is to look at the ligand-binding sites in the Crex-ORs and use reverse chemistry to synthesize compounds that are likely to bind."

"Great idea," I say and nod. What I don't say is that it probably isn't as good an idea as it may seem. The olfactory receptors we know seem to be somewhat promiscuous and bind odorants with quite different structural properties. With such weak binding affinities, it could be difficult to model for cognate ligands. But, certainly… it can be worth a try. It might even eventually help us in figuring out what the olphons are. And, of course, the Crex-ORs might differ from "normal" ORs in the way they interact with their ligands.

Don Gomez, the DHS Chief Information Officer, raises his hand. "This is probably a stupid question, but I started my position last year, and I have never seen an ORChip Array. Also, my background is in journalism, not molecular biology. I gather from the photo you showed in your presentation that the arrays are quite small, no? Like centimeter-scale? You mean you can still fit one hundred thousand copies of each receptor in such a small area?"

"Not a stupid question at all," I say. "Yes, you're right; an ORChip Array is around three square centimeters, and our current Crex-ORChips are two square centimeters. We're not sure about the size of the Crex receptors, but a typical mammalian olfactory receptor is like… five nanometers?" I look to Noa for confirmation.

"Yes," she says. "The structures we have of the mouse and human receptors show a diameter of four point nine nanometers. So, I'd say five nanometers is a good number."

"Okay," I say and open the calculator app on my phone. "Let's say, for the sake of simplicity, that we have fifty different receptors. So, one hundred thousand copies of each, with a size of five nanometers, end up being… twenty-five millimeters. So, we can pack fifty times one hundred thousand receptors on less than three square centimeters. But we wouldn't do that. We'll spread them apart to avoid allosteric modifications—structural changes—upon binding a ligand that might cause physical interactions with neighboring receptors. We also need space for the electronic circuitry at the bottom of the array. So, I'd say that these new arrays would be around four square centimeters."

"Another question to display my ignorance since I'm at it," says Don Gomez. "You said in your presentation that humans have somewhere over four hundred different olfactory receptors, no? Doesn't it seem unlikely that Fat Man"—a smile and a chuckle—"could do this mind-viewing with no more than forty-one receptors?"

"Excellent question," I say. "We certainly don't know how mind-viewing, if it existed, worked. But, as a comparison, there are only nine different opsins—eye receptors—that we know of anyhow in the human eye. And the processing of visual and mental images in the brain seems to be similar. So, considering this, it's not incredulous to think that forty-one receptors might suffice for something like mind viewing."

"Okay, thanks, that makes sense."

"Also," I continue, "we don't know what granularity mind viewing would operate at. Or, if it involves colors or just black and white."

Brad raises his hand. "Symphony, do you think—well, first," he says laughing, "I can hardly believe I'm sitting here talking about mind viewing as if it were any other science project. But… here we are. So… if these early hominids—or hominins, I don't know which is what—could 'see' what's on a person's mind, then… wouldn't there be a lot of images from different people swirling around in every head?"

"Yes, and that's probably why mind viewing would be a primitive form of communication. It worked well for Fat Man because only so many people were around at a time. In today's society, verbal language is far superior. And, by the way, I had to look up hominin and hominid some time back. Hominins are a tribe within the hominid family. So, hominins belong to a sub-group of hominids. Fat Man, as well as Neanderthals and modern humans, are all hominins."

The time is approaching three p.m. Vanessa stands up. "Symphony, I hand it to you. This has been a very informative and entertaining—and stimulating—meeting. I hope we can keep this under wraps until we meet again in three to four months' time. We also have OMICS' triennial review coming up before then, so I assume many people will be quite busy. I suggest we leave out the Crassus Project in the review. There certainly are enough other activities to discuss—though maybe not as enticing as Crassus."

Vanessa continues, "Hanne," and here she nods at me, "has booked tables for ten at McCormick & Schmick's from six o'clock. The dinner is at your own expense. Again, we want to avoid discussing Crassus in public. So, try to find something else to talk about over your seafood or steak. I cannot make it; I'm picking up my grandchildren from swimming lessons. So, try to have fun anyhow. I know it'll be tough but try your best." (Polite chuckles.) "Don't forget to turn in your badges when you leave." She looks over at me and the Crassus Team. "And safe travels."

CHAPTER 20

Fall 2024. Validation experiments.

The morning of Friday, October eighteenth, finds me in my office studying a chess move that Bryce just posted on the d4c4 app. It's another beautiful autumn day in Richland. The temperature is already approaching twenty-seven degrees. The sky is azure blue with just a few cirrus clouds. You can't open windows in this building. But if you could, I would probably hear the extensive repertoire from the starlings fluttering around in Brownian motion in the oak tree outside my office. If I had the window open, that is.

I'm telling you all this because I'm trying to forget about the chess game. Basically, my decision comes down to one of two things: either concede right now—I think "resign" is the proper term—or hold on in the off chance that Bryce develops acute retrograde amnesia and forgets about his plans. Let it be temporary; he is, after all, my friend. The situation is dire. For one, I've lost the last two games to Bryce. Second, the move I'm pondering reads *Bxf6+*, which—as the chess aficionados among you realize—means that Bryce, who is playing black, has put me in check with his bishop. In the process, he's captured my only remaining knight. I can move my king out of harm's way. But I can read the writing on the wall as well as anyone; I'm more than likely doomed. I add *0-1* in the app and shoot it off. I lean back. Fuck. Losing three games in a row eats at my confidence. Bryce texts me back immediately with a smiley face. I text back: "Don't you have work to do?"

The worst thing you can do when you're disappointed or upset is comfort eating. Anyone can tell you that. So, I just want to let you know that the reason I've now retreated to my favorite spot in the courtyard with coffee and two scones has nothing to do with the chess game; I'm not even thinking about it. I simply felt that coffee and scones were in order. And it's ten a.m., so a pretty good time for a coffee break. It's cutting it close to lunchtime for me, but… anyhow. You might be interested to learn that our cafeteria gets the scones from the Frost me Sweet bakery in town, which specializes in huckleberry scones, among other things. Delicious they are, the scones. I submit to you that if this were indeed emotional eating due to my chess defeat, I would have ordered three scones and not restrained myself to two. Just so we're clear.

Okay, that's fine, but what about the Crex-ORChips? you may ask. Well, we finished the assembly a week from yesterday, way ahead of schedule. We really have gotten this down to an art. The whole process is fully robotized. After feeding genomic information into the DNA console and entering information about the number, spacing, and distribution (random block or clustered) of the proteins, not a single person needs to be involved until we pick up the chips for inspection. Growing yeast cells, immobilizing them on alginate lattices, injecting synthesized DNA into the immobilized yeast cells, collecting translocated proteins from the extracellular matrix, threading them into artificial lipid membranes in correct topological orientation, adding a mucus-simulating layer, and inserting the electronic wafer and connecting it to the receptor proteins, are done in one continuous loop until all receptors are in place. It's quite amazing, really. And it was all my idea! I'm boasting a bit here. But what the heck? I'm worth it. When we received the funding from DHS for the ORChips, the Scientific Board at OMICS was as thrilled as it was skeptical. It was considered that our approach was too risky and that we should opt for a more conventual, albeit slower, multi-step strategy in making the chips. But I urged Ron and Laxmi, whom I've hired to lead the project, to stay firm. We funded the initial pilot of the protein assembly robot as an LDRD (that is, Laboratory-Directed Research and Development) project from the DHS grant, with Noa as the Principal Investigator. The pilot project was very successful and quickly morphed into the development of the full-scale assembly robot, which we named PATTY, for Protein Assembly with a defined Topology after Translocation from Yeast cells. The acronym was another of my ideas. I tell you, I'm a very talented guy. —Well, maybe not in chess, as it seems lately. But let's not dwell on that now.

I would be remiss if I didn't tell you that everything wasn't exactly smooth sailing with PATTY. Notably, that nosy and irritating specimen Rosy Boyd—as you know, I don't like that old cow—kept putting sticks in the wheel. She questioned the eligibility of the LDRD project. She pointed out—correctly—that the LDRD call wasn't open but, rather, was made with Noa and others in the Crassus Team in mind. I tried to argue that there were no others around who could perform the highly advanced research required for the project, so an open call would just be for show. It doesn't matter, she said; others should be able to apply; *"Rules are rules."* I wanted to tell her what she could do with her rules when the computer screen flickered; she had ended the meeting. Just as well, I thought.

So, we issued an open LDRD call for building the protein assembly pilot. Short of stating that the Principal Investigator had to be a short-statured, black-haired female Israeli scientist, we kept the scientific requirements so narrow that no one else would find it a good use of time even to apply. However, knowing old cows, and Rosy Boyd in particular, I decided to be proactive. I asked Ron to ring up some junior staff and ask them to apply. In the end, we had five applicants, including Noa. An independent committee, consisting of folks from across OMICS, made a proper evaluation and recommended Noa be awarded the LDRD grant. All this grandstanding put us back three weeks with PATTY. This was now several years ago, but it reminds me that I've promised Brad Johansen to find a way to get Rosy Boyd out of their hair. I'll talk to Bryce.

All right, enough of Rosy Boyd. I hope she gets caught in barbed wire on her way out to pasture.

So, back to the Crex-ORChips. Once we knew that the chips would be ready at or around October ninth, we planned for the next phase, chip validation. The very first thing we did, obviously, was to check if the Crex-ORChip analyzer registered something emitted by people and perform some basic tests to make sure we had data that warranted further experiments. As I already suspected that the signals Noa and her team had observed emanated from humans, I was not surprised when that turned out to be the case. This was manifested by Noa and Mike moving in and out of the line of view of the analyzer. But it was exciting, nonetheless. What was surprising—although I wouldn't have known what to think, one way or another—was that the signal was not directional; moving sideways a few decimeters did not affect the signal, close to half a meter, and the signal got weaker but was still detectable. What also was surprising—but, again, I had no preconceived notion—was the long range of the signal. When Noa moved up to ten meters away from Chip, including being on the other side of a drywall, the signal strength didn't decrease in a linear fashion; if it got weaker at one point, it picked up strength again farther away. I had a theory about that. So, we learned that the signals emitted by Noa can penetrate drywall. We also learned that they cannot go through some of the equipment in the lab. Metal and hard plastic, in particular, seemed to be a blocker. This was neither the time nor the place to launch into a full-fledged investigation of the signal transmission, so we stopped there. How far and through what material the olphons can travel "awaits further studies," to cite a statement not uncommon in science publications.

Having established that the Crex-ORs bind signals (olphons?) emitted by people, we had a few follow-up experiments to perform. First, we wanted to see if we could detect—from just looking at the signal intensity—if there's any difference if the person in the line of view looks at or thinks about something or has the eyes closed and the mind blank. We volunteered Mike for that. He has a giant poster of a green cat on the wall above one of the gene sequencers he uses frequently. We are restrictive with personal paraphernalia in the labs, but I had allowed him to put up one of the many Andy Warhol posters he has in his office— he's a huge fan, obviously. So, he chose Sam the cat. When he looked at the green cat with purple eyes—the cat's eyes, that is— the Crex-ORChip analyzer produced an obvious response. When Mike then closed his eyes (after a few minutes to rid his brain of the strange-looking cat), there was only a weak (barely detectable) response from the device. Lastly, when he visualized Sam the cat in his mind, there was a response. We first were somewhat cavalier about the results. But it dawned on us after some digestion that this small experiment, just by itself, suggested that we are, indeed, dealing with a mind-viewing device. I now shared my theory for why the signal strength did not vary as a linear function of distance. If Noa, at, say, a four-meter distance, looked at or thought about something that elicited weak signal transmission, the signal strength would mostly correlate with distance. However, if she, at a seven-meter distance—ignoring the fact that she was on the other side of the drywall at this point—

came to look at something that caused stronger emission, the signal strength would be dependent on both distance and the viewed object.

As I explained at the Gaylord meeting in August, we want to test if there's a correlation between the object someone observes or thinks about and the electrical output from the Crex-ORChips. Seems like a relatively straightforward exercise, right? Well, recording people that bring up images in their minds is rather uncomplicated as logistics go; we can do that in a conference room. But having several people look at different objects and record the output is quite a bit more involved. For one thing, we wanted to include as many people and objects as possible to make the statistical analyses robust and conclusive. But, given that we don't want to explain what we're doing to every Dick, Harry, and Mary (*"You're doing what, testing a mind-reading device!?"*), we were limited to the people already privy to the scenario, which meant the sixteen of us present at last week's Gaylord meeting.

That brings me to the second issue. Scott and Brad work closely with the National Security Agency (NSA). Before moving to DHS, they worked in the National Security Directorate at our neighboring institution, PNNL (The Pacific Northwest National Laboratory, in the likely event you've forgotten), where they were part of the Directorate's Pattern Team. The Pattern Team, or PT, provides expertise and software to the NSA. Scott and Brad, who used to spend plenty of their working days developing algorithms and approaches for finding patterns—correlations amidst background noise—strongly suggested that our continued validation experiments be performed not only inside but that we also do testing outdoors with different backgrounds and with moving objects. But a bunch of grownups taking turns staring at an object while they're seemingly operating some piece of measuring equipment might cause some raised eyebrows and an urge to investigate.

So, you see, it wasn't just a matter of rounding up some folks and starting looking at things. We needed to be vigilant. We finally decided on Wednesday, October sixteenth. There were twelve of us who could make it: The Crassus Team, Brad Johansen, Scott Krasinski, myself from OMICS, Amy Hubb, Lisa Carlson, Lisa Polkowski, Stanley Agnew, and Bryce from DHS. Vanessa wanted to come, but her husband had cataract surgery, so she couldn't make it. On Monday morning, two days before the validation event, I met with the OMICS contingency to discuss some details. For example, what should we look for in terms of objects to view?

"We should compare black-and-white with corresponding colored images, if possible," Mike said. "We can print black-and-white and color versions of the same picture. And objects in motion compared to still objects," he added. "Like a moving car compared to a parked one."

"And multi-element images compared to one or more of the elements, as you mentioned at Gaylord." That was Laxmi. "Like cows on grass versus just cows."

"Or we can just go and stare at Rosy Boyd," I proposed. No, by exercising heroic restraint, I managed not to say that. I didn't want to be a bad example to the junior staff.

"Or just grass," I said instead.

"We should probably bring two battery packs," Brad suggested.

"Excellent point," I said. The signal output from the chip analyzer is feeble as electronic signals go. So, it needs an amplifier, and the amplifier needs power. And for it to be portable, we need to have a battery pack. So as not to confuse a weak signal transmission from a subject with a low battery, the amplifier is set to operate in full mode until the battery reaches a certain point and then shut off. And the battery pack might need recharging during the day. As it turned out, that wasn't the case, but we didn't know at the time.

"We'll be in von Braun first thing tomorrow morning while we have coffee and lay out the agenda so we can do some tests there before heading out," I said. As you might infer, our conference rooms are named after prominent scientists.

"It would also be good if we could look at different people, although I realize that might be difficult—unless we just use ourselves," said Noa.

"Good idea," I said.

————

So, while I'm sitting here in the courtyard Friday morning, finishing my coffee and scones, it's not only my chess defeat that's on my mind; I'm also revisiting the chip validation event and eagerly awaiting the results—Actually, I'm not thinking about chess at all; I thought we already established that.

I'd say the validation experiment was a success—I mean, the execution of the test; we know nothing about the outcome yet. We all met in von Braun on Tuesday morning over coffee and scones (three kinds: huckleberry, cherry, and vanilla-almond). We had the Crex-ORChip analyzer on a cart and did some testing with the fixtures and furniture in the room. We also tested printed texts on documents and computer screens, like phone numbers and imaginary passwords. We looked at each other—or, rather, Lisa, Scott, and Agnew took turns looking at the rest of us. We then went outside to a hidden area of the parking lot and looked at a few cars and registration plates. We also ogled at some of the campus buildings. We headed over towards Bookwalter Winery, where we planned to have lunch. We took a circuitous route to get there, and on the way over, we stopped and got some viewings of moving cars, grazing cows, sage brushes, and an assortment of farming equipment.

We had a nice lunch. We discussed our validation experiment quite openly. No one listening in would have a clue what we were talking about. Brad and I consulted Google Maps and planned a roundabout route back to OMICS on country roads via Kiona Winery in Benton City. That would give us some more viewing opportunities without being too obvious. —I had a delicious Columbia River steelhead salad for lunch, by the way, with a Deschutes Fresh Haze IPA. Yeah, I know it's a winery, but I still chose beer. Wine not?

CHAPTER 21

Fall 2024. Possibilities and limitations.

It's Monday morning, and another exciting day awaits us. After our Crex-ORChip validation adventure last Wednesday, we sent all the data files to Sirocco. We had booked run time over the weekend. We were following a multi-pronged approach with four different software packages, two developed by PT (the Pattern Team at PNNL's National Security Directorate, I mentioned before) and two commercial programs, SPSS and STATA, commonly used at OMICS. The data points are encrypted, so the statistics and modeling crew that will eventually make the data understandable to us won't know what the results mean.

I admit that compared to our staple diet of experimental research here at OMICS, last week's validation event felt quite a bit like quasi-science or more like a school project. But, in all fairness, this is unchartered territory, and there's no protocol to follow. Now, when everything is condensed to data files for statistical analysis, it starts to feel like any other OMICS project. I think my colleagues feel the same kind of relief.

———

Well, the results are in. It's one p.m. We—the Crassus Team, Brad, Scott, and I—are sitting in my office looking at a slide deck I just downloaded. Scott and Brad, being statisticians, take the lead. They start with a cursory assessment of the thirty-five slides that have been prepared for us.

The rest of us may not be *bona fide* statisticians, but we're all reasonably familiar with looking at statistical data and assessing the correlation between variables, such as metabolite or genomic fingerprints and phenotypic traits. So, with Scott and Brad guiding us, we can all see almost immediately, at least from data produced from the SPSS and STATA, that there are strong agreements between a viewed object and the composition of the signal output from the chip device, regardless of the viewer. Results from the PT software analyses are less intuitive at face value. But once they are converted to more conventional metrics, such as Pearson and Spearman correlation coefficients, which appear in table formats in the last four slides, we see that all four software packages give a similar outcome; the Crex-ORChips can accurately reveal what a subject is looking at. The conclusion from predicting what a subject thinks about is the same, although less obvious.

Due to the complexity of the signals coming off the analyzer, they need to be deconvoluted. The deconvolution process is especially rigorous for the "thinking objects" to be able to tease out traces in the complex signal that correlate with the requested object, like a blue ball. As I mentioned at Gaylord, if I'm asked to think about a blue ball, I can do that, but a lot of other objects also pop up in my head. It seems like the other eleven subjects, to varying degrees, have the same issue. The traces of requested objects in the complex signals produced by the "seeing subjects" are easier to pick up from the background noise.

When all is said and done and tabulated, and you look at Pearson coefficients of 0.95 and above, you feel that there's no doubt about the mind-viewing theory anymore; Fat Man had a mind-viewing faculty, and the Crex-ORChip analyzer can be employed to uncover what a person looks at or is thinking about.

Scott, Brad, and I have a video conference with Vanessa and Bryce to let them know the exciting news. There's much more to unpack in the validation data set, and I promise to keep them updated.

———

In the next couple of days, we learn that upon further deconvolution and mathematical treatment of signals from the chip analyzer, they can be separated into components that reflect the different elements that constitute an image and other features that reflect adjectives, such as colors, shapes, and sizes. One exercise that Noa and Mike had fun with was teaching the chip device to recognize playing cards. They took ten cards from an ordinary deck of cards — four face cards and six numbered cards — and trained the device to respond correctly to each card when Mike or Noa looked at them. It worked pretty well as long as they kept to the same deck.

However, we also find out about the limitations of the Crex-ORChip device. Limitations, I think, might discourage DHS from pursuing the analyzer for intelligence purposes. I mentioned this briefly to Vanessa in one of our phone calls. Of course, it won't change anything about the moratorium; just the realization that the U.S. is in possession of a resource that potentially could reveal what's on people's minds is enough to sustain the moratorium *ad infinitum.*

But frankly, I don't see any way out of this. Say, for the sake of argument, that the moratorium was lifted. What would we do? Publish the research, including the development of the chip device and the ensuing results from the validation experiments, with robust statistics to back it up in supplemental figures and tables. That would cause a gigantic cluster-fuck in the research community. What do I do with John Smith's account in this whole business? There would be demand from the publishing editor to deposit relevant genomic and protein data in the public domain. At the other end of the disclosure spectrum, there would be an outcry from the NSA, DoD, DHS, DARPA, and the entire INTEL.gov to keep all these data classified. So, in effect, the moratorium is back.

Okay, but how about accepting the moratorium and publishing the Crassus Project without mentioning the mind-viewing concept? We could offer hypothetical explanations for the Crex-ORs, such as being receptive to now-extinct VOCs (volatile organic compounds), as Amy Hub suggested. That would be a high-impact publication and also satisfy our collaborator Westhoff in Leipzig. However, the data would still be public. We could request a grace period from the journal before depositing sequence information in databases, but that would only last for so long. And in any case, there's no way DHS would go for this scenario. Even with Bryce as a new Secretary, it wouldn't fly. And… I can see why. No matter how you slice the Crassus Project, with the information now at hand, there's undeniably a prominent NSNH aspect to it.

———

"If you're calling to offer a Remi, you can forget it," is how I answer Bryce when he calls. He texted me a few minutes ago, shortly after nine a.m. on Thursday, and asked if this would be a good time to call. I'm in the courtyard again. I had just finished my second scone and a cup of coffee when Bryce texted. My next meeting is at ten, so I'm just sitting here, contemplating life. I decide it's good. So, yes, this is a good time to call. By the way, if you've forgotten, "remi" is the word we use for a draw in chess.

The term is derived from the French *remettre*, which means to put back. The word is commonly used in Sweden but not so much here, but I've convinced Bryce to use it. The term is not used in France either, amusingly enough.

"No, I'm not going to offer remi. Although, frankly, that might not be a bad idea."

I'm in a strong position in this game; I have my queen and one knight down by his defense line, and I've captured both his bishops. I have a good chance here to show my superiority. Didn't you just lose three games in a row recently, you ask? Yes, I did. I know that, and there's no reason to rub it in.

"NSA and DARPA want to meet with you as soon as possible," Bryce says. "Any chance you can free up your Monday and fly to Baltimore? They want the meeting at Fort Meade."

"When you ask if I can free up my Monday, is that your way of rephrasing 'Tell him to free up his Monday'?"

"Well, sort of, I guess. There's a lot of clout accumulated in this group. They simply asked me to tell you they want the meeting on Monday."

"Fort Meade? Why not at DARPA in Arlington, or your DHS office in DC, for that matter? And why not contact me directly?"

"Beats me, but it seems like NSA is the driver here."

"Okay, I guess I'll have Hanne clear my Monday and book a flight for Sunday night—or when does it start on Monday?"

"Not sure, but I assume it's in the morning. As soon as we hang up, I'll let them know you're coming, and they'll send you an agenda and logistics info."

Well, guess I'm going to Maryland on Sunday. Julie and I had planned to go for a run with Jupiter in the morning. And stop by Coasters Coffee on the way back for coffee and scones—well, coffee for Julie and coffee and scones for me. I hope I can get a late enough flight not to ruffle these plans. I'll see what Hanne finds.

———

So, I mentioned that training the Crex-ORChip analyzer for intelligence surveillance is not our job. We sent DARPA the new software, holders, an analyzer, an upgraded amplifier, and a set of twenty chips. Although the proteins are immobilized on the chips, they are not totally fixed. At least on the ORChips, the proteins must be flexible enough for steric reconfigurations upon binding an odorant and for relaying the signal to the electronic circuitry. So, there's wear and tear. And proteins only last so long. The ORChips have a lifetime of approximately two hundred runs. That means, for chip devices installed at security checkpoints in airports, for example, chips need to be replaced on a regular basis, depending on traffic (meaning the flow rate of people in the security lines) and whether or not the device is used continuously or not. At busy airports, and if used continuously, the analyzer would need new chips as often as every thirty minutes. This, of course, is not sustainable, and most often, the chip analyzer is activated only when needed, based on previous intelligence. OMICS is providing chips to the FAA (that's the Federal Aviation Administration) through a special contract with DHS. We don't know what DARPA will do with the Crex-ORChips or how far twenty chips will last in the training efforts. But I'm sure we'll find out if they need more.

Just as I'm getting ready to head home—leaving early to run by Whole Foods—I get an email from some admin at DHS with the agenda for the Monday meeting at Fort Meads. The venue is a conference room at the NSA Headquarters. The meeting starts at nine a.m., Monday morning, and ends before lunch. Five attendees are listed: Jory Zuckerman and Bernie Rast from DoD, Laurie Thomas and Paul Fischer from NSA's Genomics

Intelligence Committee, and myself. I had no idea there's a Genomics Intelligence Committee at NSA, or anywhere else for that matter.

I have a room reserved at the Hyatt Regency, which, I found out when I checked online, is around thirteen miles from the Fort Mead complex. So, I ask Hanne to book a flight leaving Sunday afternoon and returning Monday afternoon. I'm flying first class as usual. Sometimes, I think I should fly coach or a slight upgrade of coach to convey the message that I don't think I'm better than anyone else at OMICS just because I'm the Director and that there's no need to spend tax dollars on my comfort. Sometimes I think like that. Very rarely, actually. As far as I can remember, it's happened once. That was at a celebration party for Rick Steven's Young Investigator award from DHS. Rick is a junior staff at the Computational Modeling group—a bright young guy. We were at the Atomic Ale pub, and I felt an extra surge of camaraderie with my staff, courtesy of Orbital Haze IPA. Then, after the second pint, I thought maybe I should start flying coach. I got over it, though.

Hanne, efficient as always, texted my itinerary when I parked at Whole Foods. Good! I will still have time for the planned run with coffee and scones at the finishing line.

CHAPTER 22

Fall 2024. The despicable Paul Fischer.

I f you were appointed to decorate a conference room, would you choose a room without windows, avocado-green shag carpeting, or dull puke-beige walls, bring in a random assortment of Macrame hangings and arrange them haphazardly around the wall, and then, in the midst of everything, put up a large painting depicting brightly colored circles, triangles, and polka dots? — Good grief, I hope not.

Someone did, though, because that's the environment I find myself in on Monday morning. I'm not an interior decorator, but to me, this room conveys an impossible combination of mid-century modern, 1970s, and Memphis 1980s décor. This is either a brilliant design for a singular specific purpose, or the job was handed to a psychopath.

On the way into this inspiring atmosphere, I shake hands with the hosts, Laurie Thomas and Paul Fischer, and with two sturdy guys that I would have taken for nightclub bouncers had I spotted them on the street. They introduce themselves as Jory Zuckerman and Bernie Rast. I take an immediate dislike to Paul Fischer. He has a self-importance about him that I feel disconcerting. He's medium built, maybe a little stocky, with crew-cut hair. Something about him says ex-military. When he removes his jacket and hangs it on the chair, I can see a pronounced paunch in his mid-section. He has gorgeous eyes, pale sky-blue and captivating. I wish he didn't; it detracts from his unlikable persona. Laurie Thomas could be Michelle Obama's sister, especially when she smiles. I noticed, though, that Laurie's smile never reached her eyes. Jory and Bernie stand in the back, expressionless with flat gazes, like Buddha statues.

I sit down and look around. Instead of a flatscreen monitor, there's an old-fashioned projector screen rolled up on one wall. A projector is propped up on a table with a thick Russian-English dictionary under the front feet. I halfway expect to find a slide carousel next to it. I hope their surveillance gadgetry is more up-to-date. If not, I will start losing sleep at night.

Paul Fischer takes notice as I look around for a pop-up receptacle or some other way to hook up my laptop.

"No need for laptops, my friend," he says. "We won't be needing any slide presentations. We'll just have a brief discussion and then let you off the hook in time well before lunch."

Therefore, I'm not one bit surprised when he lets me know, as I ask for the network and password, that, sorry, there's no internet access in this room. I start to suspect that the ugly wall paint not only repels aesthetic appreciation but also radio frequencies. The entire space is probably a sound-proofed Faraday's cage.

"Okay, let's get started," Paul says. "I'm Paul Fischer, and I'm the Head of NSA's Genomics Intelligence Committee, or GIC, as we call it. Laurie, here is my colleague, who is also part of GIC. Jory and Bernie are liaisons between DARPA and the GIC. We know enough about you, so we can skip further introductions and dive right into the purpose of the meeting."

Well, of course, they know about me. That's a surprise to precisely no one. They probably even know what I had for breakfast at the hotel this morning. So, I'll just put it out there; it was an omelet with peppers, mushrooms, and shrimp. And coffee *sans* scones. Not by choice but because they didn't have any.

"Okay, Symphony, Vanessa—who didn't think she needed to come—mentioned that you have some reservations about the

Crex-ORChips. So, we might take those first and get that discussion out of the way. We've been briefed about the presentation and discussion at the meeting In National Harbor last August, so there is no need to repeat any of that."

So, I assumed that the reason I was summoned to this meeting was to discuss the Crex-ORChip analyzer. Judged by what Paul Fischer just said, it seems as if the main topic is something else, something of more interest than the Crex-ORChips. What that something is, I have no idea. I'm about to find out.

"There's nothing wrong with the chips," I say. "In fact, they are fully functional and demonstrate nothing short of scientific excellence. Also, the device that records and interprets the readout signal from the Crex-ORChips is simply phenomenal. So, let me first tell you what the Crex-ORChip analyzer can do. Then, I'll describe what it can not, at least in my opinion, do."

I lay the groundwork by talking about Mike and Sam the cat and Mike and Noa's experiment with the playing cards. I hoped to use a slide presentation to illustrate what I'm about to say. But seems like I'm not.

I continue, "When Mike looks at Sam the cat, the Crex-ORChip analyzer produces a specific complex signal. We can train the analyzer to recognize the signal, link it to a photo of Sam the cat, and display that on the computer screen. When Mike looks at Sam the cat again, its picture is shown on the screen. Same thing with the ten playing cards Mike and Noa used. Again, the same thing happens when Mike looks at the number 3 written on a piece of paper. We can train the analyzer to recognize it; Mike looks at the number 3, and the digit 3 appears on the screen. We can go on with other numbers, say the numbers 8 and 0. The analyzer is now trained to recognize the numbers 3, 8, and 0. This means when Mike, or Noa, or someone else goes and looks at the number 8 on their laptop screen or a piece of paper, the digit 8 pops up on the computer display, provided the digits don't look too different from the ones used for training. Same thing if Mike thinks of Sam the cat, or numbers instead of looking at them; the Crex-ORChip analyzer can possibly be trained, but it seems much more complicated and involved, so we have given up on that."

I pause and drink from the Dasani water bottle provided.

"But," I say. "If Mike now looks at what could be the passcode for his phone, say the combination 3803—it's not, by the way—the analyzer sees that as a new object; it can't make out the four-digit combination. That the Crex-ORChip analyzer can recognize the numbers 3, 8, and 0 does not mean that it can dissect the 3803 combinations into its parts. At least not in our hands. Interestingly, though, if each one of these digits in the 3803 combinations has a different background, say red for the first 3, blue for the 8, green for the 0, and white for the second 3, then there are traces for the individual numbers in the signal. So, in this case, the signals obtained by the analyzer apparently provide information about the individual numbers as objects. Regardless, these findings suggest there are major limitations to overcome before employing Crex-ORChips to intercept intelligence. An application, which I assume has occurred to DHS, DoD, and NSA alike. But training the Crex-ORChip analyzer for intelligence purposes is not our job at OMICS. Our role is to provide information about the technology for DHS to decide how to move forward. If DARPA wants to put recourses and time into training the analyzer, it's their call." I here look at the apathetic, stone-faced DARPA duo. No response.

"The difference," I say, turning my focus to Paul Fischer and Laurie Thomas, "between the Crex-ORChip computer device and the hominin Fat Man and his contemporaries is that the Crex-ORChip device lacks the brain interface. When olphons bound to the Crex-olfactory receptors in Fat Man's nasal cavity, the signal was supposedly processed in his brain to generate an image corresponding to what his olphon-emitting friend saw or thought about. According to the former scientist we call John, and what he deduced from talking to neuroscientists, the processing would be the same as if he (Fat Man) was looking at the image himself."

"Okay, thanks, Symphony," Paul says. "I'm sure DARPA will play around with this and get some projects going with the right kind of people and funding." He doesn't look at Jory and Bernie when he says this.

"However," Paul continues, "The reason we asked you to come here is not to talk about this … chip device; it's not to discuss the computational aspect of your discovery. We're more interested in the genes themselves. Specifically, we want your opinion about using genome editing to insert the genes into humans."

"Huh… say what now?"

"Don't play coy, Symphony! You know exactly what I mean."

"Yes, I know what you mean. The reason I'm taken aback is because of the virtually impossible scope of what you're proposing."

"How so?"

"Well, the technical challenge, for one. Do you suggest inserting all genes in one single contig, which will be, like… over forty kilobases—or close to five hundred kilobases with the introns—or use several separate events where—"

Paul raises his hand. "Hey, stop right there! None of us here are familiar with genome lingo. We know what genome editing can do. We have no idea how it's done; that's not our business. Let me just say that if you're concerned about the editing being too difficult, I assure you that DARPA—and in collaboration with the GIC—is more than thirty years ahead of the curve. Have you heard about the BLUEgenes program?"

"No, I have not."

"Good, you shouldn't have. That's a DARPA-GIC program that has been running for eight years and is about to be wrapping up. If you think about the most cutting-edge methods employed today for tinkering with genomes and advancing thirty years in the future, that's where the BLUEgenes technology stands today."

"Well, okay, but then you also have to get the DNA constructs into every neuron in the olfactory epithelium—"

"That does not impress me one bit. I don't know where that epithelium is or what it does. And I don't fucking care. If the genes need to go there, we can make it happen. Anything else?"

"Yeah, how about FDA approval? There's no way you'll—"

"Don't be a fucking imbecile, Symphony! FDA approval!! Do you think countries like Russia or China are worried about regulatory approval? Oh sure, China said they didn't provide the legal basis for the experiment with the edited twin girls back in 2018. Bullshit! It's just a façade. There's a battle going on, and if we sit on our asses waiting for some little Jack-in-office to make decisions, we've lost."

Paul, now red in the face, takes a deep breath. "What we need to know from you, Symphony, is if you guys have all the information—genes and whatnot—for this to be possible."

"Well, if you mean—"

"Yes, or no? It's a simple question: do you have what is needed?"

"It's not a simple question, and if you stop interrupting me, I will answer." I'm starting to get really annoyed with Paul's bullish behavior. "Yes, we have the genetic information required for making the receptors—the Crex-olfactory receptors—and having the genes being expressed in the proper cells. What we don't have are the DNA elements necessary for assembling the genes into constructs for delivery to the cells."

"That's a technical problem, right? And nothing you need to worry about. Okay, good! That's what we needed to know. Now, here's another question for you. If Fat Man were here today—or… rather, say that there are some people here today where the deletion of Fat Man's receptors hasn't happened. They still have this mind-viewing capacity. Would you agree that these people could be remarkable assets for intelligence gathering?"

"Assuming that they were otherwise normal, yes, I would tend to agree."

"All right, so if you agree with that, I assume you also agree that if we transfer the genes to Laurie here"—he taps on her shoulder, pretty hard, it seems to me—"she would also be a remarkable asset for intelligence gathering."

"You mean she isn't already? Then, why is she here?" No, I didn't say that, but I wanted to. I can tell Laurie has the same thoughts because she turns a little red and looks annoyed.

"Well," I say, "given that the genome editing itself—"

Paul gets agitated again and waves his hands. "We've been through this already. The genome editing part is no problem. Now, answer the question! It's a simple yes or no."

"It's not a simple yes or no question," I counter. We don't know, but it seems reasonable that Fat Man acquired the skills of mind viewing while growing up. The same way we learn a language. So, if you or Laurie suddenly possessed the biological ability for mind viewing, there might be a steep learning curve to master it. The same we learn to read or write a new language as an adult. Say that you wanted to learn Russian—

"I already know Russian," Paul says with a smirk.

"Well, okay, that's beside the point, but… good for you. So, then say that you wanted to learn Swedish—I bet you don't know that—a very useful language in international espionage." For a fleeting moment, it looked as if he was going to smile, but he quickly caught himself.

"If you wanted to learn Swedish," I continue, "It's not instantaneous; it's a process. And it might be similar to mind viewing. We don't know. Or… it might also be that you don't need any training at all."

"Okay, that's fine. So now, when this is settled, how would you go about getting this show on the road?"

"I'm not sure what—"

Paul throws out his hands in the air. "What is the first thing that needs to be done to start the process of getting these genes into humans?"

"Well, the normal thing—but I guess there's nothing normal about this—so… well, the logical way to proceed, in my mind, would be to set up experiments in mice. They have olfactory systems similar to humans and many other animals. This would allow you to make sure the genes are installed correctly, that they are expressed at the mRNA and protein levels, and that the proteins are produced in the right neurons."

"Okay, so let's do that then. You pick some people, as few as possible, and—"

"Hey, whoa, whoa! Wait a minute. I'm not getting involved in this. No way! And I'm not a lab scientist anymore. You need to pick a Principal Investigator with the appropriate credentials, and let him or her—"

"Paul gets more agitated and impatient. "I don't mean that you should do the work. I want you to select one or two people from OMICS who can assist the team and provide the info they need. We'll put together the team."

"Even so, I really don't want to be part of this proposal. Also, I have other—"

"You already are part of this. DHS is also part of this. You do well to remember that DHS has classified the Crassus research in the interest of U.S. national security. Yours refusing to serve in this matter goes against the grain of the OMICS mission, wouldn't you say?"

I'm quietly mulling over his harangue. He's right, of course. Fuck!

"Okay," I say finally. "I have one person in mind."

"All right then. The research will be performed at the BLUEgenes facility. You provide sequence information and whatnot. Mice are already used as experimental systems there, so they should have what they need in terms of materials and supplies. And if they don't, we'll get it. I'll set up a meeting for you with DARPA, DoD, and Anne Leiden, the BLUEgenes team lead. This needs to be your highest priority right now."

"Well, I—

"Sorry, I have to prepare for my next meeting," says Paul, and he holds up the door for me.

I gave him a hard punch right in his solar plexus on the way out. Well, not really. But in my mind, I did.

CHAPTER 23

Winter 2024. The BLUEgenes project. A clandestine program.

What do you know about Paul Fischer?" I ask Bryce as I take a seat by the chessboard. Bryce is looking at the d4c4 app on his phone and is setting up the pieces accordingly. When he's done, he takes a good look at the chessboard. I can tell he's nervous; his hands are shaking, his eyes twitching, and there are drops of sweat on his forehead. He can hardly control—

Sorry, sorry, of course not. Just kidding! No, Bryce, with his calm brown eyes, is his usual well-composed self. He takes a sip of his beer (Deschutes Oatmeal Stout) and looks at me.

By the way, I should mention that we are at Betty's Books and Bar in the town of Danville, in the San Ramone Valley in California. And Danville is one of the municipalities in CA that uses "town" instead of "city" in its name. Bryce and I, together with our wives, are invited to a retirement party tomorrow evening for one of our friends and colleagues from our Berkeley time, Roger Hazen, at their home in Walnut Creek. All three of our families used to live in Walnut Creek. We attended the same church—Saint Matthews Lutheran—and used to hang out together on many occasions.

Julie and I arrived yesterday, October thirty-first. We were driving and brought Jupiter along. We spent a good time hiking Mount Diablo and reminiscing about our many previous hikes in the area. Then, we participated in Halloween trick-or-treating in the Hazen neighborhood. I was Olaf from Frozen II, if you're interested, and Julie was Elsa. Now, Julie (and Jupiter) and Bryce's wife, Lucy, are over at the Hazen's to help Rogers's wife, Sarah, with arrangements for the party tomorrow. Bryce and I took the chance to drive to Danville for the afternoon, just ten minutes down Interstate 680, and go to Betty's, a place we've frequented often during our Berkeley years. Betty's Books and Bar is a rarity in that it's a bookstore that also hosts a full bar. Another of Betty's amenities is that it has four tables set up with marble chessboards. It's at one of these chess tables where I now sit with Bryce.

"Ah, so you've met Paul," Bryce smiles. "As I guess he told you, he's the Head of the GIC, the Genome Intelligence Committee. Very little public information is available about the GIC, and that's probably per design. I know they are administratively affiliated with NSA. But with a separate budget appropriated directly from Congress. Activity-wise, they have close ties to NSA, DHS, and DoD via DARPA. Their interactions with DHS seem limited to participation in various meetings."

Bryce takes another sip of his beer. I go up to the bar and come back with a Lagunitas IPA. Bryce continues. "Paul Fischer is a former Army—Colonel rank. He received a General Discharge (honorable) after repeatedly mistreating his staff, having them run his personal errands, and consistently disregarding their schedules. He's known to be difficult to work with."

"He's the epitome of an asshole, is what he is."

"Language Symphony, language."

"Well, he's a bully, anyhow. I hope his wife deserts him and that he hooks up with Rosy Boyd. Those two fuckups deserve each other."

I go on to tell Bryce what transpired during my meeting with Paul Fischer *et consortes*.

"But, he's right, you know," Bryce concludes. "He might be a bully, but he's spot on when forecasting the future in the rivalry for human enhancement performance—or HEP. As you probably know, using genome editing to endow soldiers with extra powers has been openly discussed for many years. Pentagon published a report in 2021 describing how genetic modifications and AI" (he refers to artificial intelligence) "can be employed for HEP. And remember that DARPA announced already in 2019 that they plan to explore genome editing of soldiers and intelligence agents. They have plunged hundreds of millions of dollars into genome editing technologies. Most of these projects are open and solicited through competitive grants. But then there are others, like the BLUEgenes program you mentioned, that are classified."

"So, what do you know about this BLUE—"

"Sorry," Bryce interrupts, "I just want to add that countries like China and Russia are doing the same thing. The U.K. is also heavily involved in HEP research. For all we know, China and Russia may be ahead of us; there's evidence that China has already implemented some of its results on soldiers. And this race for dominance doesn't stop at HEP and AI; it also includes genome editing of microbes and plants, chemical warfare, cyber warfare, and—at least with China—economic warfare. So… Paul the Bully Fischer is correct. If the U.S. were to slow down and wait for legislation to keep up, we would lose our grip."

Bryce takes another sip of his stout. "But you were saying…?"

"Well, I was going to ask what you know about the BLUEgenes technology."

"Not much. And you would probably understand more about it than I do. To my knowledge, it's far beyond what's openly known about genome editing. It's apparently not gene-based per se but more of a chromosomal-building approach. I'm not sure about the acronym, but they managed to come up with a string of words that fit. It's something like Beyond Limitations and with Unprecedented Efficiency in genome editing strategies. Not exactly, but along those lines. And, I don't doubt Paul when he says that they can achieve pretty much what they want in genome editing using the BLUEgenes protocols."

"But what mandate does this guy, or the GIC, have? He talks as if he singlehandedly decided the agenda in this space. Don't you guys in DHS keep an eye on them? Or DoD? I mean, for all I know, Fischer could be a rogue agent."

"I'm not sure how they exert their control. But it seems as if even the notion of refusing to comply with their agenda is tantamount to treason. That's how they manage to put themselves on the itinerary for federal meetings. I've asked Vanessa about the GIC, but she doesn't know much. Says they always keep a low profile. DoD, I'm not sure. However, the GIC is subject to congressional oversight. I'm not sure how strong or efficient. But at least there's some degree of control."

"And...," he adds. "For you wishing Paul Fischer and Rosy Boyd ending up together, that's not likely to happen. Rumors say he's gay. And unattached. That might be one reason it's difficult to extract information about him. Not that he's gay, but that he's unattached, I mean."

Bryce, who plays white, moves his remaining bishop and enters *Be5* in the app. I was hoping I would have a chance to offer him another beer before he made his move to slow down his neural traffic a bit. But... didn't happen. I really shouldn't scheme like that, right? I think I'm losing my moral compass. Anyhow, I'll let you know that I'm in excellent shape in this game. It's mine to lose. I just need to focus. If I don't win this one, I'll start growing a beard and not shave until I've won another game. Of course, Julie won't let me, so it's just me talking.

"You want another one?" Bryce asks as he gets up. Hmm... is he thinking what I did? He wants me to drink some more before responding to his move.

"Sure," I say. "I'll take a Hazy Wonder." I intend to let the head settle—I'm talking beer here—while considering my move and not drinking more until I decide on my strategy.

Bryce comes back with another pint of stout and a Hazy Ale for me. He looks around and then at me.

"There's another thing you should know," he says in a low voice. "Not necessarily related to Paul Fischer and the GIC or the NSA. It's all rumors, but I've heard enough of them to believe there's substance here. If rumors are correct, there's an operation deep within the government called '46+'. It's a highly stealthy program; it's not even classified. It simply doesn't exist—except it most likely does. I don't know their budget or where it comes from. You ask senators about 46+, they either don't know or pretend they don't know. Most likely, the former. I'm not sure even an act of Congress would suffice to expose 46+, maybe not even a presidential decree. It seems it has taken on a life of its own and is freewheeling. You can trace 46+ until 9/11 in 2001, and theories are that it's part of the Patriot Act that still remains after most of the provisions of the Act were abandoned in 2005. At that time, the program was known as 'Reform.' Supposedly, the purpose of Reform was to use any possible means across disciplines—AI, genomics, computation, financing—to reform U.S. intelligence gathering to make sure something like 9/11 never happened again."

"Then, in 2018, rumors started that China had generated genome-edited soldiers with reptilian genes to give them infra-red vision, something that's been discussed for many years. They purportedly had also introduced a mutation—a mutation that bestows some women with the ability to see in UV—in operatives to allow for UV communication. That put a scare across the entire U.S. intelligence landscape. DARPA started to invest heavily in genome editing for HEP applications. The GIC was established as an independent offshoot of the NSA. And the agenda of the Reform operation seems to have shifted to focus solely on HEP genomics. And, about the same time, the name 'Reform' disappeared from our interceptions, and the name '46+' popped up."

"What's with the 46+ name?" I ask, although I have a pretty good idea.

"Well, probably what you'd expect. The mission of 46+ seems to be to implement HEP research, with the ultimate aim of adding extra, custom-made chromosomes to soldiers and agents. And all this involves the BLUEgenes technology. So, of course, if there's a gene package that confers a mind-viewing faculty, 46+ would be all over it."

"Could Paul Fischer be part of this 46+ operation?"

"Possibly. The way I look at it is that the GIC is the visible and legit—albeit still shady—front that funnels information to 46+, which operates completely in the dark. And Paul Fischer swims in both waters. Of course, if you were to ask him, there's no such thing as 46+. It's just people watching too many spy films."

"So where does it have its base—46+, I mean—or I assume that's not known."

"Well, my guess is that the think tank is at Liberty Crossing, but where—"

"Liberty Crossing…?"

"Sorry, Liberty Crossing Intelligence Campus in Virginia, where many other secret intelligence organizations are housed. However, where the actual research is carried out, I have no idea."

"So, Paul Fischer told me that the Crex-OR research on mice that I apparently have been dragged into is to be performed at the BLUEgenes site, wherever that is. Do you think that might be the same place where 46+ does its business?"

"No, definitely not. I don't see how they would let you in there if that were the case."

"Will you keep trying to learn more about this guy and 46+, or will you drop your domestic terrorism role when you transition into the DHS Secretary position next year?"

"I'll keep dual appointments, at least for the first year. No, I'll keep looking into the operation. But there are a lot of firewalls in place. And, honestly, I'm not so concerned about the 46+ as such when it comes to HEP; if the purpose is to strengthen U.S. national security, I'm all for it, even if it's covert and shifty."

Bryce pauses and looks around again. "What I *am* concerned about," he says and looks back at me, "is that terrorist groups, including well-organized and well-funded domestic terrorist organizations, are very adept at adopting front-edge technologies. And—and I'm probably telling you more than I should here—there are indications that secret forces involved in conspiring against the U.S. government are employing products developed or acquired by 46+, or possibly, are part of 46+."

Bryce stops, looks at the chess board, and then at me. "We came here to play chess," he says and delivers one of his jovial smiles. "I have at least made one move; you have made none. But I noticed that you've glanced at the board every now and then."

That's true. I have half-heartedly been trying to decide the merits of placing my knight on *h4* so that I, with my next move, can put him in check. But it's challenging to devote brain power to chess when you're amidst a discussion on covert intelligence operations in the U.S. government. Not to mention that I'm no longer *compos mentis* after two pints of beer; I finished my second glass already at Liberty Crossing. My intentions were good—not to drink before my move. The execution, not so much. But I'm a very smart person, nonetheless. And likable and good-looking. So, a few faults here and there are okay.

Well, Bryce has had two pints of beer as well. So, here goes nothing, I think, and move my knight. I enter *Kh4* in the app.

We decide that one move each suffices to say that we've been playing chess in case someone asks what we've been doing. And it's getting late in the afternoon, anyhow.

While we're walking to Bryce's car—we went together in his Tesla—I ask him if he can promote the old cow Rosy Boyd sideways, out of harm's way, when he takes over as the DHS Secretary.

I'm saying, "She's disruptive, and people are complaining. Maybe you can find a corral somewhere where the grass looks greener and where she can roam without disturbing people."

Bryce smiles and says he will look into it.

By the way, before I forget, the Triennial Review that Vanessa Ashby mentioned at the Gaylord meeting in August went very well. No surprise there. I got a lot of accolades for my leadership. No surprise there, either. I received a lot of jeer for my scone consumption. Again, no surprise. And they don't bite on me anyhow. I'm a Swede.

CHAPTER 24

Winter 2024. The BLUEgenes lab. Meeting at the Pump House.

Jalle's Research Enterprises in Longmont, Colorado, doesn't have a website. It doesn't even have an address. Tucked away behind a Brothers Equipment Rental and a nondescript warehouse on the industrial end of Main Street, JRE enjoys a secluded and anonymous existence. If you go online and try to find out what kind of research JRE is engaged in, you're more likely than not to give up after following links that take you back and forth to non-informative sites. However, if you've decided, come hell or high water, you're not going to give up until you've tracked down JRE's line of business, you'll eventually—after hours of agonizing detective work— find out that JRE specializes in renting laboratory space for start-up companies. You'll also learn that the business is still in development and that *More information about our services and rental policy will be provided shortly.* What you probably won't know is that JRE has been in this development phase for the last eight years. If you—against all odds—would be able to find the entrance to the JRE facility, which goes through the warehouse, and get inside the JRE building non-invited, you'll find a lobby filled with boxes containing all sorts of hi-tech equipment, apparently poised to be installed somewhere in emergent laboratories. However, suppose you went further into the building. In that case, you'd find three big and fully furnished laboratories, offices equipped with computers, printers, and other paraphernalia, as well as a big conference room with a table, chairs, and a large wall monitor. At this point, you'd probably scratch your head and ask yourself, *What the fuck?* And no one would blame you; JRE is anything but in development. In fact, JRE is a fully functional, cutting-edge, and sophisticated research facility.

JRE is the site for the BLUEgenes project, funded by DARPA to secretly develop beyond state-of-the-art technologies for genome editing. The mission of BLUEgenes is to advance the field of genome engineering to a state where there are no limitations for adding, modifying, or deleting DNA—including inserting *in vitro* synthesized chromosomes—into an organism with unprecedented efficiency and precision.

Locating the BLUEgenes laboratory in a relatively unknown town in northern Colorado was triggered by two factors. First, the DARPA folks behind BLUEgenes, for whom the preferred state of presence is "incognito," grew uneasy about the aggressive political and media climate in DC. Second, and more importantly, the research teams selected by DARPA for the BLUEgenes program, based on expertise and previous interactions with DARPA, happened to be the University of Colorado in Boulder and Colorado State University in Fort Collins. Boulder and Fort Collins are each less than an hour's drive from Longmont, allowing frequent and convenient visits for the research teams to the secluded and specially designed laboratories at JRE.

I know these things about the BLUEgenes operation because I'm sitting in the JRE conference room talking to Professor Anne Leiden from UC Boulder, the lead for the two research teams working on the project. Deputy Director Dr. Sheila Wright from DARPA, and Chairman of the Joint Chiefs of Staff, Army General Ralph O'Connor-Salih from DoD, are also present. Anne is in her early forties. Trim with blond hair, alert blue-green eyes, and a clean and wholesome look about her. She is originally from Germany and still has a slight accent. Sheila is probably a few years younger than I am, medium-built on the slim side, with prematurely grey hair. There's some Mexican or Native American in her face that reminds me of Joan Baez, a folksinger and political activist from the 1960s to 70s. Ralph seems to be in his fifties. He has a dark complexion with a Mid-Eastern look. A soft-spoken man but with a mannerism that conveys authority. He takes the lead after a short introduction. Although I've never met any of them personally before, they all know me as Symphony.

"The Fat Man and BLUEgenes projects have both been declared top secret on a need-to-know basis," Ralph says. The Fat Man project refers to the mice research with the Crex-OR genes.

"DoD will issue top secret clearance for the Fat Man project to those in OMICS directly involved," Ralph continues. "The clearance does not cover BLUEgenes. And vice versa: the BLUEgenes teams have clearance strictly for their scope of work, which does not include the ultimate goal of the Fat Man project. You will still all have to sign NDAs." (That's Non-Disclosure Agreements). Director Paul Fischer at the NSA and the GIC will also sign them.

Ralph continues, "Symphony, can you please define the work scope for the Fat Man project, which will be added to the existing clearances and entered into the NDAs."

"It will be something like 'Demonstrating that the assembly of the forty-one selected genes can be inserted into mice and expressed at the protein levels in the olfactory cells and correctly inserted into the plasma membrane.' I'll send you an email."

"Thanks, I'd rather you just write it down for me. I'll have you proof the text before it goes into the documents."

So, I do. We sit around a while longer and make small talk. Paul Fischer's name comes up a few times, and I get the impression he is not everybody's cuddle bunny. Especially, Anne's body language reveals that the less she needs to interact with him, the better. I play it safe and remain neutral on the topic. No need to expose yourself, even among like-minded folks.

As we part, Ralph says, "I'm sorry, Symphony. I know you are on the dispensing side in this collaboration without getting anything back."

"No worries at all," I assure him. And I mean it. I'd rather not be here at all. In fact, I most likely will not be here at all after today. I've appointed Mike to assist with information and advice. So, he will come and go on a regular basis.

———

"Well, I can see why Fischer goes apeshit over this."

"Is that a technical term?" I ask him.

He looks at me. He actually blushes. "Sorry, Symphony, but you know what I mean, right?"

Yes, I know what he means, and I agree. I'm talking to Mike, by the way. I have just summarized my meetings with Paul Fischer and the GIC last month and my discussion with Anne, Sheila, and Ralph a few days ago for Ron, Laxmi, Noa, and Mike, a.k.a. the Crassus Team. I don't mention anything about 46+. It's just rumors, although I trust Bryce in assuming that they are rooted in truth. Obviously, given the potential impact of the Fat Man project for 46+, it's easy to see why Paul Fischer is so anxious to get it started, more so than Mike and the rest of the Crassus Team realize.

It's Wednesday afternoon, November sixth, and we've just gotten back from a meeting with the BLUEgenes team, where I introduced Mike and the rest of us, explaining that Mike will be the go-to person for questions and that he will work together with BLUEgenes on the Fat Man project. After that, Mike sat down with Anne Leiden for a one-on-one to discuss some housekeeping issues. Anne is not privy to the details or ultimate goal of the Fat Man project, and I had cautioned Mike beforehand to be careful with what he says. He promised me it went well.

We're sitting at the Pumphouse, a brewery and eatery establishment on Main Street in Longmont, not far from the concealed location of the BLUEgenes operation, having a late lunch. We have a table far in the back, away from the Hump-day crowd. The atmosphere at the bar is loud and vibrant. And is dominated by, what seems to be a rather friendly discourse about the potential outcome and impact of yesterday's presidential election. However, I also hear the word "insurrection" being floated from time to time. So, probably not necessary, but we're still keeping our voices down. We're all sharing a bunch of starters, stellar among which are the cauliflower wings. Mike and I each nurture an unfiltered Flashpoint IPA; the rest drink Kombucha.

There's another reason we're sitting here, apart from me giving meeting updates. Mike wanted to talk to me about some recent sequencing results he discovered when he accessed the OMICS computer network yesterday evening.

"Remember you asked me to try to extend the five-prime sequencing of Crex-OR4 at a Crassus meeting last year?" Mike talks about "Noa's Crex-OR," which has since been formally annotated with the rest of the Crex-OR genes.

"Well, I did that," he continues, boots up his laptop, and shows the screen. "We now have another, close to four hundred base pairs, sequence, including putative promoter and enhancer elements."

"And…?" I say when Mike pauses and looks uncomfortable.

"Well, the good news is that we now have a full-length Crassus-OR gene, with two exons, one intron, promoter, and other upstream and downstream cis-elements. The bad news is that comparative analyses suggest that this gene was not expressed in the main olfactory neurons in the nasal cavity but in the vomeronasal organ."

I know the vomeronasal organ has been implicated in pheromone reception in mice and other animals. And I remember Bryce mentioning the vomeronasal organ when talking about Ronda Trueblood's work. Apart from that, I have only a faint recollection of the vomeronasal organ, and from the look of it, so do Noa, Ron, and Laxmi. But that is about to change; Mike, who has obviously done his research and is used to giving presentations, now goes into lecture mode. He explains that the vomeronasal organ (or Jacobson's organ after a Danish surgeon in the 1800s) is part of the accessory olfactory system. It's located in the anteroinferior portion of the nasal chamber and is designed to detect certain moisture-borne odor particles, such as pheromones. Thus, the vomeronasal olfactory receptors are sensitive to a different set of chemicals than the primary sense of smell. Amphibians and reptiles use this system, and also many mammals. However, the presence or function of the vomeronasal organ in modern-day humans is controversial. From some research publications, it can be concluded that in today's humans, the vomeronasal organ is a vestigial system; either because we lack the organ altogether or because we lack the necessary nervous connection to the brain's limbic system. Then, there are other data to suggest that modern humans do have a functional vomeronasal system.

"Hm… interesting but problematic," I say. "Thanks, Mike. Obviously, we need to assess this information carefully. Mike, I suggest that you and Noa sit down with Ron and Laxmi tomorrow and confirm—as best as you can—that the vomeronasal organ, rather than the main olfactory system, is the target for the Crassus-ORs. Meanwhile, Mike, can you give me a list of the current authorities on the vomeronasal organ? I will set up a web meeting with one or more of them. We need to get clarity on whether or not the organ is functional in humans."

This is critical. I'm not about to have Mike spending valuable time on a goose chase pursuing Paul Fischer's brainchild project just to find out they're building expression systems—or entire chromosomes, or whatever they do—for the wrong cells.

Noa, who has also opened her laptop, shows us a slide of the Fat Man's cranium. "This might explain," she says, "why the ORs we found are located so far down in the nasal cavity."

"Good point," I say. It adds to Mike's conclusion that the receptors were located in the vomeronasal organ.

I continue, "Well, we still have some time until the top secret clearances and the NDAs are issued and signed, so let's try to get this done before that happens."

In some incongruous way, I'm hoping Mike's discovery will be a showstopper for Fischer's Fat Man project. But not really. Anyhow, of course, it won't. I assume there are fewer olfactory neurons in the vomeronasal organ compared to the main olfactory system. So, if anything, this should make the project easier to carry out. Although, given the implicitly advertised performance of the BLUEgenes technology, it probably doesn't matter. No, I'm not against the Fat Man project as such. I think it's exciting, and it aims to enhance our national security. All good. Right? It's Paul Fischer himself I dislike, the shifty way he goes about the project and how it was thrust in my lap.

CHAPTER 25

Winter 2024. The Fat Man project.

It's been a few weeks since we returned to OMICS from Longmont. I've been dealing with a lot of non-Crassus-related activities. I am the Director of this place, after all. Although I've outsourced most of the administrative duties to various appointees, my engagement in the Crassus Projects leaves me with a heavy backlog from time to time.

I'm sitting in the courtyard again. It's nine in the morning on November twenty-eighth. Still pleasant weather this late in the fall, twenty-four degrees, and just a few cirrus clouds above my head. I'm savoring my third scone. I'm in celebratory mode— Why? Yesterday, I made an elegant trap with my rook that rendered Bryce checkmate in two subsequent moves. That was still the game we worked on at Betty's Books and Bar earlier this month—November first, the day after Halloween, to be exact. Bryce is a good loser; he sent me a thumbs-up on the phone. Since I'm now playing white, I enter *d4* in the chess app, starting the next game. My app dings immediately, displaying *d5*. I finish the scone and enter *c4*. That's a Queen's gambit, folks. Now, let's see if Bryce accepts it or not. There's no activity on the app for several minutes while I finish my scone, so I assume Bryce has diverted his attention to other things—like hunting down domestic terrorists.

Lemon juice and white vinegar is my recommendation. At least to start with. Then, you might need to follow up with hand or machine washing. I'm talking about the jelly stains on my shirt that I see now as I brush off scone crumbles and get ready to go back inside for a meeting. Huckleberry stains are one of the most difficult to get rid of. If Julie is home in the afternoons when I get back from work, she often spots the jelly stains on my shirt as she comes running towards me overfull with joy and engulfs me in hugs and kisses. —Okay, maybe not exactly. But if she is home, she sees the stains. Otherwise, she'll notice them in the hamper after I treat the shirt with lemon juice and vinegar, a staple stash in our household. *"I don't understand why you can't eat scones without getting stains on your shirt. And if you refuse to learn, my dear, why don't you wear one of your huckleberry-colored shirts?"* Yes, I do have a couple of shirts in blue-red shades. But I don't like to wear them. I think I look better in white or light-colored shirts. Especially in the summer or fall when they show off my tan. *"My dear, I love you, but you're so, so vain!"* She's right, of course. Now, being called vain by your wife and a moron by your admin (and receiving invectives from your dog) may give some men pause and cause for reflection. Not me. I'm a Swede.

Since we are on the subject, another reason Julie often complains about my scone diet is because she's of the opinion that I eat too many. *"Having two scones at a time—let alone three, as is sometimes the case—don't you think that's a bit excessive, my dear?"* Well, she's right; I know that. And, it might seem odd to have such a scone-rich diet for an epicure like me, who is very health conscious. I can cut down, of course. All it takes is a character, which I have. I'm not sure what kind, but I'm sure I have one. But then again, the way I see it, if you're going to have a vice, then scone extravagance ought to be counted as a fairly guiltless one. Right? That's my reasoning anyhow, and I stick to it.

―――――

"Fuck it, man; just because she is gone, you have to leave too?"

"It's a very important meeting," I explain. "I have to sign documents that concern national security."

"Well, if you're such a hotshot, you can arrange to have me come with you."

I'm talking to Jupiter. Tomorrow, I'm taking the Crassus Team to DC, to the DHS headquarters, to sign five-year, limited top secret clearances and NDAs issued by DoD and NSA. I reviewed the documents beforehand and made some minor edits. After the visit to DHS, I will drive over to Bryce and Lucy in Arlington, who have invited me to spend the weekend. Julie is away at a veterinary conference until Tuesday. I'll board Jupiter today since I'm leaving early tomorrow morning. We don't like to have to board her. And she doesn't take lightly to it, either. But, it's a wonderful kennel, with lovely staff and a lot of playtimes with other dogs. She actually likes the kennel, and she spends weekdays there on a regular basis. It's the overnight boarding she's against, and that's why she has an attitude. But, when I pick her up on Monday morning, she'll jump all over me, wiggling her whole body, letting me know how much she loves me. She can be resentful, but she doesn't keep grudges.

Yesterday, we had a webinar meeting with Jakob Rasmussen from the University of Southern Denmark in Odense. Rasmussen is a professor in Chemosensory Systems and a world-leading expert in human vomeronasal function and disorders. He holds a dual position as a rhinologist at the University Hospital in Odense. We've told Rasmussen that OMICS is evaluating research proposals for genomic studies of the human vomeronasal organ. Given the controversy surrounding this organ in humans, we wanted to find out if these proposals had merits and warranted evaluation in the first place. And this is precisely what we are doing with the Fat Man project at the BLUEgenes lab in Longmont. I mean, if we can conclude that the vomeronasal organ is defunct in humans, then the Fat Man project is a non-starter. So, Rasmussen had agreed to talk to us after work, so we called him at noon our time. He said he had recent results, not yet published, that he was willing to share—not the details, but the outcome and conclusions.

"I will not tell you about the experimental setup or individual results," Rasmussen said in excellent English and with a typical Danish thickness. Rasmussen is a clean-shaven man in his fities with a round and pleasant face, blue eyes, and strikingly blond hair for his age. He was sitting in what looked like his living room, propped up on a couch with his laptop. We spotted a shot glass with an amber-colored liquid on a table nearby. Whiskey?

"What I can tell you, though—since you're asking me if I think the proposals you're referring to deserve consideration—is that, yes, they do! The results we will publish in due course show conclusively that Jacobson's organ in humans comprises a fully functional system. I can afford some details, for example, that a substance such as estratetraenol, a typical pheromone, binds to receptors in Jacobson's organ and transmits information through the vomeronasal tract across the cribriform plate through the olfactory bulb—specifically the accessory section of the bulb—and tract, and on to the amygdala in the brain. Now, these are results obtained from both clinical studies and molecular analyses. If you're still interested when the publications are out, I'd be happy to revisit this topic."

I thought for not wanting to disclose details, Rasmussen offered quite a bit of specific information. We thanked him. It had been a very instructive forty-five-minute consultation. However, I had made up my mind and decided to move forward with the vomeronasal route already before the meeting with Rasmussen. Why? Because I remembered what Bryce had told me some time ago about Professor Ronda Trueblood at UC Berkeley and her—

still unpublished—studies on the effect of pheromones on vomeronasal gene expression in human subjects.

So, I made additional changes in the top secret clearances and NDAs to reflect the new target cells. I realize I should probably notify Paul Fischer about the shift in the gene venue. I had no desire to do so, but I figured it would be prudent. I will tell Anne Leiden as well. I don't have a phone number for Fischer, and I don't expect to be able to find one—well, Bryce, if anyone, could help out. However, I used my contact info for the NSA and sent an email saying that I wanted to have a word with Paul Fischer and asked if I could get a number to call.

A couple of hours later, when I'm in the flour section at Whole Foods picking up 0-0 flour, I get an email back from NSA. No, Paul Fischer doesn't do phone calls; he wants to meet in person. I send an email back with the suggestion that Fischer arrange a meeting with Anne Leiden instead. I'll have Mike inform her. I haven't heard anything back. But I figure I've done due diligence and move on.

———

Italian 0-0 flour is the secret behind an elastic and amenable Napolitano pizza dough, in case you're interested. The ultra-fine grind (0-0 is the finest, and 2 is the most course) and high gluten content in semolina flour make kneading pizza dough into smooth balls such a joyful and therapeutic exercise, I often start singing Dean Martin's Amore, with a crooning baritone. When I do, Julie's face usually takes on a tortured expression, and Jupiter runs away. Today, I'm alone in the kitchen, and I don't really feel like singing when no one else is around to depreciate it.

While I'm working on the dough, I'm thinking about the Fat Man project that I'm now in the midst of. From my limited vantage point, and after talking to Bryce, it seems the project is headed by the GIC (the Genome Intelligence Committee), which apparently is talking to the NSA, DARPA/DoD, and DHS. There's also some kind of congressional committee overseeing the GIC's activities. Thus, although the GIC maintains and strives for low posture and secrecy, it is—at least partly—a visible operation. So, say that the mice experiments (the Fat Man project) become a beaming success. It's hard for me to see what the next steps would be. I mean, they can't very well start working on humans, right? Even if Paul Fischer boasts of casting legal codes and guidelines on the wayside, there's enough light shining on the GIC to rein him in. Certainly, a successful Fat Man project with mice as experimental systems could be used to leverage legislation toward FDA approvals on humans. But that's a process. And a lengthy and controversial one at that. But, as Bryce alluded to, in the interest of national security, the process could be fast-tracked by congressional intervention and without public scrutiny. I think I can agree with that.

Now, if the GIC and its various operations are shrouded by a tangled web, the 46+ group, if it even exists, is cloaked in a black cape. Is there a link between 46+ and the GIC, possibly through Paul Fischer? Given the purported agenda of 46+, to build extra chromosomes to use in HEP (that's short for human enhancement performance, remember) for intelligence applications, they would have a field day with the Fat Man project. My concern here is my own involvement and how insulated or exposed I am from any fallout that might come my way if anything goes terribly wrong. My involvement is two-fold. I'm responsible for the Crassus Project and for discovering the Crex-OR genes and their presumed role in mind viewing. I'm also responsible for supporting and assisting the GIC's Fat Man project. If something goes south through the operation of 46+ behind closed doors, I might be implicated as an accessory. But, then again, the 46+ group may not exist at all. And even if it does, their genome editing would merely pop thousands of copies of forty-one large receptor proteins, totally unknown to today's humans, up the nasal cavity in a bunch of people. I mean, what could possibly go wrong?

Do I lose sleep over this? No, but I would feel better if I learned that 46+ is just a fabrication based on false rumors. But, no smoke without fire. And Bryce smells smoke.

Well, that's it. I stroke the silky surface of the second dough ball. I put the dough balls in the fridge. When Julie comes home on Tuesday, I'll make pizza for dinner. I told you that I'm partial to pickles on my pizza. Other toppings I'll try this time are pistachios and thin-sliced potatoes. An idea I got from our daughter Inga and that she and her family enjoy on their homemade pizzas. To be adventurous, I'll also throw on sauerkraut. Not kidding. In fact, one of my favorite pizzas is the Beer Garden Combo Pizza from one of our local pizzerias, with salami, linguica, sauerkraut, dill pickle, onion, and sweet hot mustard. It's not strictly vegan, but very good.

CHAPTER 26

Spring – Summer 2025. A fatal outbreak.

Starting apple cuttings for planting is quite an intricate process that needs to be initiated one year before planting. Luckily for me, all this preparation was done by John Smith. I have twelve ready-to-plant cuttings of the Flower of Kent apple variety in a box that came last week.

It's spring again, and I'm sweating in the afternoon sun as I'm digging holes at the south end of our linear fruit orchard. Julie and Jupiter are over by the garden, cleaning up the raspberry patch. Well, Julie is. Jupiter is lying by her side with an annoyed look. *"Why doesn't the woman throw the fucking ball? It's right there in front of her nose!"* Like I said before, Jupiter is a gentle soul but with an attitude.

I will plant some cuttings in our yard and the rest in the OMICS' courtyard. And, yes, in case you wonder, I do have the proper USDA permits. I've been communicating with John Smith regularly since I visited the U.K. last summer. He kept me updated on the cuttings, and I've told him about the progress with the Crex-ORs, stopping short of mentioning anything about the classified Fat Man project. Mostly, though, we've been discussing the Qumran texts and if there's been any news about recent excavations in the Qumran Canyon. There hasn't. Valerie, the sweetheart, sent me a box of her quince scones for Christmas, which I devoured during the Holidays. Julie and I plan to go to the U.K. next summer to visit Jessica and her family, which now includes our new grandson. I will schedule visits with John Smith and Valerie as well as with the McIntoshes. I've had a few communications with Julius and Molly just to touch base. They haven't inquired much about the Crex-ORs, probably because they realize it's a sensitive matter.

It's mid-March, but not much has happened with the Fat Man project since it started last November. Why? Well, there were a few reasons. One was housekeeping matters, such as arranging an apartment for Mike in Longmont. Another was the lengthy process of getting top secret clearances for Noa, Ron, and Laxmi. However, by far, the most significant roadblock to getting the project started was that bovine creature, Rosy Boyd—I really, really don't like that old cow. Because Mike's work on the Fat Man project is offsite, he needs fieldwork approval from DHS. And since the project is classified, there are so many fascinating ways for Rosy to find sticks to throw in the wheel and delay the project. I can just imagine her stomping her hoofs in excitement. I left it to my CSO, Kirsten Anjou, to deal with Rosy. Thanks to Kirsten's authoritative diplomacy, we were only put back a little over three weeks instead of... well, who knows?

So, anyhow, the Fat Man project is just now about to commence. All the necessary paperwork is in place, and Mike is at the BLUEgenes lab in Colorado right now. I've scheduled an informal meeting with the Crassus Team and Anne Leiden in my office for Friday next week.

———

"We have a decision to make," Mike says and looks at us. We're in my office. The whole Crassus Team and Anne Leiden from the BLUEgenes project is here. It's Friday morning. We're sitting around the oak table that I personally purchased when I started as Director of OMICS. There's coffee and tea on the table and two saucers with scones, huckleberry, and almond butter. Hanne—

who is on spring vacation—instructed her substitute, Ramsey, to set the table. *"Make sure the moron has at least two kinds of scones."* Apparently, Ramsey didn't bat an eye at hearing me be referred to as a moron by my admin. This makes me believe that the epithet is rather widespread around OMICS, something I already suspected. It doesn't bother me; I know I'm very liked and respected as the Director. Not to mention that I'm a Swede. Poor guy, though. Our cafeteria only had huckleberry scones left, so he had to run all over town to find another kind. But he did it in good spirits.

Some background here. When I interviewed Hanne for the admin position back in 2014, I was quickly impressed by her directness, married with a slightly mischievous look. This was another beautiful spring day in mid-May. We were sitting in the courtyard. When she saw me eating my third scone, she commented that only a fucking moron would have three scones with his morning coffee. There was a twinkle in her eye when she said it. That sealed the deal for me. I hired her on the spot.

I got off on a tangent here. Sorry about that. —So, Mike looks at me. He continues, "There doesn't seem to be any restrictions on the length of DNA cargo that can be delivered with the BLUEgenes technology. The transfer is through systemic injection. And, although it's not an issue here, the carrier system allows for transport across the blood-brain barrier." Mike looks at Anne, who nods in confirmation.

"So," Mike continues, "we have forty-one genes. Using the Crex-OR4 as a template, we arrive at a payload of a little over four hundred sixteen kb. Which, in itself, is no problem. But we're thinking of using cDNAs instead, which cuts down the cargo to forty-one-point-five kb, and using a constitutive promoter for each cDNA. We wouldn't get a full readthrough with a single promoter driving all genes."

Mike is referring to complementary DNA. Such cDNAs are made from mRNA, which eliminates all introns. So, if your focus is to demonstrate that the genes can be expressed and the encoded proteins synthesized in the target cells, then cDNA seems logical. If you're also interested in the regulatory aspects of gene expression, then you might want to include the introns, as they often harbor cis-elements responsible for gene activity. In our case, the former scenario is more relevant. So, I agree that a cDNA approach makes sense.

I'm thinking about what Bryce told me about the 46+ group and the manufacturing of tailored chromosomes. I Look at Anne. "So, not prying into the BLUEgenes intricacies, but what you'll be inserting is normal, quote-on-quote DNA cassettes, right, not anything like artificial chromosomes?"

"Yes, it is. The extension of the BLUEgenes project is to allow for the synthesis and delivery of chromosome pairs. There's another DARPA project working on that. I'm not privy to any details, but I think they're several years out from having that implemented."

Anne doesn't seem one bit surprised by my inquiry. And there's no reason she should be. The concept of custom-made chromosomes for HEP applications is not exactly novel, although it's still in its infancy. However, if the rumors about 46+ hold true, the DARPA project she's referring to is bound to be significantly farther ahead than she seems to think.

I say, "Okay, I agree with using cDNA. Our objective is to determine if the OR genes are expressed in the vomeronasal organ and if the ORs are inserted into the epithelium cells."

Ron, who has had a whispering conversation with Noa, comments. "Another thing worth considering; I think you should gauge the promoter strength and, if needed, lower it so as not to overflow the cells."

I nod. "Good idea; you can titrate the promoter activity to mimic the effect of the negative feedback loop you saw in the yeast experiments."

I should explain here that what Mike found out in the yeast studies was that the produced OR4 binds to a site in the OR4 gene promoter as a negative regulator, impeding the activity of a positive transcription factor. So, in essence, the more OR4 that was produced, the more the activity of the OR4 gene was inhibited. This is an example of a negative feedback loop mechanism that aims to keep the gene product at an optimal level. Instead of going through the trouble of installing this feedback loop system for the rest of the forty genes, Mike suggested using another kind of promoter that is not sensitive to the gene product.

I continued, "So, how long do you think this project, the Fat Man project, will take?" I look at Mike and Anne.

Mike throws a glance at Anne. "Well," he says, "We have agreed that we should be able to complete the project within three months, four tops. And we can get started right away."

———

But, as it turned out, they couldn't. The hiatus this time was due to seemingly unrelated outbreaks of a severe and fatal disease that occurred two weeks after Easter in several places around Washington DC Early symptoms included loss of smell and extreme headache, so it was first thought that a new COVID strain was on the horizon. However, examinations showed no retrovirus or any other infectious agent. A total of five cases were reported. All were hospitalized, and they died within two weeks after being symptomatic. Although the mysterious disease was deemed non-contagious, several workplaces and schools closed down as a precautionary measure, especially given the severe nature of the disease. Because of the frequent travels between OMICS and DC, it was no surprise that DHS closed down the lab for most personnel. We were in lockdown and remote-working mode, with travel restrictions from the end of April to June first. The cause and origin of the outbreaks were never found—at least, to my knowledge, nothing was disclosed—and the story soon faded in favor of all other "Breaking News!" that nowadays are flooding streaming platforms and social media.

Similar to what happened during the OMICS lockdown due to the COVID pandemic some years back, the closure this time saw a dramatic increase in cyber attacks on OMICS' computer network, particularly from China and Russia. It's a well-known fact among hackers that when the routine is changed, you're less vigilant. For example, if you start working remotely, you're more inclined to wander off from the computer compared to being on-site. All data files in Sirocco and the entire OMICS' computer ecosystem are encrypted. However, just as in many other computational-heavy organizations, OMICS is consistently involved in fighting off breaching attempts, planning, developing and implementing vulnerability management programs, and updating counter-attack measures. A significant share of the research in our National Security Directorate is devoted to strategies for countering cyber threats.

In late May, I had an all-hands meeting with OMICS staff to discuss how to increase our efforts in cyber-attack prevention. I also had a private meeting with the Crassus Team over an Easter lunch in our home to discuss how to deal with potential cyber-attacks related explicitly to the Fat Man project and the overall Crassus research.

So, on June fifth, which also happens to be my birthday, Mike is finally back in Colorado, and the Fat Man project could get started in earnest.

My birthday? It was really nice. Julie had made a Swedish strawberry shortcake, a fluffy composition of light spongecakes topped with whipped cream and fresh strawberries. I got thoughtful gifts from Julie and our kids, like olive oils, red wine, dark chocolate infused with chili peppers, and a twenty-pack of to-go instant stain-remover sticks. Hanne—probably the only one at work who knows my birth date—had sent over a box with three kinds of scones; almond butter, huckleberry, and vanilla cream. Jupiter gave me a waistband with lights front and back. I look at Jupiter as Julie hands over the gift.

"What is this," I ask.

"Fuck it, man, you know what it is. You always cut our walks short in wintertime when you tell me it's getting too dark. No excuses now to—"

"Okay, okay, I get it. Thank you, Jupiter!"

CHAPTER 27

Summer 2025. Problems. Suspicions of foul play.

The problems with the Fat Man project started in mid-July It's nine on a new Monday morning. July fourteenth, to be precise. There's a slight overcast on the horizon, but the forecast promises a sunny and pleasantly warm day. In other words, not too hot. I'm in my office looking through emails while drinking my coffee. I'm finishing my second scone—and using the stain-remover stick I got from Inga to clear my shirt from huckleberry evidence—when Mike calls. He's back from Colorado for a few days and wants to have a meeting as soon as possible.

An hour later, Mike, Ron, Laxmi, and I are sitting at my conference table. Noa is on a vacation trip to Tel Aviv with her fiancé. Mike has opened his laptop, and we're looking at some gruesome pictures.

"So," he says, "everything looks okay with the constructs. We synthesized three versions with different promoter strengths. We tested the constructs in yeast cells, and they all behaved as expected. This was all done in early March, before the lockdown. We now injected each of the three constructs into six mice." Mike points at the first picture. "This is on day one."

What we see are mice under severe stress. I'm not fond of experiments on animals. But I'm also not a hypocrite. I realize the significant importance of animal testing in the medical and pharmaceutical sciences. But I hate to see animals suffer in the process. I can tell that Mike feels the same. He looks disgusted.

"So," he continues, "almost immediately after the injections of the DNA constructs, the mice showed symptoms of extreme headache. And, we could tell that they lost their sense of smell." He points to another picture that starts a short video clip. "They obviously cannot find their food. After two days, they seemed to have lost their vision as well, and… after six days, they were all dead." He points to another picture.

Action potentials are suddenly firing up in my brain, and chemical neurotransmitters start swimming around my axon terminals. I look at the others to see if they make the same connection I do. They don't seem to. I opt to say nothing.

Mike continues, "Expression analyses of biopsy samples of the sensory epithelium in the vomeronasal organ revealed that all neurons—and there are several thousands of them—accumulated loads of Crex-ORs. So, there's nothing wrong with the transcriptional activity. But, none of the proteins were embedded in the plasma membranes. In fact, the cell cytoplasm was so stock-full of receptor proteins, they were like bloating." He shows a series of cell and tissue pictures. "As you can see, the entire epithelium looked inflamed. That held true also for the constructs with the lowest promoter strength."

We're quiet for a while. "Yuck!" I say finally. "Well, I assume that even if we incorporate the negative feedback loop in the constructs—which I think we should test, by the way—but what I'm saying is that even if we do, I don't think the Crex-ORs will insert into the membranes. However, the problems with ballooned cells and inflammation may be avoided."

"I agree," says Mike. Ron and Laxmi are both nodding.

Laxmi points to one of the high-magnification cell pictures. "Could it be that the tension pressure in the cell disrupts the ER and the whole co-translational process?"

ER stands for the endoplasmic reticulum, a cell structure involved in threading synthesized proteins into the plasma membrane. This is referred to as co-translational translocation of proteins. Laxmi has a good point. If that process is disturbed, it will interfere with getting the receptor proteins into the cell membrane.

I nod in agreement. "Could very well be."

I continue, "So, let's see what happens with the feedback loop in the constructs. It's a lot of extra work, of course; you also need to change back to the Crex-OR4 promoter, but something we need to check out."

"It's not that bad," Mike says. "The DNA synthesis pipeline they have over there is fantastic. I'll head back over there tomorrow and let them know."

Ron has his laptop up and swivels it around for us to see. He displays the Crex-OR4 sequence schematics on the screen. "Maybe we should include the intron," he says and points to the red section of the gene. "For one, it might have a regulatory function that modulates gene expression similar to the feedback loop mechanism. Second, there might be alternative splicing that results in a modified OR protein. We could start by checking the sequence to see if that's a possibility." As he says that, he feeds the Crex-OR4 intron sequence into software on his computer and lets it run.

"That's an excellent suggestion," Mike says. "We may start by testing just the Crex-OR4 gene."

While waiting for Ron's program to run, we chitchat about summer plans and vacations. Mike is going to an Andy Warhol exhibit in San Diego—shocker. Ron and Laxmi will visit friends and family in Mumbai in early August.

"Well, this program doesn't suggest any alternative splice sites," Ron says after about twenty minutes and shows the results from the search. "But it's still worth a try."

I'm summarizing. "OK, let's test Crex-OR4 constructs with or without the feedback loop and with or without the intron. I suggest trying different permutations of one-, three-, and five-gene constructs."

———

It's Sunday. Bryce and Lucy are on their way back from San Francisco and a Psychology conference, and we invited them to stay with us over the weekend. Lucy is a child psychologist specializing in treating children from abused homes or who are otherwise traumatized. Julie and Lucy are very good friends from our time in California and have remained close also after we moved apart. They have much in common, and they communicate almost weekly. For example, they're both highly empathetic people who can compartmentalize their emotions and often stressful experiences from work when off duty.

I'm also empathetic and good at compartmentalizing, by the way. Like right now, I feel very empathetic for my queen, and I have compartmentalized myself into the singular objective of saving her from being captured without getting in check. Bryce and I are sitting in the shade of our lilac grove, deep in thought, pondering our chess moves. We still have a game ongoing in the d4c4 app, but we started a new one *in natura* yesterday night. Unfortunately, the end is near and doesn't look good for me. An ordinary chess player would have conceded by now. But, in the spirit of "It ain't over till the Fat Lady sings," I hang on to the thin thread that Bryce might fall off the chair and topple over the chess board, and we would call it remi. I kick slightly on his chair to see if it's balanced or not. He looks up at me.

"Hey! No dirty tricks." He makes his move. I struggle for a bit, queen-less, but to no avail. There's no fat lady around, let alone one who sings, but the game is over nonetheless.

"Well played," I say and kick his chair so it falls backward. But by then, Bryce had already gotten up and was stretching his arms.

The four of us got back from church a couple of hours ago. We'll soon have a late lunch, and then I'll take Bryce and Lucy to the airport. Yesterday, before dinner, Bryce and I sat with our wine—a 2021 California Orin Swift, a red blend of such odd bedfellows as Grenache, Petite Sirah, and Syrah—in the blue Amish swing, a birthday gift from Julie several years back. I wanted to talk to Bryce about something that bothered me.

"You remember the DC cases in April? Five people came down with COVID-like symptoms—extreme headache and loss of smell—and they all died within a week."

Bryce takes a sip of wine. "Yes, I do. Strange. And they never found out what was going on, right?"

"No, but that's what I want to ask you about. Any chance you could use your network to find out more? I'll tell you why."

I refill our glasses, take a mouthful, and savor the flavors of raspberry and blackberry jam—it's like the filling in a scone but with an undertone of leather.

Bryce knows about the Fat Man project. I recount the details from the meeting with Mike last week. "So, hearing about the symptoms in the mice reminded me about the DC cases. In both instances, there were severe headaches, loss of smell, and—within a week—death. What seems to be the difference is that the mice also experienced impaired vision. So, I'm wondering—"

Bryce interrupts, "Hey! Are you suggesting that the DC cases were due to the Crex-OR constructs? That's wild!"

"Well, think about it. That despicable idiot Paul Fischer would easily have access to the constructs and could have handed them over to the 46+ group. Maybe through some DARPA collaboration. The time from March to the end of April would suffice to perform human injections."

"But, how the hell would they find people that would volunteer to be subjects?"

"No idea. Maybe they weren't aware of being subjects?"

"Whoa," Bryce says after a while, "That's one hell of an accusation!"

"Well, one thing I wonder if you could do is find out if the DC cases also involved loss of vision and if there's any common denominator between the cases that could explain what happened."

Bryce thinks. "I don't think the FBI was ever involved. So, this would have landed in the DC Metropolitan Police Department. I can try to do some fishing. But, what would you do with this information, anyway?"

"Well, I bet that if the bodies were exhumed, a simple PCR test of the nasal cavities would reveal the presence of Crex-OR DNA."

"Symphony, come on! This would require a court order. And there's no way you would get one without evidence. And you have none. There's no proof that 46+ exists or that any other group has used the Crex-OR gene package for HEP purposes. Even if you're technically right—and I think you might be— there's no proof that Paul Fischer is the mediator; it might as well be people within DARPA. Fischer would say that the GIC is investigating the potential for using the genes for HEP applications, nothing more and that he has no knowledge about a secret 46+ operation. I suggest you focus on trying to see if and how the problem with the project can be fixed. As I mentioned before, I have a team looking into Fischer and the 46+ rumors."

That was yesterday. Now I'm on my way back from taking Bryce and Lucy to the airport. I think that Bryce is right; there's no concrete evidence implicating Paul Fischer in the DC cases. Be that as it may, I still strongly suspect he is somehow involved. The purpose of the Fat Man project in Colorado is to ensure everything works as intended and pave the way for genome editing in humans in the future. If Fischer was so intent on doing tests on humans that he couldn't wait for the mice experiments to be completed, that's extremely reckless. He should be exposed and held responsible. But, putting my feelings for Fischer aside, I agree with Bryce that even more important than trying to find incriminating evidence of wrongdoing is to figure out how to remedy the issues with the Fat Man project.

Meanwhile, Mike and the BLUEgenes team are making new constructs that include the negative feedback loop and the intron. As I told Mike, I don't think the feedback loop will solve the core problem of getting the receptor proteins incorporated into the plasma membrane of the vomeronasal neurons unless Laxmi's idea is correct. But it might alleviate the unintended—and seemingly fatal—consequences of cell stress and tissue inflammation. As for the intron—well… let's see.

As we're having our Sunday dinner—Mid-Eastern chickpea salad with sautéed spinach, tahini dressing, and pita chips, since you're curious—Julie makes some interesting comments. We're talking about the Fat Man project. I'm saying, regarding the agenda of a hypothetical 46+ operation, "What if engineered mind-viewing people turn up as chess players? That would be the end of my future career as a chess master after I retire from OMICS."

Julie, whose mind is going elsewhere to more practical concerns, rolls her eyes and comments, "Let me suggest a less absurd scenario. What if also dogs and cats emit these olphons? Then, a mind viewer at a vet clinic might be able to assist with diagnosis. Say, a dog that produces an image of something she's eaten and that made her sick. Or, in more general terms, helping understand what's bothering a dog or a cat. Dogs and cats keep multi-modal mental imageries of objects they encounter in their daily lives."

Julie is on a roll now. She continues, "Or, say that a blind person gets injected with these genes—the Crex-OR genes—then he or she could view images generated in the guide dog's brain. So, in essence, the blind person could have partial vision through the dog."

I'm getting excited. I haven't even touched my second glass of wine. If you're guessing we're drinking Columbia Valley 2016 Ethos Reserve Merlot, you wouldn't be far off. We're enjoying the 2014 vintage, which is superior in taste and bouquet. I got two bottles from a neighbor for my birthday.

So, Julie's comments open up a whole array of possibilities for Fat Man applications, also within the realm of national security. For example, a dog could be used for reconnaissance, inconspicuously snooping around in targeted territories and absorbing images of people or other assets that could later be "harvested" by a mind-viewing agent. Of course, all this is contingent on dogs producing olphons as part of their visual processing. It's easily testable, of course.

I'll be in a meeting off-site all of tomorrow. So, after dinner, I emailed my COO (Chief Operations Officer), Laura Waters, telling her that Noa would come to her with a request to bring a dog to the premises and that this was okay. I also send an explanatory email to Noa.

CHAPTER 28

Fall 2025. Suspicions confirmed.

It's early August and another warm day. The mercury hits thirty-two degrees already at nine-thirty a.m. I'm in the OMICS courtyard again, watching an extrovert house finch, picking scone crumbles right off the table I'm sitting at. I'm covering my remaining third scone with my hand; I don't want to give this gregarious guy any ideas.

This is my favorite spot in the courtyard. It's next to the lawn and a group of old oak trees where the squirrels like to hang around. They run up and down the trees and out on the lawn to bury their loot. For some reason, I still don't comprehend, it's not acorns they hide, but walnuts. There are no walnut trees anywhere near OMICS. So, this is one of life's many mysteries I have to deal with. But I need to prioritize; I must get to the bottom of whatever is screwing up the Fat Man project. So, I can only spend so much time trying to figure out the logistics of busy squirrels.

By the way, since I spend a great deal of my time in the courtyard, I don't want to give you the false impression that I'm alone here. At this time of day, for example, several people are scattered around, drinking coffee, having breakfast, talking, and/or working on their laptops. I'm often left alone, though. Why? Well, it should be no secret to you by now that I'm an affable chap; I'm extremely well-liked by everyone who knows me. That obviously includes the OMICS staff. Still, only a few are audacious enough to come and sit down next to the Director. I like it that way. Not that I want to sit here in splendid isolation to emphasize my status, but because I don't want to feel pressured to share my scones. Also, I do enjoy the solitude.

The finch is gone, so I can now savor my third scone. He knew I was hiding it. He tilted his little head, gave me a look with a peppercorn eye that I prefer not to interpret, and took off. I'm cleaning off some reddish spots on my shirt with a stain-remover stick when I get a phone call. It's Bryce.

Bryce and I usually start our conversations with some insults referring to an ongoing chess game. Not this time. "Well, you were right," Bryce says. "Turns out the five DC case patients lost their vision just a day or so before they passed away. Interestingly, they were all five athletes—or, at least, athletic people—and they had recently been to health clubs for intravenous, or IV, therapy with electrolytes and vitamins. Different clubs—"

"Sorry," I say. "IV therapy, is that a thing?"

"Yes, apparently it is. I didn't know that either. Anyhow, these were different clubs around DC The electrolyte-vitamin cocktails were all from the same company, Health Solutions, Inc., in Pennsylvania. The company denied all accusations. And examinations of the Health Solutions cocktails that the clubs routinely use revealed nothing suspicious. But to avoid negative exposure, Health Club Solutions Inc. quickly filed pretrial motions and negotiated settlements with the families. And, no— since you're going to ask—the cocktails and injection needles used for these five people are all gone. So, there's nothing left there to investigate."

"So, if Paul Fischer is involved in one way or another, he's not only careless. This points to intent. Someone entered these health clubs and deliberately manipulated the IV bags to add the Crex-OR genes."

"If that's what happened, yes. Or, maybe add the genes to the needles. But, of course, there's no evidence that implicates Fischer or anyone else."

"Oh boy, what a clusterfuck!"

"Sums it up about right."

We're quiet for a while. Then Bryce asks, "So what's up at your end? Any progress?"

"They're running experiments with amended constructs." I give Bryce a rundown of the modified approach. "I have a meeting with Mike tomorrow to discuss the most recent results."

Back in my office, I send another email to the GIC requesting a meeting with Paul Fischer. I did the same last month, right after I found out about the problems Mike and the BLUEgenes team had run into. That time, Paul just sent me an email back saying he knew what had happened and instructed me to "Focus on fixing this shit as soon as possible!" This time around, I insist on a meeting in person. I'll be in DC, at the DHS Headquarters, Thursday through Friday, and I recommend we meet on Friday after ten a.m. I'll ask Bryce to join if he's available.

Fischer surprised me with a quick email back, suggesting lunch on Friday at Schemalis, a Mediterranean restaurant. If I didn't know better, I would almost think he was being considerate by choosing a place within walking distance from DHS.

––––––––

The next day, Mike is in my office. "OK, he says, "We made the different combinations we talked about—or that you suggested. As expected, adding the negative feedback loops to the constructs didn't help get the ORs into the cell membrane. Also, we saw a clear correlation between the number of genes in the construct, the level of ORs in the cytoplasm, and the intracellular and physiological stress symptoms; the less free OR accumulation in the cytoplasm, the lower the stress effects. I would state that this was also something we expected. I have pictures, but I don't know if—"

"No, that's fine. Well, at least we confirmed that suspicion. Okay, what about the intron?"

"Well, we didn't notice any effect of the intron, at least not to start with. But, and I don't know if there's a correlation or if it's even relevant, but it seemed as if the subjects that received the intron—whether one, three, or five—were less stressed than the rest of the test subjects, as far as pain, and smell and vision impairment go, but instead they appeared to develop a mild cold. Not sure what to make of this. It's a preliminary observation, at best."

So, we still don't know the root of the problem. I ask Mike to tell the BLUEgenes team to keep as many of the mice as possible under surveillance for a while, at least those that don't suffer too much, in case there are long-term physiological and or metabolic adjustments needed in the vomeronasal organ for the ORs to get inserted into the plasma membrane of the neurons.

The rest of the day goes by with a few meetings. I leave early to go by Whole Foods to get ingredients for dinner. I'm making Shakshuka, a Tunisian dish. The foodies among you may frown and argue that Shakshuka is more of a breakfast or lunch thing. And you'd be right. But… we'll have it for dinner tonight. So there. I pick up a few things I need for dinner, plus some extras you can never have too many of in the kitchen, like avocados, lemons, garlic, and extra virgin, first cold press olive oil.

Julie will be home late tonight. The Shakshuka comes together in a breeze, so I have time to spare. I decide to pick up Jupiter early from the kennel and take her for a long walk on Badger Mountain. Jupiter, of course, is all for it. I'm well-licked when we jump in the car. Well … you know. She does, anyhow. Jump in the car.

It's still hot, so we first drive home, where I change into shorts and a T-shirt and don a cap. I usually get my best ideas for research programs, grant proposals, or other initiatives when walking—or sitting down with coffee and scones. So, I'm hoping that hiking Badger will get the neurons in my brain talking to each other and come up with a thread to pull in the Fat Man project.

I'm operating under the fair assumption that Badger Mountain is not your go-to hiking spot. So let me just say that it's a small mountain by any standards, just a little under five hundred meters tall (sixteen hundred feet for non-metrics folks). It's a top-rated hiking destination for people in the Tri-Cities area. Two trails are leading to the summit. The shortest one is the Canyon trail, and that's our choice. Or, I should say, that's *my* choice. Jupiter is of a different mind and wants to take the longer trail, the Skyline trail, where—she knows from experience—she's more likely to encounter jackrabbits. Last time we hiked Skyline, Julie and I let Jupiter off leach for a while since no other people were around. She got nose of a jackrabbit and chased it off trail until the poor lagomorph found a hiding place. She completely ignored our commands to "Stay" and "Come."

"I know you want to take the Skyline trail because you think you'll get an opportunity to chase another jackrabbit. Fat chance, lady. You should not disturb the wildlife. It says so explicitly at the trailhead."

"Bullshit, it's good for the rabbits to get chased. It keeps them from becoming complacent. And it's good for their stamina, too, like the squirrels at home. I keep them in pretty good shape, I would say. 'Disturb the wildlife?' Well, kiss my ass!"

"I'd rather not, but I get your point. So, let's just leave it at that. We're taking the Canyon trail. Skyline is almost three times as long. It's too hot, and I must get back in time to start the Shakshuka."

We have a nice hike. We see no other hikers on the trail. It's three p.m., so people are either at work or in school. The rest are too smart to go hiking in this hot weather. It's cooled down a little bit, but it's still hot (thirty-six degrees), and I'm dripping with sweat when we reach the summit. Julie and most of my colleagues would grade the difficulty level of the Canyon trail as easy. I call it moderate. Give me a few years, and I'll call it difficult. We rest for a while, and I tell Jupiter about the Fat Man project and the snag we've run into. She is usually an excellent sounding board, as you may have inferred. But now she is frantically looking around for jackrabbits, so she's not very communicative.

We have a good view of central Richland from our vantage point. I'm looking down at the new TRI-CITY GAME CENTER, TCGC for short. Its symbol is a colossal icosahedron—a twenty-sided die—located on the roof. It's the kind of die you find in games like Dungeons and Dragons or Nintendo. TCGC has become a water hole for game-thirsty people from all over Washington. It also has good conference capabilities, and OMICS has had meetings there on a few occasions.

"It's not what you look at; it's what you see that matters." Someone coined that piece of wisdom. I think it was Henry David Thoreau. You can look it up. —So, what I look at is the game symbol, prominently exposed on the TCGC roof and easily spotted from the Badger Mountain summit. But what I see in my mind is something different. Something I should have thought about a long time ago.

Jupiter has given up on jackrabbits and suggests we head back. I agree, and we start our descent. But not before I email Mike and explain what I want him to do. And that I will meet him in his office as soon as possible on Monday morning after I return from DC.

245

CHAPTER 29

Fall 2025. Meeting with Paul Fischer at Schemalis.

Life is full of surprises. Here's one for you: Paul Fischer, the scumbag, is vegan. We're at Schemalis on Friday, a little before noon. Fischer met us here shortly after we had secured a table in an area where we wouldn't be overheard. Bryce and I had been in a meeting where I updated DHS and DOE on OMICS' overall project portfolio. This was in preparation for our annual financial reports by the end of the fiscal year. When we were seated, the waiter announced that today's lunch special was a beef and chicken kabob platter in Greek yogurt sauce.

"I certainly don't want that," Fischer says with an almost indignant voice, totally uncalled for. "Meat and dairy are toxic. I'll have the vegetarian platter."

"Certainly, Sir," says the waiter, unfazed. He turns to Bryce and me. "And you, gentlemen?" I detect an ever so slight emphasis on "gentlemen," by which I think the waiter subtly suggests that Fischer doesn't qualify for this distinction.

"I'll have the same, thanks," I say.

"And I'll take the lunch special," says Bryce.

Bryce looks at Fischer. "Well, you have a kindred spirit in Symphony here."

Just the thought of being considered a kindred spirit to Fischer makes me shiver. I certainly have no desire to expand on Bryce's comment, but since I'm prompted, I do.

"I prefer to eat and cook vegan, or at least vegetarian," I explain. "My Achilles heel is cheese and other fermented milk products like yogurt and kefir, which I have a hard time being without. Although, more and more acceptable plant-derived alternatives are coming offline."

"Milk is for babies and kids that need to grow," argues Fischer. "As adults, we don't need that shit. I have a brother who is a prostate-cancer survivor, and his doctor told him to stop drinking milk. Humans are the only species that is fucked up enough to drink milk as adults."

"Well, first of all, that's simply not true; we give our dog kefir every morning, and she loves it. And put some milk in front of a cat or a hedgehog, and you'll—"

"We are the only species that deliberately drink milk," snarls Fischer.

"Yes, animals like orangutans and chimpanzees don't go out in the fields and milk cows and goats, let alone do they operate dairy pipelines for the production of cheese. Is that because they have dietary concerns about drinking milk? No, if humans are the only species that intentionally drink milk as adults, it's because we're the only species that can."

I realize I'm arguing against myself here, but before I have a chance to develop my reasoning further (I was going to mention my visit to the R Farm), the food arrives. Although it's early in the day, it's warm, and I was hoping for a cold beer to go with the food. I see nothing on the menu, but I ask the waiter anyhow. But sadly, they don't serve any alcoholic drinks. Nor do they have non-alcoholic beer.

"Alcohol is another toxin," exclaims Fischer. "I never touch the stuff."

"It kills your neurons," he continues.

"Not to mention the liver," he adds as a punchline.

"You just did," I say.

Fischer stares at me.

"You said not to mention the liver, but you did—mention the liver."

For a fraction of a picosecond, I thought I saw a tremor on Fischer's lips as if he was going to acknowledge the joke. But, no, that didn't happen.

Bryce, meanwhile, who shares my interest in good food—but doesn't have any specific restrictions other than high quality and large enough portions—looks at his watch.

"This is fascinating and all," he says. "But I have to leave soon. And you, Symphony, have a plane to catch. I don't want you wandering around here in town longer than necessary."

I drink some water. "Okay, yes. So, Paul, the five people who died here in DC last spring, experienced the same symptoms as the mice in the Fat Man project: splitting headache, loss of smell, and, soon thereafter, death. This was in the news. What wasn't in the papers, and that Bryce found out, was that they also claimed to have impaired vision just before they died, which is also what the mice did. So, the five people, who were all athletic and in excellent shape, followed the exact same pattern as the Fat Man mice."

I look directly at Fischer. "These five people were clients at health clubs where they were given IV therapy with electrolytes and vitamins. A common enough procedure, as it seems. There's no doubt in my mind that those five people died because someone had substituted the Crex-OR DNA constructs for the electrolyte and vitamin mix or added it to the mix."

"And?" Fischer looks at me.

"And someone did this, and that someone must have gotten hold of the DNA construct!"

"DARPA, for one, has full access. I haven't been to the BLUEgenes lab in over a year. And, besides, what you have are allegations. There's no proof."

"If we get a court order to have the bodies exhumed, a quick PCR test would confirm that they have the Crex-OR genes."

"We? Who are you, the FBI?"

"I guess my message here is that whatever influence you have over what's happening on the human genome-editing side of things, you use that to make sure that no more experiments be performed until we have successful results in the mice."

"That's what you should use your time for," Fischer argues, "instead of trying to incriminate me."

"Check!" he orders as the waiter goes by.

Bryce and I hang around for a while after Fischer's abrupt departure.

"He has a very agreeable personality, that guy," I say. "I wish more people could be like him."

"But he does have beautiful eyes," I add.

Bryce looks at me.

"He does," I say. "I wish he didn't, but he does."

"I think eyes are interesting," I continue. "They say something about your personality. Your eyes, for example, are very ordinary." In fact, Bryce's brown eyes have an exceptionally pleasant and soft appeal. Of course, I don't tell him that.

Instead, I say, "I find that people often consider my eyes to have an attractive cobalt-blue charisma that gives me a youthful appearance."

"Where do you find people who say that?"

"Well, they not directly say it, as much as I sense that's what they're thinking."

"Of course," I add, "Fischer has the personality of a slug. So, I assume he must have a redeeming streak somewhere deep inside him."

———

When I walk into Mike's office Monday morning, the first thing I see is a monstrous-size version of a Shot Blue Marylin poster. Just one of twelve Andy Warhol art pieces in various sizes he has displayed on his walls. I've been here several times, of course, but the decoration looks different each time; he replaces the paintings on a regular basis from what must be an endless supply he keeps at home. Mike lives alone. There probably is no space for another person, or even a pet, in his apartment because of all his Andy Warhol paraphernalia.

Mike's dating history is famous among his friends and colleagues. He's had several girlfriends, all very short-lived relationships. He has two interests in life: Andy Warhol and computational genomics, a.k.a. work. Every attempt to strike up a conversation with him on any topic outside of Andy Warhol or work, you find yourself within a minute talking about Andy Warhol. There's either a painting or a story that relates and that he effortlessly uses as a segue. It's quite impressive, actually. Any girl who aspires to maintain a sustainable bond with Mike must be a stout Warhol fan or strong enough to force his attention in other directions.

He is a very nice and good-looking person, Mike—albeit with a somewhat lonesome look about him—with dark hair and clear, blue eyes and an athletic build. Although he never exercises or does sports. Unless, of course, there was to be an Andy Warhol tournament. I hope he eventually finds the right woman. In fact, ever since he started working with the BLUEgenes team, there's been a certain luster to Mike. I'm guessing here, but I wonder if he might be infatuated with Anne Leiden, the PI who leads the work. She is older than him by probably five years—Mike is thirty-eight. Whether Anne is available or married with five kids, a dog, and a cat, I have no idea. I leave that to Mike to sort out.

Speaking of Mike, this is a good time to mention that Mike and Noa made staff earlier this year. I strongly supported their promotion, which I considered long overdue. And, as long as we're talking about changes, I should also point out that neither Ron nor Laxmi is longer involved in the Crassus or Fat Man project. They are both fully occupied by leading different aspects of a new big thirty-five million dollar-project on non-invasive phenomics (NonPhen) jointly funded by DHS and DOE. This started with another idea I had—my intellect is the dynamo that drives the lives of many—and that I asked Ron and Laxmi to develop. NonPhen rests on the premise that DNA can be found in particles scattered or shed from a human body: dandruff, skin flakes, hair. Such particles can be collected non-conspicuously from a person using a harvesting device. Ron's and Laxmi's team are now setting up research where the aim is to allow for airborne particles to be collected, sampled, processed, and analyzed within minutes. The goal is to be able to non-invasively get a genomic identification of a person basically in real time as he or she walks by a security check. So, Ron and Laxmi nowadays spend the lion's share of their working hours in the Genome Synthesis and Sequencing (GSS) wing of OMICS. Noa is still, to a limited extent, part of the Crassus Team, but she is six months pregnant and is gradually transitioning into another chapter in her life.

Finally, on the staffing side, I'm happy to let you know that Rosy Boyd is no longer with us. I mean, she's still alive, but she's not alive in OMICS. Bryce, true to his word, has promoted her sideways to the Interagency Office within DHS. Good riddance, I say.

When Mike comes into his office, he carries a tray with two coffees and a plate with three scones and a muffin. What a marvelous young guy! I'm afraid to ask if all three scones are for me or if he wants me to share. But I need not worry; he takes the muffin and puts the plate with scones in front of me.

"We had the sequence for the intron a long time ago, of course," he says when he sits down and wakes up his computers. "But nothing popped up that made us suspect anything. However, we were focused entirely on the protein sequence to compare with other olfactory receptors. We didn't pay attention to the intron."

Mike brings up a slide on one of the computer screens. "But you were right. I did as you suggested and made a low-stringency search. And, lo and behold, I can see the integration sites and other hallmarks of a virus." He points to different elements in the sequence. "Nothing that is recognized in any database but some kind of unknown retrovirus."

He looks at me. "So, eighty-six percent of the intron is occupied by this unfamiliar virus. How the hell did you come to think about this?"

"Well, I'm incredibly smart, as you know."

Mike laughs. "Yes, we all know. And an incredible scone consumer." He nods at my empty plate. "Do you even chew them?"

"Oh yes, I savor every bite of them."

I look with satisfaction at my spotless shirt. Not a single huckleberry stain in sight. But then, these were vanilla-cream scones.

I say, "But also, I hiked Badger with Jupiter yesterday. And when we looked down over the Tri-Cities from the summit, I saw the TCGC logo—the icosahedron. That triggered a signal transduction cascade from two outposts in my powerful brain: the mice with a slight cold and the icosahedron, and with laser-sharp deduction, I came to think about a virus."

"Must feel good to have such a superior intellect. Not to rain on your parade, but you're not the first one—to make this connection between TCGC and a virus I mean. And, of course, this is not what a retrovirus looks like. But you should still feel proud of yourself!"

"Thanks, I do—often."

When I leave Mike's office, I realize I forgot to ask him for any news about the cold-inflicted mice. I think of going back, but I'm already late for a couple of back-to-back meetings. I'm confident he will contact me with any updates as they unravel.

CHAPTER 30

Fall 2025. The mouse model.

Which he does the following day when I meet him in the parking lot.

"Hoy," he shouts when he sees me a couple of cars away.

"Hoy yourself," I say, ever the conversationalist.

"Do you have a few minutes?"

"If it's about the Fat Man project, yes, I do. If it's about Andy Warhol, I have a meeting starting right now."

"Not to worry. Although I have some interesting news on that front too that I can share later if you're curious."

"Maybe in another universe, I would be. Now stop wasting my precious valuable time and tell me about the mice."

"So, I spoke with Anne yesterday," he says as we walk towards the building. (Anne, not Dr. Leiden or even Anne Leiden!)

"Okay?"

"Confusing but intriguing stuff; the mice with a slight cold — those with the intron — now seem fully recovered. But all other mice, including the control mice, have nasty colds and seem to have lost their sense of smell. And — here's the weird stuff — they are very aggressive and have an uncontrollable sexual appetite. Like… they never stop."

"And this fits," he continues. "Social and mating behavior are things the vomeronasal organ controls. At least in mice."

"It also squares with a virus being involved," I say while we're walking in the corridor towards my office. "The virus must have spread from the intron mice to the rest of the population. Are they all kept in the same area?"

"Fairly close, yes."

"Can we meet later today, say after lunch? And, can you contact a virologist and ask if retroviruses can get out of a cell without causing harm? So, no lytic cycle. Preferably, no budding either."

"Okidoc, I'll come to your office around 2."

"Bloody hell, Symphony! People are waiting for you. You're supposed to be in Pasteur for the mass spec meeting twenty minutes ago."

This is Hanne, my admin, as you might have guessed, who comes running towards us."

Mike lets out a chuckle. "So, you really did have a meeting after all."

"Apparently, but I forgot about it."

I look at Hanne. "Tell them to start, I'll be in soon."

"You're the one leading the meeting, pretty boy!"

"Oh, crap, I can't even remember what the meeting is about."

"Well, fuck me sideways! Just go in there, Symphony, and do your thing. You never disappoint an audience. I'll brief you on the agenda on the way over."

"But, I haven't even—"

"I already put coffee and scones for you in there."

"You're an angel, Hanne. Foul-mouthed, but an angel."

———

You know I'm a terrific mentor. I've shown you that. Here's another example. I'm pretty confident about what's happening with the Fat Man mice. I figure Mike does, too. So, I'll first ask him to explain what might be going on. I know him well enough to expect he's already made a slide or two.

"So, what's your theory, young man?" I ask him as he walks into my office a little after two p.m.

Mike opens his laptop and shows me a colorful figure with red and blue mice.

"First," he says, "I checked online, and I also talked to Louis Paterson, a virologist over at UW" (which he pronounces *"UDUB,"* which is short for the University of Washington) "about how retrovirus can exit cells without harming them. And, yes, there are examples of naked virus DNA getting out of a cell without causing damage. Paterson said that in some cases, the viral genome may encode a translocase. In other cases, the mechanisms are unknown. He also suggested budding as another route, although that might eventually deprive the cell of the plasma membrane. And, of course, this is an unknown virus, so who knows what kind of exit strategy it has."

"Now," he continues and points at a neuron cell in his figure, "here's a plausible scenario. Once in the neurons, this unknown retrovirus is reactivated. In the cells, the virus might somehow facilitate the Crex-ORs to be threaded into the membrane during the co-translational process. For example, it might interact with membrane lipids, as has been shown for other viruses. Or, it might encode some kind of chaperone."

"Then the virus exits the neurons," he says and points to an epithelium cell, "and enters the epithelium cells, where it replicates and undergoes a lytic cycle. This, in turn, leads to a cold response in the mouse and the release of a virus that can infect other mice."

"Excellent deduction, dear Watson," I say. "Possibly, the virus might also help with the OR insertion from the outside by 'lubricating' the neurons through all the extra mucus being produced when the epithelium cells burst."

"Good idea," says Mike.

"Only ones I have," I counter.

There's one crucial question remaining, and I'm waiting for Mike to get to it before I mention it. And, as I assumed he would, Mike soon delivers.

"So, I assume that Fat Man and his contemporaries walked around with a persistent slight cold, or they developed immunity, which is more likely. But the key question is why control mice, and other mice without the intron, develop these horrible symptoms, whereas mice with the intron do not." He shows a second slide. "One possible explanation is that neurons containing the Crex-ORs in their membrane are resistant to the virions coming out of the epithelial cells, while neurons without the ORs are not. And, once in the vomeronasal neurons, the virus runs amok with the cellular machinery, resulting in pathological behavior."

"I think you paint an excellent scenario for the situation. My thinking is that the Crex-OR receptors function like defensins, interacting with viral glycoproteins and or the cell membrane to protect against viral infections."

I look at him. "Now, this is a virus, not to mention an unknown one. And given the awful symptoms in the mice, there's a potential for a scary outbreak in the human population. So, if you aren't already, I suggest you start wearing masks over at the BLUEgenes lab and take every other precaution possible. For example, get rid of all infected mice as soon as possible."

"We are already wearing masks as a routine safety measure. I'll call Anne as soon as we're done."

"Good. Well, as fascinating as this is from a basic science perspective, we now need to focus on making another generation of constructs. By the way, do you know yet if all the Crex-OR genes are expressed in every neuron or if only one gene is selected for each neuron, like in the main olfactory system?"

"Yes, I thought about that, and our data suggest that all genes are expressed in every neuron, at least the cells we've looked at so far. I also emailed Jakob Rasmussen about this, and he said that orphaned ORs don't seem to be the norm for the vomeronasal neurons."

I now have Paul Fischer's email address. So, after Mike left, I sent an email saying that we needed to talk.

"We did talk," he sends back immediately.

"We need to talk again!"

"Why?"

"Because! Don't you guys have a secure phone line? You're NSA, for crying out loud!"

"I try to avoid phones."

"Well, make an exception."

Nothing. And then my office phone rings.

"This has better be good!" Fischer says, clearly annoyed.

"No, it's not. In fact, it's bad. Really bad! So can I talk freely on this line?"

"Make it short."

So, I give him a brief summary of what we think is the problem with the Fat Man project and how we are moving forward.

"So, it's extremely important that you let whomever you're interacting with that they need to shut down all human experimentation until we have demonstrated a successful outcome of the mice project."

"Like I said, I'm not calling the shots here."

"No, but—"

Click.

CHAPTER 31

*Spring – Summer 2026. The Fat Man project concluded.
The FBI.*

It's now six months after the successful conclusion of the DARPA-funded initial phase of the Fat Man project. When I asked Paul Fischer about the ongoing process and ensuing steps of the project, he simply announced that what happens next is compartmentalized information on a need-to-know basis, which is not covered by our top secret clearances. For all intents and purposes, the OMICS contribution to the project is now over. From talking to Bryce—who is now the DHS Secretary but still maintains his role as Head of Domestic Terrorism—no one outside of the NSA and the GIC seems to know anything for certain about the continuation of the Fat Man project. Of course, very few know about the project at all. Congressional inquiries into information that seeped out about the Fat Man project were addressed in a written statement from the GIG, declaring that *The results from the Fat Man project are now being evaluated for future HEP applications. The project remains top secret, and no public dissemination of the project is planned at this time.*

Do we now have any humans around us with extra chromosomes harboring the Crex-OR gene package, and do they possess mind-viewing powers? Bryce, Lucy, Julie, and I are probably the only people asking these questions. Paul Fischer wouldn't ask because he most likely already knows the answer. Anyone associated with whatever 46+ might be also wouldn't ask since if there are mind viewers on the street, they're the ones who put them there. I remain undecided whether or not to inform Mike and the rest of the former Crassus Team about the 46+ rumors. But, as for now, they have no reason to ask these questions either.

So, do we have mind viewers out and about that have the Crex-OR genes edited into their genome? Considering that I believe that five of them were created already last year, my gut feeling says yes.

Now, there is a potential way to find out if people have been engineered with Crex-OR-containing chromosomes. You might be way ahead of me here. But I doubt it; this requires a very creative brain with exceptional deduction ability. So that's what I wanted to talk to Bryce about as we meet for an afternoon Guinness at Bryce's favorite pub in DC, The Dubliner.

"What are you doing all day, you haven't responded to my brilliant queen move?" I ask him by way of greeting.

"This may come as a surprise to you, but my life doesn't revolve around your haphazard chess moves."

"I think you're in shock over my aggressive attack and fumble to find a graceful exit strategy."

"Whenever I have a minute or two to spare, I'll consider your desperate move."

"Well, you can at least buy me a beer to celebrate my upcoming victory."

Bryce doesn't answer but gets up and returns with two Smithwicks in twenty-ounce glasses.

Having gotten our insults out of the way, I get down to business.

"Any news on Paul Fischer or 46+?" I ask him.

"Not really. I've asked the FBI to keep a tab on Fisher's movements. He's been to Boston a few times and had a trip to Sarasota in Florida—nothing out of the ordinary. We have no claims that warrant an in-depth investigation of him at this time. 46+? Nothing."

"Well, this may change. I think I know how we can find out if the new Crex-OR construct has been used in genome-editing of humans."

"Do tell."

"Well, assume that the symptoms the mice displayed, the ones that were infected by the intron mice—loss of smell, grave aggression, and insatiable sexual appetite—are the same for humans, which, I would say, is a reasonable assumption. Then, finding people with indications of such behavior would tell us that they have been infected by the Crex-OR virus. In other words, by a mind viewer. And, again, if the infection pattern is the same for mice and humans, only people directly infected by a mind viewer would show obvious symptoms. Secondary infections would be mild to nonexistent."

So far, no such cases have been reported, at least not in public media. But as the old saying goes, "The lack of evidence for infection is not evidence for lack of infection." —No, I just made that up. Sorry! But it's true, though. Just because we haven't heard of any such infections doesn't necessarily mean they have not occurred. If we know what to look for, which we do, we can make a targeted search. And that's precisely what I'm asking Bryce to initiate.

"So, could you use your authority to have the FBI check for incidences that fit this hypothesis?"

———

Life is like chess; you make a move, and that move dictates subsequent moves by those around you and by yourself. I'm not sure exactly where I'm going with this, but if not for anything else, I like to think I'm dispensing profound wisdom. Actually, I'm not just trying to be philosophical; the move I took by asking Bryce to arrange for a search of Crex virus infections elicited a cascade of actions that eventually led to the unveiling of the 46+ operation.

Two months after I met with Bryce at the Dubliner, he called me back. Although it was not obvious to start with, there were, in fact, several cases of aggression coupled with sudden abnormal sexual behavior and loss of smell among a small cadre of the population in and around one particular city, Boston, Massachusetts. Taken together, information that the FBI could extract from episodes of hospitalizations, police records, and reports of violent behavior painted a telling picture of Crex virus symptoms. The development led me to breach my NDA with DARPA/DoD and inform the FBI about the Fat Man project. Given the unusual nature of the infection pattern and how it completely matched that of the mice in the BLUEgenes lab, the FBI had no problems getting search warrants for premises of interest. Using a "guilt by association" approach, the FBI could encircle an area where the epicenter for the infections seemed to be a suburb of Boston, Belmont.

At about the same time the FBI agents started to descend on Belmont, the DHS received an anonymous phone call from someone claiming to have intimate knowledge about the 46+ group. The phone call was directed to Bryce Vogel.

Shortly afterward, two people from Belmont fled the country.

Two days later, the FBI carried out two raids in Belmont. One in an erected trailer-like building on Concord Avenue, with a neon sign in the front identifying it as an IV therapy clinic with the name VitaMin. The other was in a modern brick-and-glass complex on the nearby Sumner Lane, part of which housed a biotech company called FutureGenome.

CHAPTER 32

Spring 2027. Congressional hearing.

A nd I assume we have a name for the whistleblower at this time?"

It's been one year and a half since the completion of the Fat Man project in the BLUEgenes lab in Colorado. It's Monday, April fifth, and we're in a congressional hearing behind closed doors in one of the rooms in the Dirksen Senate Office Building on Constitution Ave. More specifically, it's a hearing before a select committee on Emerging Threats and Spending Oversight, the Senate Committee on Homeland Security and Governmental Affairs. Senator Paula Sanderson is chairing the hearing, and she's the one who just posed the question.

"Yes, Senator; it's Colonel Paul Fischer, the Director of the Genomics Intelligence Committee within the NSA, who initially unveiled the information."

The one who answers the question is FBI agent Sam Peters. There are nine other people in the room. Senator Sanderson (D) is flanked by Senator Randy Long (R) and Senator Steve Lofquist (D) at the head of the rectangular table. On one side of the table, next to FBI agent Peters, is Bryce Vogel, the DHS Secretary and, until the end of the fiscal year, Head of Domestic Terrorism. Next to Bryce are Paul Fischer and myself. On the other side of the table are FBI Director Walter Graham, NSA Director General Lionel Schwartz, and NSA Deputy Chief, Central Security Service Admiral Sheryl Barnes. Seated at a desk up front in the room is the clerk, Roland McGown.

The hearing started two hours ago. Senator Sanderson greeted us and explained the purpose of the hearing. She is a tall woman in her upper fifties with ash-blond hair. Her voice is husky and low but carries well across the room.

"Welcome, and thanks for coming," she started out. "This hearing is closed and, at least for the time being, what is disclosed and discussed here today is classified as top secret. You all have the necessary security clearances, as do I. This Committee has exercised its power to subpoena testimonies and documents. And I remind you that all of you answering questions here today, which we will refer to as 'witnesses,' do so under oath."

She paused and took a sip of water. Then looked at the notes in front of her and continued. "The reason we're here today is to discuss genome editing for human enhancement performance or HEP. Specifically, we are reviewing the alleged creation of genome-edited human subjects with mind-viewing faculties." Everyone in the room is aware of the topic. So, the concept of mind viewing is not as startling as it might otherwise have been.

Sanderson then led us through an introduction to the people assembled in the room. Senators Long and Lofquist, whom I saw jokingly boxing each other's shoulders when they walked in—a gratifying display of across-the-aisle comradery—are friendly-looking guys about the same age as Sanderson. The NSA folks are in full uniform, decorated with an impressive assembly of service ribbons on their chest—"chest candy," as I've heard them referred to, possibly by those who don't have any but want some. Paul Fischer has the rank "Colonel" printed on the nameplate in front of him. I don't know if that's a concession on the part of the Committee. I didn't think you kept your rank after being generally discharged, even if it's under honorable conditions, as was the case with Fischer. Anyhow, he doesn't wear a uniform.

And when he introduces himself, he just mentions his title as the Director of the GIC.

FBI agent Peters wears a dark suit. He can't be much older mid-thirties. Sand-colored hair and a face that could easily blend in anywhere. Probably a good trait in his line of work. When Sanderson commences the questioning by asking Peters if he would please explain how the Fat Man case—as it's become known—got to the attention of the Senate Committee on Homeland Security and Governmental Affairs, he answers in an easy-going style but with a noticeable gravitas.

"Certainly, Senator. Rumors about a secret operation under the name 46+ were substantiated when a whistleblower with first-hand knowledge about the operation anonymously contacted the DHS Secretary with information crucial to U.S. national security. This was on August eleventh last year. From the material provided by the whistleblower, it seems as if 46+ have been engaged in covert activities toward genome engineering of people with a novel technology called BLUEgenes that was developed through DARPA-funded research. The whistleblower conceded that he was associated with the 46+ group and privy to their agenda. And that he was instrumental in providing necessary data for their genome-engineering efforts. According to the whistleblower, the sole purpose of 46+ was to keep the U.S. at the forefront of utilizing genome engineering for national intelligence in fighting international and domestic terrorism. However, when it became obvious that 46+ also had other ambitions, the whistleblower decided to get in touch with DHS in the form of an anonymous text message from a burner phone."

When Peters responds to Sanderson's prompt by identifying the whistleblower as Paul Fischer, none of us in the room are surprised as we had been informed beforehand. Since I'm seated next to Fischer, I can sense that he's tense, but he looks defiant. I also notice he's sweating, although, in all fairness, it's unnecessarily warm in the room.

It's also ten a.m., and we've been sitting here for three hours. We have coffee and water but nothing else. I'm hoping for a break to get out and chase down some scones.

"Thank you, Agent Peters." Sanderson looks around. "Also, as I come to understand, the initial … unveiling, if you want, of the 46+ operation was precipitated by circumstantial evidence collected by DHS Secretary Vogel and Dr. Thovén?"

"Yes, Senator, that's correct."

Sanderson takes another sip of water. "Before we hear from Colonel Fischer about the details that led him to contact DHS, I think we will benefit from having Dr. Thovén describe the sequence of events that led to the Fat Man case, and the… intriguing, to say the least, mind-viewing genes."

The NSA folks looked at each other when Sanderson mentioned Fischer. He takes the cue. "Senator, just to be clear, I no longer carry the rank of Colonel."

"Oh, sorry. My bad. Well then, Director Fisher has agreed to explain what transpired in his interactions with the 46+ operation and what finally made him inform DHS. But we will first hear from Dr. Thovén." She looks at the big round-the-clock above the door. It's a hideous contraption with a blue fish head in the middle; it seems totally out of place in this environment. Anyhow, the ugly clock shows five minutes past ten. "But before doing that, I suggest we stretch our legs and have some bio breaks as needed. Let's be back here at eleven sharp."

"Is there a cafeteria nearby?" I ask Sanderson as I walk up to her.

Bryce joins us. He smiles. "This guy's main fuel is scones," he says to Sanderson. "So, what he's really asking is if there's any chance to find a place around here that serves scones."

Sanderson laughs. "Well, there's Dirksen Café down the corridor. Not sure they have scones, but you can try it."

Bryce and Sanderson continue to chat, and I see that the other senators are joining. I find the men's room and then take off for the café. Sadly, they don't have scones. They have muffins—which I don't like—and croissants. I can lower myself and eat a croissant without much hesitation. I mean, I'm not an elitist. But, of course, a croissant is not a scone. For me, anyhow, the hallmark of a scone is a hard surface and soft center. Pretty much like me, with a tough appearance with a gentle inside. Well... I'll let you be the judge here. Anyhow, the feeling of biting down on a scone, cracking the surface, and reaching the soft, jelly- or cream-filled center is special, something a croissant does not live up to. So, I tell myself, if this establishment doesn't have scones, it's their loss, and I'll show my displeasure by leaving with nothing.

On the way back to the hearing room, I finish the croissant before going inside. When I get there, I see Bryce still in conversation with Sanderson and the other senators, The brass from NSA is there as well. Graham and Peters are having a discussion nearby. Fischer remains on his chair, looking through some documents. He doesn't look up when I enter. The others take notice, however, and Sanderson says, "Welcome back, Dr. Thovén. But I've now learned that you go by Symphony, and Bryce has explained why." She laughs, and others chuckle or smile. There must have been a cordial atmosphere in here while I was gone. Well, except for Fischer, he's not smiling and still staring at his papers. Sanderson continues, "But for the sake of the transcripts, we'll use your formal name and title for the hearing."

When we're all seated, Sanderson nods at the clerk. "The hearing is back in session. Dr. Thovén, can you please provide some background to the Fat Man case."

"Yes, Senator." I lean back in the chair. "The conception of the Fat Man case was an organized bird-watching tour in Morocco back in 1967. One of the tour members—who was jokingly called "Fat Man" by the others because his stature was the opposite; he was meager and gangly—fell and accidentally uncovered a hominin fossil. The site, which was later referred to as Fat Man's Cave, was excavated and found to contain several hominin fossils. One of those was a well-preserved cranium of a five-hundred-thousand-plus-year-old male hominin, which became known as Fat Man or *Homo Crassus* in Latin. The cranium and other artifacts from the site were transferred to the Moroccan National Archeology Museum in Rabat. Max Planck Institute for Evolutionary Anthropology in Leipzig, Germany, carried out the initial dating and examination of the Fat Man cranium. Subsequently, they sent it to OMICS for DNA and protein analyses. At OMICS, we were able to extract and sequence intact or close-to-intact proteins, as well as several DNA fragments, some of which encompassed full-length genes.

"Sequence analyses of some of the proteins and genes revealed a novel kind of olfactory receptors. They bear a resemblance to olfactory receptors in modern-day humans and several other animals, like mice. But they are also distinctly different, indicating that their function involved being receptive to something different than the odorants that bind to our contemporary olfactory receptors. We call these receptors Crassus extra olfactory receptors, or Crex-olfactory receptors for short, or Crex-ORs for shorter."

I pause and drink some water. I proceed by summarizing my first meeting with Derek Tyne-Callaghan in Greece, how I tracked him down in the U.K., and what he told me regarding his research on the evolution of language and olfaction in hominins and his hypothesis about hitherto unknown perception receptors used by early hominins in mind viewing as a primitive communication faculty. Obviously, I don't mention anything about Derek's Qumran escapades.

I go on. "We have previously designed an electronic device, an OlfactoryChip, or ORChip analyzer, by which we can measure and identify volatile organic compounds being emitted from humans or other animals as indicators of emotions or diseases. We have made a similar device with the Crex-ORs, and with this Crex-ORChip analyzer, we could confirm that the Crex-ORs do indeed respond to images we look at or see in our minds."

I stop and look at Paul Fischer. "The potential for using the Crex-ORChip analyzer for intelligence gathering was assessed by DARPA. Not sure what came out of that. At the same time, the research was picked up by the Genomics Intelligence Committee, or GIC, at NSA, which is headed by Director Paul Fischer. The mission of GIC is to identify and promote genome editing projects that can be evaluated for applications in national security. The GIC quickly initiated the Fat Man project, which aimed to evaluate the prospects for producing genome-edited humans with mind-viewing abilities, using mice as model systems."

I look at Sanderson. "I think that about covers it."

"Thank you, Dr. Thovén."

CHAPTER 33

Spring 2027. Paul Fischer's testimony.

Sanderson directs her attention to Fischer. "Director Fischer, could you please elaborate on the sequence of events that eventually led you to contact the DHS."

Fischer clears his throat and looks up. "One of the frontmen for the 46+ group is Professor Georg Steed. Steed is affiliated with the Wyss Institute, where he was a full professor until 2019. He then took a leave of absence to start a gene-synthesis company, FutureGenome, with some colleagues. He has since returned to the Wyss Institute as a part-time employee while continuing to build and expand his company. George's opinion was that we couldn't wait for the U.S. government to develop HEP programs. As a private company, he could bypass lengthy legislative steps and devote all energy to human genome editing. FutureGenome attracted funding from DARPA and several commercial entities. As I understand, DARPA has now provided full disclosure of their interactions with George Steed. I knew George from my time in Fort Devens. He came up from Boston a few times as an invited speaker to talk about the potential for genome engineering of soldiers. We clicked and realized we had the same vision for how the U.S. should attain and maintain leadership in the HEP space. I was soon invited to sit on the FutureGenome's Advisory Board."

Fisher's voice is getting scratchy, and he pauses for some water. He continues, "George spent considerable time with two people from DARPA, Bernie Whats and Simon Launders, who were also on his Advisory Board. He also knew people within the political establishment in Massachusetts who shared his view of avoiding unnecessary hurdles in moving the U.S. forward in the war against terrorism. From there, he made inroads into think tanks in DC, where he found some like-minded people. He eventually had a group of fifteen people, including the seven of us on the FutureGenome's Advisory Board, that had regular meetings in DC and Boston.

"In 2020, George was contacted by someone—I later learned it was a member of Congress—who asked him to join a rather furtive operation called 46+. Turned out that the mission of 46+ was to empower the U.S. national security efforts by taking bold steps toward creating and employing genome-edited humans for intelligence gathering. They had their roots in a covert operation that started way back after 9/11, known as 'Reform.' 46+ had contacts with DARPA-funded projects to identify suitable genes for HEP. I met a few of the 46+ members at meetings, but I never knew all the names behind 46+ or who was in charge. We signed NDAs concerning our interactions with the group. The only contact I had with 46+ was through FutureGenome, which became very much the front for 46+."

Sanderson, who has been listening intently, interrupts with a question. "So, from your perspective at that time, what was your impression about the objectives for 46+ and FutureGenome?"

"The sole aim and the mission of the 46+ operation was to create genome-edited operatives with superior abilities that could propel U.S. intelligence gathering into the next generation."

"Was it your understanding that this ambition would meet with significant pushback if it were to follow set rules or guidance for genomics research?"

"Yes, it was clear to all of us that we might operate in unethical or even illegal territories." Fischer looks around with a rebellious expression. "But it was also obvious to us that there's an ongoing warfare on several fronts—HEP through genome engineering as one example, AI is another — that the public, and probably most politicians, are unaware of. We viewed what we were engaged in as absolutely critical to not lose this war to China and Russia, and other adversaries."

"Now, Director Fischer, I'll take you back to May sixth, two years ago, 2025. There were seemingly unexplained cases of a short outbreak of a severe and fatal affliction that struck five people here in DC The symptoms and progression of this sudden sickness were eerily similar to those of the experimental mice in the BLUEgenes lab. Dr. Thovén has alleged that these five people died from being injected with DNA constructs synthesized at the BLUEgenes lab. You claimed no knowledge of the cause of this incident at the time. What's your response to these allegations under oath today?"

Fischer drinks some more water and loosens his tie a bit. "Yes, these people were injected with the Crex-OR constructs. This was ordered and arranged by George Steed and some colleagues. I'm not sure exactly how they pulled it off. But I know they had planted surveillance cameras in the clinics, or health clubs, so they know the routines and where solutions and other stuff were stored. So, when the time was right, I assume they tricked the staff away under the guise of some fictitious urgency and then went inside and did their thing — added the constructs to the vials."

I'm not surprised Fischer confesses to this under oath today. Due to the unraveling of the 46+ and the fact that there's a congressional hearing, it's evident that, if needed, the FBI could get a court order to exhume of the DC cases. A PCR test or DNA sequencing would then confirm the presence of the Crex-OR constructs.

"Were you complicit in this decision?" Sanderson asks.

"I was aware of what was going on, yes. I was responsible for the Fat Man project at the BLUEgenes lab. My view was that any experiments on human subjects should wait until we had completed this project. I voiced my concern to George. He claimed that it was necessary to quickly find out how humans—healthy humans—reacted to the extra chromosomes with the Crex-OR genes."

"So… extra chromosomes? Can you elaborate here?"

"It's not really my area. However, the ultimate goal of the BLUEgenes technology was to be able to have custom-made chromosomes inserted into organisms. Maybe Symph—Dr. Thovén can explain."

"Dr. Thovén?"

"Yes, so like Director Fischer said, the BLUEgenes technology allows for the synthesis of tailored chromosome pairs that can be systematically injected into all cells—or selected cells—of an organism. This was supposedly accomplished in two phases. The first phase was carried out at the BLUEgenes lab in Longmont, Colorado, and was started by DARPA in 2016. The work there focused on DNA synthesis of extremely long constructs and the delivery targets and efficiency. The so-called second phase was performed at another lab, which we now know is the FutureGenome lab in Boston, and started in 2019. So, it wasn't really a second phase of the Longmont project; it was conducted very much in parallel. When the Fat Man project was concluded, it could already be phased in with the chromosome-building technology that had been developed after six years of research at FutureGenome. This project was also funded by DARPA. Possibly, after 2020, when FutureGenome got in cahoots with the 46+ group, funding of the chromosome-building project might have gotten entangled with the 46+ budget. I don't know if Secretary Vogel wants to add something in this context?"

Sanderson looks at Bryce. "Secretary Vogel?"

"Well, let me first say there's nothing covert or secret about DARPA or DoD funding research for HEP applications or even chromosome synthesis. There are several ongoing projects in this space with proper oversight and accountability in federal contracting. The BLUEgenes projects, however, were kept under wraps and carried out as top-secret projects. It's been estimated that the BLUEgenes technology is decades ahead of what is publicly known or approved today in genome-editing research. As for the funding of 46+, our probe into this confirms that the 46+ operation was continuously funded directly from the president's budget on an annual basis and prior to Congress passing appropriation bills. I assume this is something for Congress to grapple with."

"Thank you."

Sanderson looks back at Fischer. "So, Director Fischer, did you try to convince Dr. Steed not to go ahead with his plan?"

"As I said, I told him I was worried. For one thing, I thought it might lead to unnecessary exposure of the 46+ operation."

"So, today, and considering what happened, what are your thoughts about the decision to execute Dr. Steed's plan?"

Fischer raises his hands in the air. "Well, obviously, I think it's unfortunate. But, in every war, there are casualties and collateral damage."

"That's how you look at this incident, as collateral damage?"

"As I said, it's unfortunate, but… yes."

"Were there other attempts to inject the Crex-OR genes into humans before the initial phase of this BLUEgenes project—the Fat Man project that is—was successfully completed?"

"No. I told George that, based on information provided by Dr. Thovén, it was imperative that the HEP phase be put on hold until we had positive results from the Fat Man project in the Colorado lab."

"And this was in mid-August of 2025?"

"That's correct, yes. I was informed by Dr. Thovén on August twelfth."

"And then in November of the same year, the Fat Man project was completed, right?"

"Yes, it was."

"And this was a top-secret project funded by DARPA under the auspices of NSA, and particularly the GIC, is that correct?"

"Yes."

"And this was not an open-ended project, was it?"

"Ehr… Sorry, I'm not sure I understand what—"

"In the documents signed by DARPA, the Department of Defense, Dr. Thovén, and yourself in late November 2024, the NDAs included a statement formulated by Dr. Thovén that defined the Fat Man project. It reads, and I quote, 'The purpose of the Fat Man project is to use mouse models to demonstrate that the package of 41 Crex-OR genes can be expressed in the entirety of the vomeronasal neurons and that the produced receptors can be correctly inserted into the plasma membrane. The results from the Fat Man project will be used to evaluate the prospects for future HEP applications.'"

Sanderson continues, "There's nothing in the signed agreements—the NDAs or the top secret clearance documents— suggesting that the Fat Man project should directly transition into HEP experiments, correct?"

"Well, the whole purpose of the Fat Man project, as far as national intelligence goes, was to investigate the potential for generating a cadre of intelligence operatives with mind-viewing capabilities. That's what the last clause in the statement is all about."

"Yes, but the key word here is *evaluate*. Which entails scientific as well as legal and ethical considerations."

Fischer gets agitated again. "So, while countries like China and Russia are moving ahead with actually producing genome-edited soldiers and agents, the U.S. will remain in the back wagon, in the research and evaluation stage?"

"This hearing is not about what the U.S. should or should not do in regards to genome-editing of operatives in the interest of national security; it's about illegal genome-editing experiments on humans carried out by an underground campaign."

Sanderson takes a deep breath before continuing. "So, Director Fischer, somehow, the 46+ group got hold of the necessary data and biologicals to replicate the Fat Man project in humans. Were you involved in this dissemination?"

"No, what I did, was tell George about how the problems with the project had been solved and that it now was producing genome-engineered mice that fully complied with the goal of the project and that the mice also seemed healthy."

"So, who provided the 46+ movement with the material?"

"Well, DARPA had full access."

"Are you suggesting that Bernie Whats and Simon Launders might have been involved?"

"I have no evidence one way or another. I just note that they were also part of the FutureGenome Advisory Board."

"So, the 46+ group somehow got hold of the material used in the Fat Man project. Can you please take us through what happened then?"

"George was in charge of the second BLUEgenes project through FutureGenome, which, as Dr. Thovén explained, was aimed at synthesizing chromosomes for genome-editing purposes. Now, and this was February last year, the Crex-OR gene construct developed as part of the Fat Man project was being used in the chromosome synthesis effort. Later, in March, George engaged a physician, Dr. Randolph Kulak, who registered a new IV therapy clinic, VitaMin, in Belmont, a suburb of Boston, that advertised IV injections of vitamins and minerals. Dr. Kulak hired a small staff and, as I understand it, performed legit IV therapy. Some of VitaMin's patients—or customers, I guess—were selected by George and given the Crex-OR cocktail instead, or together with the vitamins and minerals, I'm not sure. Only George and Kulak knew who these persons were. They were referred to as Larry or Sally; so, Larry 1, 2, 3 and Sally 1, 2, 3, and so on. Collectively, they became known as LarSal agents or LarSals. The first one was created on April fifth, George's birthday." Fischer shrugs his shoulders. "Not sure if there was any specific thinking behind that date."

"What made these people agree to get this treatment? I mean, even if the mice experiments were satisfactory, it's a far cry from having these extra chromosomes inserted into your own body."

"It was money and prestige. Each LarSal was paid fifty thousand dollars per month. And they were told they would perform highly sensitive and covert operations in the interest of galvanizing U.S. national security. The later LarSals were paid even more. Not sure how much."

"How many of these people, these LarSals, were created?"

"Not sure exactly, but there were at least three hundred of them at the end. Like I said, only George and Kulak knew who they were. Possibly others in the inner circle of 46+ or FutureGenome—which I guess was the same at that point—had more insight, but I wasn't privy to this information."

"And what did the LarSal agents do?"

"They were put in training. That consisted of infiltrating the society at different levels—the Capitol Building, state senates, banks, restaurants, and several other places. They were put in positions such as janitors, servants, substitute admins, or delivery personnel. Or they were hanging around people in public places. Most of them, more than half anyhow, were assigned to the Capitol and its surroundings. The purpose was to covertly obtain as much personal information as possible and then report back to George and the rest of the 46+ group."

"And you never met any of these LarSals?"

"I could have met hundreds of them. I wouldn't know. But none was identified to me."

Sanderson looks at Peters. "Agent Peters, after the FBI's raid against the FutureGenome facility and the VitaMin clinic in Boston on August twenty-sixth, 2026, three LarSal agents came forward. Can you please comment on that?"

"Yes, three individuals contacted us. They provided their names and claimed to be three of the early LarSals, Larry 2 and 3, and Sally 3. We, in turn, contacted the Department of Homeland Security. Due to the top-secret nature of the case, we went directly to Secretary Vogel."

"Secretary Vogel," Sanderson says, "can you please take over."

"Yes, I asked Dr. Thovén to join me in interviewing the three LarSals. The Committee has been notified and received an audio recording of the interview."

Sanderson looks at the ugly clock. It shows ten minutes past twelve.

"Yes, and we will play that after lunch. We now take a one-hour break, and we'll reconvene at ten past one. You have restaurant options listed on your agendas. I would recommend The American Grill in this building, but feel free to explore other options."

CHAPTER 34

Spring 2027. The LarSals interview.

S anderson looks at the clerk. "Roland, can you please play the recording of the LarSals interview from the Department of Homeland Security provided by Secretary Vogel."

The clerk presses a button. We hear some clatter and then Bryce's voice.

"This is Friday twenty-seventh, 2026. Present in this interview are the interviewees, Mindy Dahlberg, Douglas Hess, and Tom Stahl, referred to as Sally 3, Larry 2, and Larry 3, respectively. The interviewers are Dr. Ludvig Thovén, Director of the OMICS laboratory, and myself, Bryce Vogel, Secretary and Acting Head of Domestic Terrorism of the Department of Homeland Security."

Bryce: *"First, let me thank you for coming forward. And, on that note, what made you contact the FBI in the first place?"*

Larry 3: *"Well, for all of us early LarSals, I would say the first twenty to thirty, the training, which was supposed to be one to two weeks, just seemed to continue. Most of us were stationed in the Capitol or at restaurants or banks nearby. We were still getting paid fifty grand a week. I thought it meant that our training was not yet complete and that we eventually would be assigned locations where we could intercept information critical to U.S. national security. Then, after the raid, I figured that whatever was going on must have been illegal."*

Sally 2: *"Also, personally, I was getting tired of the mind-viewing ability. It's strenuous to try and keep tuning it down when surrounded by people. It gets better with time, but even now, after a little over a year, it's still a significant effort, at least for me, to keep the noise level down. So, I'm hoping there might be a way for me to get these genes removed."*

Larry 3: *"Yes, I wouldn't mind getting rid of them."*

Larry 2: *"Same here. But I'm getting pretty well adapted. And, not sure I should mention this, but we were encouraged to test our powers for fun as long as we didn't expose ourselves. So, I had a stint at the poker and blackjack tables in Vegas. One-on-one with the blackjack dealer was very interesting. I could have won more often than I chose to, but I held off so as not to be too obvious. Still, I left the table five thousand dollars richer. Same with Texas Hold'em; once I got the targeting in place, I had a major advantage. Got close to another five thousand there."*

Me: *"So, how would you describe this extra sense of yours, your mind-viewing faculty? How efficient is it when you view what someone is thinking of or looking at?"*

Larry 2: *"It's pretty cool, I would say. It took some time, a week or so, before you learned to target a person in a group, what position and angle to use for the best reception. And also to learn how to shut off or tune down reception. But after that, mind viewing works quite well. But I agree with Mindy, it can be tiresome; it's like you have background noise in your brain most of the time. Like visual tinnitus."*

Me: *"How far is the reach, and what materials can block these olphons?"*

Larry 2: *"Olphons? Is that what they're called? We never knew they had a name. I would say the reach is around one hundred feet. The longer, the weaker the signal. I noticed that the wind doesn't affect the reception at all. Neither do trees or other vegetation. But metal and hard plastic are impenetrable. That's why the guys wore plastic helmets when they met with us."*

Me: *"They had plastic helmets? The people who gave you assignments?"*

Larry 2: *"Yes, they covered the head and forehead. They said they needed that to protect themselves from being mind viewed."*

Bryce: *"Tom, you said that you started to realize after the raid of FutureGenome that what you were engaged in might have been illegal. Did any of you ever before at any time perceive what you were asked to do as illegal?"*

Larry 2: *"No. I mean, it seemed a little odd that the training went on for so long and that the purpose was to extract information from members of Congress and others at the Capitol. And to have to report our viewings in such a detailed manner. But I think we all still assumed that it was a training exercise and that we would later be asked to perform similar tasks at security checkpoints, or embassies, or during interrogation of suspects, or something like that."*

Bryce: *"Why do you think that didn't happen?"*

Larry 3: *"I don't know for sure. The three of us—I mean Mindy, Doug, and myself—have known each other since before. I never knew and I still don't know any of the other agents. We heard rumors, though, that training assignments we were given, which mainly focused on intercepting information in and around the Congress Building, more and more became the real mission for the LarSal agents."*

Me: *"Personal questions; don't any of the LarSal agents have spouses and families with kids? Or were you all required to be single? And how about your previous jobs?"*

Larry 3: *"Yes, as I understand, all LarSal agents that were recruited were single or would agree to end ongoing relationships. I don't think any of us have kids, but I'm not sure. Jobs? Yes, we were asked to resign from our jobs. We were told this would be full-time assignments for a long time—several years. And the pay, fifty grand per month, was much better, at least for me. Also, we were told not to report the income, and no taxes were withheld."*

The clerk stops the recording.

"There's more in this recording, but we heard the essential portion," Sanderson says. "We listened to three of the early LarSal agents. Now, Director Fischer, as you alluded to in your testimony this morning, the scope and purpose of recruitment shifted with the later agents. Is that right?"

Fischer, who had been listening with great interest to the recording, clears his throat. "The training of the first fifty or so LarSal agents consisted of taking low-level positions—janitors, waiters, gardeners, what have you—at the Capitol, or at restaurants, banks, or other places where members of Congress milled around, or just to try to get close to them in public places. And then try to extract and memorize as much personal information as possible. The newer LarSal agents—the remaining two hundred fifty or so, I don't know the exact number—were groomed for more advanced positions; they could be couriers, admins, or even staffers—and were told that the intelligence they gathered was to be used to secure the safety of the United States, the 'Homeland,' as George often said."

"It was at a meeting last February," Fischer continues, "we were at a beach house in Sarasota, Florida, that one of the 46+ people owned, when it became clear to me that the deployment of LarSal agents now was almost entirely aimed for Congress, the White House, state legislatures, and the Pentagon. George shared some of the information that had been obtained by the LarSals so far—incriminating or embarrassing intelligence: illness history, passcodes, and other personal details. It was obvious to all of us that the extent and nature of this information amounted to a treasure trove for anyone intent on coercing members of Congress, the states, or the Pentagon into following specified directions. This could entail signing documents, voting against party lines, constituent interests, or conscience, or giving false confessions, or supporting constitutional amendments, or, for the Pentagon, to sign up for military support."

Fischer stops and drinks some coffee. He still looks defiant, but I can tell the veneer is starting to wear off. He takes a deep breath. "George and I had always shared the view that the U.S. Government does not properly prioritize or recognize the importance of winning the war against terrorism; there are too many obstacles or too much precaution, and not enough resources allocated for AI, computational technology, or genome editing for military and intelligence applications. And that resources ought to be reallocated from what George called 'soft areas,' like climate change, renewables, and other environmental issues, to 'hard areas,' such as intelligence and military. George, from time to time, used to say things like, 'The safety and prosperity of the Homeland rests on winning the war against terrorism and having a government strong enough to allow us to do so.' And this was a sentiment that was tossed around plenty at the Sarasota meeting."

Fischer pauses again. He now gives off a feeling of resignment and fatigue. "The outcome of the Sarasota meeting was a mission statement and an action plan for the 46+ operation. The mission statement mirrored pretty much George's vision to 'Secure U.S. safety and prosperity in the international arena by dominating the development and employment of HEP for intelligence applications.' It was agreed that to reform the U.S. intelligence gathering, we need to reform the U.S. Government. Here, the employment of LarSal agents offered an unprecedented opportunity to provide information allowing the 46+ group to control Congress, other legislative processes, and the military. So, it was determined to prepare the LarSals for various assignments in Congress, the White House, the Pentagon, and their surroundings."

Fischer looks up, some of the insolence back on his face. "The first step in the action plan was to abolish the Senate."

Fischer stops and seems to absorb some of the tension that has suddenly enveloped the session. He then goes on, "The sentiment was that we should side with the late House Representative John Dingell; that the Senate is an antiqued legacy that is the reason for much of the dysfunction that plagues Congress. —And I agree; considering the vast difference in population that exists between states, equal representation in the Senate is right down stupid. I'm all for a reformation of our government; I'm not impressed by what I see."

"But how would this even be feasible?" Sanderson looks confused and deeply concerned. "I mean, eliminating this body would require a constitutional amendment. Article five of the U.S. Constitution mandates that 'no state, without its consent, shall be deprived of its equal suffrage in the Senate.' I realize that one singular amendment could be used to eliminate this requirement, but I don't see how getting support for the passage of such an amendment would be possible. Is this where the information gathered by the LarSal agents was supposed to be used?" She looks back at Fischer.

"Yes, the 46+ group, or the 46+ Movement as they started to call themselves—I should mention here that there was, or is, rather, a burgeoning support for the 46+ mission statement among large cadres of politicians and the military—so, they considered they now had enough intelligence from Congress, and from state legislatures, to be able to strongarm at least two-thirds of both the House and the Senate to support the proposal of a constitutional amendment for annulling Article five, and to have it ratified."

Sanderson now seems aggravated. "So, you mean, states and senators would vote to reduce or abolish their own influence?"

"There were four approaches to this first step that we discussed. The first one was to simply try to win over senators and house representatives by presenting convincing arguments for how wrong and skewed the Senate representation is. The second approach was to use intimidating information to convince select members of Congress to vote as instructed. And there was plenty of material here that the LarSal agents had collected that was followed up on by others in the operation. We had a whole suite of computer hackers, moles, investigators with cameras and video equipment, and various performers. So, if a LarSal agent obtained a mind view indicative of, for example, an improper relationship, a sexual preference, visiting a porn site, gambling habits or debts, Alcohol Anonymous meetings, embellishments of various kinds, or something else of value, this could be quickly confirmed and expanded on by these other 46+ operatives.

"Another approach was bribing. The LarSal agents had accumulated an extensive amount of passcodes, bank accounts, credit card numbers, and CVV codes to be used in embezzling several millions of dollars. I heard in one meeting that we had enough information to obtain four billion dollars in one concerted action. The money was supposed to be used to compensate people for following proposed directives. The fourth approach was to use this same information in extortion attempts. You lift a couple hundred thousand dollars from an account and notify the account holder—say a congressman—that he will get the money back if he casts a vote a certain way."

Sanderson lets the information sink in before continuing.

"So, when did you decide to take action and reach out to the Department of Homeland Security?" she asks.

"I would say that I gradually started having second thoughts about the whole scenario. And as the action plan for the 46+ operation took shape during the next few months, it became clear that subsequent steps — after getting rid of the Senate — included a non-hostile but effective replacement of the President and the entire administration with a military-supported leadership. I continued to be part of the operation for a few more months. But I finally realized I had to do something; I had not signed up for a takeover of the U.S. Government, not even a non-hostile one. So, yes, I contacted Secretary Vogel at DHS, whom I had met before. I know he was in the loop with the Fat Man project and already involved in investigating 46+."

"Thank you, Director Fischer."

The atmosphere in the room is heavy and solemn. And for a good reason. From what Fischer has described about the 46+ agenda, it's obvious that what they planned was nothing short of a *coup d'état*. I remember with chilling clarity the insurrection after the 2020 election and what might have happened if the military had supported it. And how concerns for another insurrection were on people's minds prior to the 2024 election. What the 46+ Movement was planning was, in a way, more dangerous and effective than a violent insurrection in that it would have overthrown the U.S. Government by — seemingly consensual — legislation. With the amount and type of personal information the LarSal agents have acquired and would continue to acquire in the new administration, it's conceivable that the 46+ movement would have succeeded in their long-term goal of drastically reshaping U.S. domestic and international politics through what would have appeared to be, a democratic process.

Funny to think how the stumble of an Austrian car salesman during a birding trip in the Moroccan desert in 1967 could have resulted in the overthrow of the U.S. Government several decades later. —Well, maybe funny is not the best word, but… you know what I mean.

CHAPTER 35

Spring 2027. A Different Paul Fischer.

Agent Peters, as we mentioned yesterday, on August nineteenth, last year, the FBI conducted a raid at two locations in Belmont, a suburb of Boston. Can you please tell us what precipitated the raid and what you found at these locations?"

It's the second and final day of the congressional hearing, Tuesday, April sixth. We're back in the Dirksen building, the same room as yesterday. The ugly clock above the door says it's nine ten a.m., and Sanderson has just started the session.

"Certainly, Senator. In late July last year, DHS Secretary Vogel requested a meeting with the FBI. Secretary Vogel and Dr. Thovén described the so-called Fat Man project and the mind-viewing concept, its background and supportive, albeit circumstantial, evidence for the allegations that a covert operation was involved in engineering humans with the mind-viewing genes. This all took some getting used to; mind-viewing sounded like science fiction. However, given the credibility of Secretary Vogel and Dr. Thovén and the background to the Fat Man project, as explained by Dr. Thovén, the FBI decided to move on with the information. Because of the top-secret nature of this task, we looped in the Director of National Intelligence, Alice Weingarten.

"We started to search for cases with the pathology pattern as described to us by Dr. Thovén: acute and violent aggression, uncontrollable sexual appetite, and loss of smell. We collaborated with several police precincts, and it was mainly through their support we were able to identify eleven different reported and non-reported instances, all in and around the Boston area, that fit the expected symptoms. Since, as explained by Dr. Thovén, secondary infections are mild to non-existent, we could rather quickly determine the epicenter of the primary infection. By triangulation, we were able to zoom in on the Belmont suburb, where we identified the VitaMin IV clinic and FutureGenome laboratory as sites of interest. This was now August third. At the same time, or a week later, rather, DHS received the call from the whistleblower. I should add that the information provided by Secretary Vogel and Dr. Thovén also implicated Paul Fischer as a suspect, and a surveillance team was deployed to monitor Director Fischer's movements and daily routines. At about the same time, DARPA volunteered information that conclusively linked FutureGenomics to the second BLUEgenes project."

"And what did you find at the raid of the two buildings in Belmont?"

"We found crushed vials and discarded needles in a waste deposit at the VitaMin clinic. Per Dr. Thovén's suggestion, we took those materials to the OMICS Lab for analysis. I would like to ask Dr. Thovén to explain the results."

Sanderson nods at me. "Dr. Thovén."

"Yes, when we received the assortment of glass fragments and needles from the FBI, we opted for a batch procedure rather than analyzing individual glass fragments and needles. We incubated the entire collection in a minimal volume of solution to extract any attached DNA. We then concentrated the solution, amplified the DNA, and ran a test. Through this procedure, we could conclusively show that some of the glass vials or needles found by the FBI had contained the Crex-OR genes."

"Thank you. Agent Peters?"

"Apart from this evidence material, very little of value was found at the VitaMin clinic. At the FutureGenome Lab, we seized a laptop that our digital forensic team is currently trying to unlock and study. We also gathered a variety of documents that are being analyzed."

"What do we know regarding the whereabouts of Dr.s George Steed and Randolph Kulak?"

"They were last seen on Monday, August seventeenth. Since then, we have had no information as to where they are. Dr. Steed's private airplane, a Beechcraft G36 Bonanza, is missing from the Worcester Regional Airport. We have no information about a filed flight plan. We have talked to Dr. Steed's ex-wife. She has not communicated with him for three weeks and claims no knowledge about where he might be. She said they have a condo in Key West, and we have deployed a team there and by his house in Belmont. We have no information about Dr. Kulak as of yet."

Sanderson looks at Fischer. "Director Fischer, do you have any insight that could help locate Drs. Steeds or Kulak?"

"I do not."

———

The hearing ends with a summary statement from Sanderson, where Paul Fischer's dual role as a conspirator through his interactions with the 46+ Movement and as an informant, providing critical intelligence that helped uncover the 46+ movement, took center place. Obviously, the committee report will not be made public at this stage.

When we leave the hearing room, the ugly clock shows eleven a.m. Senator Sanderson asks me to join Bryce, FBI Director Walter Graham, and NSA Director General Lionel Schwartz III for a luncheon meeting tomorrow at noon, in the Hart Senate Office Building, a few steps from the Dirksen Building. This is a reminder; I was informed about this meeting before yesterday's hearing. I'm told that also Barbara McCarthy, the Director of ICE (U.S. Immigration and Customs Enforcement), and General Alexander Soros, the Secretary of DoD, will attend.

Bryce and I head over to Union Pub, a stone toss away. We find a table outside, and Bryce takes out the chess board from his briefcase and unfolds it on the table. We look at the score in the d4c4 app and start setting up the pieces. When a waiter comes by, we both order Union Pub Pils and then a plate of fried pickles to share as a starter. As I turn around to take in the scenery, I see Paul Fischer stepping out of a church,

"This individual puzzles me," I say. "I had him pegged as a beer and burger kind of guy, and he turns out to be a vegan and a teetotaler. And now I see him coming out of a church."

"What does the church have to do with anything?"

"Well, I just have a hard time reconciling that obnoxious and rude Paul Fischer that I've become attached to with this new image."

"A lot of church-goers are obnoxious and rude people."

"No, they're not; people who attend church are all very nice and polite. They never curse and never say bad things about people. Just look at the two of us."

Bryce ignores me. "Maybe we should wave him over," he says.

"Huh?"

"I feel for him. He knew where to draw the line for what he believed in. And he helped in cracking the 46+ case."

"Okay, wave away. But when he comes, take a look at his eyes; they're remarkably beautiful."

"You really have a thing for his eyes, don't you?"

"Not just his eyes; I study a lot of peoples' eyes."

Bryce holds up his hand and waves. After a while, Fischer looks up, sees us, and starts walking hesitantly toward our table.

"Come and grab some lunch," Bryce greets him and pulls out a chair.

"You guys chess players?" Fischer says with raised eyebrows.

"I'm teaching Bryce how to play," I say before Bryce has the chance to say the same thing about me. I move the board and pieces toward the side.

"Take a pickle," I say. "They're great, and they're vegan. And alcohol-free," I add.

Fischer actually smiles, and that changes his whole face. His stunning clear-blue eyes, which seem to flicker, and a wide grin that displays even white teeth transform him into an altogether attractive appearance—*wow, did I really say that?*

Thinking that we've somehow broken the ice, I look at him. "What did you do in the church? Seeking penance?" I hold my breath, thinking I might have gone too far.

But Fischer just smiles while he's nibbling on the pickle. "I thought going to church after my testimony might be worthwhile. It's a beautiful church, by the way."

"It's the Senate church," says Bryce, "St. Joseph's."

The waiter comes by again. Fischer orders a black bean burger without cheese. I take pasta linguini and Bryce a turkey Reuben.

On behalf of Fischer, but also because I'm interested, I ask the waiter if they have any non-alcoholic beer.

"We have an excellent low-alcoholic IPA, the Athletic run wild. Only 0.4% alcohol. It's from the Athletic brewing company in Connecticut.""

"I'll take that," Fischer says. "And I order one for myself and Bryce as well."

We have a pleasant chat. We mostly try to avoid touching on the hearing, but I ask Fischer what the status is on the Belmont BLUEgenes project. "As I understand, the Longmont project is completed. It was basically finished already before DARPA extended it as part of the Fat Man project. But how about the BLUEgenes project at the FutureGenome lab in Belmont? Was that also finished when Steed disappeared?"

"I don't know the specific scientific lingo, but, no, it wasn't over. What was injected into the LarSals were small chromosomes—mini-chromosomes. The research was supposed to go on with the construct of larger chromosomes. I also heard talk about controlling the activity of the chromosomes by modifying the ends. George explained it at some point, but I forget the exact words."

"They probably wanted to control the replication by altering the telomeres," I explain.

"Yeah, that sounds familiar. Well, we'll see what happens. If I have anything to say about this—if I were still leading the GIC, I would strongly argue for DARPA to fucking quickly find a replacement for George and make sure the project continues. This is not the time to be complacent just because the 46+ Movement has stopped moving—pardon the pun." This is the feisty Fischer I'm used to. But I also get the feeling that he is relieved that the whole 46+ business is now busted open.

We hang around for a while longer and make small talk. We learn that Fischer is a devout catholic. And—I know you won't believe this, but it's true—he said he's singing in the church choir in St. Lawrence Martyr, his home parish. Nothing about Paul Fischer will no longer surprise me. If he told us he was shortlisted for the position of the Pope, I might hesitate, but I wouldn't completely discount it at face value.

"Where is that?" I ask him.

"Oh, it's less than an hour away from here. I live on Argonne Hills, kind of between Ft. Mead and the church."

Fischer looks pensive for a while. Then he chuckles. "In my twenties, I was singing and playing bass guitar—my role model was Paul McCartney—in a small band, the Chocolatiers. Later on, it became a duo with me and… my boyfriend at the time, John. I assume you know I'm gay from all your surveillance shit."

"We do," Bryce says. "But that hasn't factored in one way or another in the investigation."

"Whatever. We called ourselves Paul and John, very original, and we had a stint for a year or so, playing mostly at bars. Then… John died. Car accident. This was the time, mid-90s, when the vegan movement started to be front-page news. John got engaged quickly and was soon a stout vegan advocate. He had a bumper sticker that said Meat kills our planet. One day, some fucking sicko who didn't like that message rear-ended John's car. John lost control of the car and was sided by a semi. He didn't stand a chance. The sicko claimed it was an accident, but enough people had seen what happened, so he was charged. Not that it helped John. Or me."

Fischer takes a break. I first thought he would stop talking, but then he continued, "I tried to get a grip on my life, and I joined the army. I was forced to quit, as you know, but it was a good time. I got a lot of contacts, and I formulated and cemented my political view on national security. That's how I got to the NSA. I wasn't hired by the NSA—possibly they didn't want a homosexual in their midst, I'm not sure—but I was tasked with organizing the Genomics Intelligence Committee, the GIC. This was a year after a tremor went through the entire Intel.gov after we suspected that China had successfully genome-edited soldiers and spies with super-powers, like infra-red vision."

"So, is that how the BLUEgenes project started?" I ask.

"Yes, I was appointed Director of the GIC, with the specific aim of identifying and initiating projects that conceivably could be used for human-editing of intelligence agents. I worked with DARPA and got the BLUEgenes started as a platform technology for future genome engineering. DARPA also supported projects more focused on the military and genome-edited soldiers. Our motivation in the GIC was solely on intelligence."

Fischer looks almost embarrassed. "I didn't mean to open up like this. But, well. I did."

"I'm glad you did," says Bryce, and I nod.

Fischer looks at his watch. "Well, I'd better be leaving. I need to find a suitable birthday gift for my brother's granddaughter."

"What age," Bryce and I say almost simultaneously.

"Eight."

"How about a book, something educational," Bryce says.

"Genome editing for dummies," I suggest.

Bryce and Fischer both laugh. In Fischer, I again see the change in his face: an amazing makeover. I noticed something comparable when I confronted Derek Tyne-Callaghan—or John Smith, rather—three years ago in England, but not to this extent. Bryce's face doesn't change much; he seems to have a permanent benevolent smile plastered on his face, even when he's frustrated—like all the times I beat him in chess.

After Fischer left, we packed away the chess. I say, "Good thing you waved Fischer over; it saved you from losing another game."

"Another? Who won the last two games?"

"Well, you did, but—"

"But what?"

"But I will win this one."

"And you say that based on…?"

"Intuition and the fact that you're facing a fork." I have one of his knights and the remaining rook in a pawn fork.

"True, but let's see how this unfolds next time we play." I don't like the upbeat sound of his voice.

As Bryce and I are strolling back, Bryce says, "You're right; Fischer of today is a different person than the one from a year ago."

"Did you see his eyes?"

"No, Symphony, I didn't pay attention to his eyes."

"Too bad, they're remarkable."

When we come to St. Joseph, we stop and look at the exterior. We're considering going inside and poking around but decide against it. We both have some work to do for the rest of the afternoon.

"If St. Joseph is the Senate church," I say, "it stands to reason that there's also a House church, right?"

"You figured that out all by yourself?"

"Yep! I'm the eagle on the fence post."

"What are you talking about?"

"Haven't you heard about the turtle on the fence post? If you see a turtle on a fence post, you know he must have had some help, right? He couldn't have climbed up himself."

"So?"

"So, I'm the eagle on the fence post; I didn't need any help; I got up there all by myself. So, yes, thank you very much; I figured out about the House church all by myself."

Bryce sighs. "It's exasperating to be around you sometimes; you know that?"

"Well, you don't have my flexible and powerful brain. But you do have knowledge. So maybe you can tell us the name of the House church."

"St. Peters."

"That's what I thought."

"Well, then, why did you ask?"

"I mean, I thought that you would know, not that I knew."

"Can we please go the rest of the way in silence?"

CHAPTER 36

Spring 2027. The meeting of the seven on April seventh.

The luncheon the next day is buffet style, with an excellent selection of meat and non-meat dishes. All dishes are labeled by name and a short list of ingredients. Very upmarket. I opt for vegetarian stroganoff with halloumi. A separate table offers coffee, tea, pastries, and—I kid you not—scones! Two varieties. They are on saucers with small labels reading SCONES: VANILLA BEAN and SCONES: CHERRY-ALMOND. Wonderful words. When I scan the scones, I sense Bryce looking at me. When I see him, he gives me a conspiratorial smile. He's behind this, of course. I decide to be nicer to him when we play chess.

"Thank you for attending." It's Sanderson. "This is a follow-up discussion to the congressional hearing we just concluded. The matter we will be considering is classified as top secret. Before we start, let me introduce Alexander Soros, the U.S. Secretary of the Department of Defense, and Barbara McCarthy, the Director of ICE, who were not at the Senate hearing. They have both been briefed on the matter at hand." Sanderson indicates Soros and McCarthy and then introduces the rest of us. She goes through some housekeeping issues and hands out agendas. "This meeting will not be recorded, but a transcript will be made for limited distribution." She smiles at Roland McGown, who just entered the room, and then introduces him. "If need be, we will have dinner served here at around six p.m."

After we dish up from the buffet, Sanderson continues, "When we planned the congressional hearing back in March, the U.S. Secretary of the Department of Homeland Security"—she nods at Bryce—"and I discussed the importance of a satellite meeting directly after the hearing as necessary to quickly decide on how to move forward with the information and knowledge we now—after the hearing— have about the mind-viewing capability and its potential, and about the existing mind-viewing LarSal agents."

She continues, "What we decide here today will be recommendations. The next step is to brief the Secretary of State and the National Security Council, who will advise the President. Because of the urgency of the situation, I have already alerted the Council that a matter of grave importance is forthcoming."

She looks at Bryce. "Secretary Vogel, will you please take the helm and kickstart the discussion."

"Thank you, Senator. We are now at the juncture of two main pathways; we could try to keep the discovery of the mind-viewing genes—the Crex-OR genes—and the generation and employment of mind-viewing operatives—LarSal agents as they're currently called—as a secret from the outside world, and an exclusive asset to the U.S. Whether this is even possible is unclear, given close to three hundred existing LarSal agents with unknown identities and whereabouts, and Drs. Steed and Kulak still at large. We also don't know who the mastermind behind 46+ is, but supposedly, it's a member of Congress.

"The other option is to go public, to describe how this hominid was found and how analyses of proteins and DNA led to the conclusion that this hominid—*Homo Crassus*—exhibited some unusual, and hitherto unknown, olfactory receptors. Protein and DNA sequences would be published and available in public databases. This would, obviously, be considered a major achievement for U.S. science and for OMICS science in particular. In addition, this scenario would also satisfy an important OMICS collaborator on the project—the Crassus Project—Professor Elke

Westhoff at Max Planck Institute for Evolutionary Anthropology in Leipzig, Germany. Without her, the Crex-OR genes would never have been identified."

"I know you feel very strongly about this," Bryce continues and looks at me. I nod.

"With this second pathway in mind, we come to another fork; we either let researchers around the world try to figure out the function of these new olfactory receptors in the early hominids. While we—the U.S. intelligence community—continue to exploit the mind-viewing genes to strengthen our war against terrorism. That is, we would continue to construct and make use of genome-edited operatives. The necessary legal and ethical framework, including FDA approvals, could be grandfathered in."

Bryce pauses and looks around. "Or, we go public with all of the results, explaining the purported role of the Crex-ORs in mind viewing and how this hypothesis was validated using the Crex-ORChip device. The technology for generating mind-viewing people and the chip device will be patented and become the property of the U.S. Government. The challenge here is, how do we do that without implicating the scientist who postulated the idea of mind viewing in early hominids."

Bryce pauses again and drinks some water—La Croix, nonetheless. "I'll pause here for questions."

"You're talking about Dr. Thovén's science connection, correct?" asks Sanderson.

Bryce nods. "Yes, that's right."

Lionel Schwartz, the decorated NSA Director, puts on his readers and looks down at his notes. He seems to be in his upper fifties, possibly lower sixties. When he clasps his brown hands in front of him, I notice his fingers are very long and elegant-looking. I wonder if he plays the piano. He's clearly going to say something, but he's quiet for an almost uncomfortably long time.

When he speaks, he does so slowly and with distinct, almost staccato pronunciation.

"Regarding the second track from the second road, let's call it the 2.2 route, where we would go public with all the data. Are the genes in question even patentable? I thought the U.S. Supreme Court stroke down patents of human genes many years ago."

Bryce looks at me. "Symphony?"

I've been studying the scones on the coffee table and was caught off guard. Before I had a chance to recover, Bryce stepped in. He looks at Sanderson. "I guess we might as well help ourselves to some coffee while we're talking?" He's a very good friend, Bryce. I must let him win in chess more often. Sanderson explains the "Symphony" epithet to the newcomers, who look puzzled.

Once we're seated again, Bryce looks at me. "So, Symphony, what's your take on the patentability of the Crex-OR genes?"

The vanilla-bean scone was very crisp with a pleasing glaze. It's not nice to talk with food in your mouth, so I'll leave the cherry-almond scone alone for a while.

I wondered if Bryce's use of "Symphony" meant that we now had transitioned into a first-name basis at the meeting. But I hesitate to call the NSA Director by his first name without knowing him. Not to mention that the guy is a four-star general, as judged by his shoulder loops. So, better safe than sorry.

Anyhow, I now have the wits with me again. "As General Schwartz correctly alluded to, the U.S. Supreme Court ruled in 2013 that human genes are not patentable. However, genes organized in unique constructs, as is the case with the Crex-OR constructs, can be patented. And the technology utilizing these genes, or corresponding proteins, for whatever purpose, can also be patented. That being said, there's no legal governance framework in place for utilizing genome-edited humans for specific tasks. This is unchartered waters."

"Bryce, you mentioned that it would be difficult to go down this route without diving into details about Symphony's science connection. Can you elaborate on that?" It's Barbara McCarthy, the Director of ICE. She's a stately woman in her early sixties.

Bryce again looks at me. I'm in the mid-chew of the cherry-almond scone. Bryce rolls his eyes but politely waits until I'm done.

"Symphony, I think you'd better explain."

"Yes, so the concept of a mind-viewing in early hominids, as a primitive faculty predating the development of speech, was first proposed by this scientist, who prefers to be anonymous, so I'll just call him John. He's now in his upper eighties." I go on to describe my first meeting with John, his postulation of finding an unknown kind of olfactory-like receptors in early hominids, and how I tracked him down in the U.K., where he told me his story. I don't mention anything about the Qumran episode.

"So," I continue, "If John wants to remain in the dark, we can say that our Crassus Team came up with the notion that mind viewing would be a reasonable capability to test. Now that I've gotten used to the idea, it doesn't seem that farfetched. Of course, we would check with John, and I think he would approve. So, we would do it in good faith."

Barbara says, "You say that mind viewing is a primitive form of communication. It seems to me it's a more advanced skill set compared to speech."

"Well, it's primitive in the sense that it works well between two people or in smaller tribes with just a few members. You can direct your viewing or emission of the image-generated olphons to identify with whom you're communicating. We still don't know what the olphons are, by the way, but we have confirmed their presence. Now, in larger groups of people, like in today's society, it's probably much more difficult to use mind-viewing efficiently; you're limited to environments where you can fairly easily target individual people. That's a training experience, as we learned from interviewing LarSal agents. Also, with speech, you can modulate your communication; you can whisper or you can scream. That ability is probably not included in the mind-viewing faculty. Finally, from an evolutionary perspective, spoken communication is nowadays used over the internet or in cellular traffic. We might not have seen such an advancement in communication technology had mind-viewing persisted."

Alexander Soros, another four-star Army General, raises his hand. He's probably around fifty, a little stocky with dark, curly hair, noticeably big, dark eyes, and a wide mouth. His voice is soft but commanding. "In the military, we do a lot of war gaming to ferret out what might happen." He looks at Schwartz, who nods in agreement. "So, assume that we take the second track from the second road, the 2.2 route as Lionel calls it; how would the world look in a few years? First off, and to be frank, I don't think a U.S. patent on the technology or the gene constructs would be worth even the paper they're written on. The technology obviously has intel gathering written all over it. Anyone who wants to use it will have less than zilch concerns about patents. Terrorist organizations come to mind, as do our enemy countries and shadow governments. Now, this begs the question of who has the availability to use it." He looks at me. "Symphony, and I like your name, by the way. Lionel here could play it on the piano." *See, what did I tell you?* "What's your opinion? How accessible are these genes and the technology for anyone who wants to use it?"

"So, say that the U.S. Government has a proprietary interest in the Crex-OR gene constructs and the technology to utilize them. And assume we will continue using it for creating mind-viewing agents, like the LarSals. Then, all it takes is a DNA sample from such a person to obtain the sequence information for the Crex-OR genes. I'd say that just by simple diffusion, anyone who wants to get hold of the sequence will be able to do so sooner or later.

"Then, of course, computer hackers will use phishing and other hacker techniques to try and get the sequence. I don't know about DARPA and NSA, but all sequences that can be remotely identified as Crex-OR in the OMICS computer ecosystem are variants of something completely different. In fact, if you use any of these constructs in the genome editing of a person, he or she will end up having skin tones in one of several colors: red, blue, green, red, or purple. These are constructs developed at OMICS in collaboration with Princeton University for tagging mice used in population genetic courses. We had some fun planting those decoys. The Crex-OR files in OMICS are only stored on computers that are off the network."

People are laughing and smiling. I'm such an entertainer.

I continue, "Now, for the technology—to engineer human individuals with the Crex-OR constructs, this requires DNA elements, software, hardware, and protocols that are way more advanced than are currently considered state of the art at our research institutions. It's encapsulated in the so-called BLUEgenes technology; to synthesize extremely long constructs that can be introduced into all or selected cells of a human (or other animals) as part of custom-made chromosomes. We certainly don't know where countries like Russia and China—and possibly Iran—are in this space, but I wouldn't hold it against them that they are at a similar level—or will be in a few years."

"I would add well-funded terrorist groups to that list," says Bryce.

Soros nods. "I agree with Bryce."

"It's a valid point." It's Schwartz. "Terrorist groups have an uncanny way of accessing the newest technologies."

"So, to summarize then," says Soros. In the world five years from now —

"Sorry for interrupting," I say. "I just need to add that it's the development of the BLUEgenes technologies that are intricate. Once it is developed, it's fairly straightforward to perform the genome editing by getting access to the constructs and protocols and whatever software and hardware are required. So, I think that we need to consider the possibility that the ability to produce mind-viewers will be widespread. Sorry again, but I think this is important to realize."

"Absolutely," says Schwartz. "Thanks for pointing this out. So, it seems then like many countries on our enemy list, in or outside collaboration with terrorist groups, will have mind-viewing agents or other operatives. Any way to stop this?"

People look at me for answers. "Well," I say, "If we could round up all LarSal agents and disengage their mind-viewing ability, and then abstain from further human genome editing with the Crex-OR constructs. And hide the sequence and the entire Fat Man technology as top-secret classified material for the time being. That would help."

"Except that George Steed is still unaccounted for," interjects FBI Director Graham. "Same with this Kulak guy."

"Yeah, there's that," I say.

NSA Deputy Chief Sheryl Barnes is a stout woman with a round, beautiful, almost angelical face. She has a way of squinting her eyes that makes her whole persona seem radiant. I noticed some of that before, during the hearing. Surprisingly, when she raises her hand, I see an American flag tattooed on her right upper arm. "Two questions; you mentioned something about rounding up and disengaging the mind-viewing ability in the LarSal agents.

So, I wonder, how is that done: the rounding up and the disengaging? The rounding up, I assume, needs to be preceded by identification. So, I guess my real questions are, how do you identify existing LarSal agents, and how do you remove their mind-viewing capacity?"

Before I can answer, there's a knock on the door, and a catered dinner is rolled in. It's close to six thirty p.m. Based on the luncheon, I have high expectations. And I'm not disappointed. Well, I am disappointed because there's no wine or beer on the carts. Sanderson explains.

"I'm sure you all can drink responsibly, but the optics here is critical. If it's found out that we're sitting here discussing the future of the U.S. national security while imbibing, it would look really bad. But we have a variety of still and mineral water, as well as sodas."

I was hoping they might have had Beck's Blue or something similar, but no such luck. Well, pan-sheered swordfish with garlicky mashed potatoes and Perrier is not bad. Quite good, actually.

CHAPTER 37

Spring 2027. Presidential recommendations.

P.G. Woodhouse.

So, Symphony," Bryce says after we've had a chance to organize ourselves with food and drinks, "regarding Sheryl's question, how do we identify LarSal agents, and how can we deactivate the Crex-OR gene function?"

"To confirm that a person possesses the Crex-OR genes is straightforward. As I mentioned before, you can get the sequence information by a blood sample or simply by taking a nose swab. Now, that requires that the person is willing to be sampled unless it's done with force. However, there is a way to screen for individuals with the constructs. At OMICS, we developed a technology called Non-invasive Phenomics, or NonPhen, a couple of years ago. It's based on the principle that humans shed debris—skin fragments, hair, dandruff—that contain DNA. Also, secretions such as sweat can oftentimes contain DNA. These fragments and droplets can be sampled covertly from a person when he or she passes by the collector device, for example, at a security checkpoint. Collection can be aided by a faint airstream from the other side of the passing individual. The software in the device can instantaneously analyze the DNA and compare it with a suite of public and non-public databases, and—within seconds—come up with an ID. We can easily reprogram the device to look for Crex-OR information. So, this offers a way to find LarSal agents. It would require deploying the NonPhen devices at several places. It's not an all that satisfactory strategy, but it is something."

"It's certainly an approach worth taking," Bryce says.

"Now, deactivating the mind-viewing capability may or may not be tricky. We may need to involve someone with more expertise in genome editing than I have. We need to look at the sequence in these mini-chromosomes to see if there are enough flanking sequences to allow for the deletion of the entire Crex-OR constructs. If not, it can be at least partly deleted, and what remains would most likely be defunct. Whether this truncation of the chromosomes would result in any deleterious effects down the road is unclear to me. If the telomeres in this twenty-fourth chromosome—the ends of the chromosomes— are different enough from those of the rest of the chromosomes, then these could potentially be used to remove most of the chromosome. At any rate, it shouldn't be too difficult to excise enough of the constructs to deactivate the mind-viewing function."

"What if the mind-viewing capability is inheritable?" Sheryl Barnes asks.

"It's not," I say. "We're talking about somatic engineering, where the Crex-OR constructs are targeted to the vomeronasal organ."

Schwartz pushes his plate away and spreads his hands. We're all looking at him, waiting. "This is starting to get confusing," he says finally. "I think we need to revisit the four scenarios again, one by one, and do what Alex suggested, try to tally up pros and cons, and picture what the U.S. and world would look like."

I raise my hand. "Before doing that, there is another aspect to this. And I'm sorry, but it will make things even more confusing. There are potential medical benefits to the mind-viewing technology. We now know that also dogs and cats emit olphons." I'm thinking back on a few experiments the Crassus Team performed on dogs and cats using the Crex-ORChip device. "As a mind viewer, you are likely to be able to view images generated by a dog. This could be useful for intelligence gathering; the dog could be trained to look for specific items in a room or at a site and then 'report back,' so to speak. And, similarly, if a blind person receives the Crex-OR constructs, he or she could perceive images from a guide dog as long as the blindness does not interfere with the signal transduction pathway for the mind viewing. Also, the dog would probably need to be trained to look up at the person to get the right line of view. But it doesn't have to be a guide dog. It could be a guide person; the blind could obtain images of the surroundings through a companion."

I drink some Perrier. "Also, a mind-viewing pediatrician might be able to discern images from a toddler that screams in pain and figure out what's wrong. A mind-viewing psychiatrist could diagnose a person with psychosis. Or a mind-viewing veterinarian could diagnose a dog in pain. We obviously don't know since we haven't tried. But I do think there might be medical-related benefits with the mind-viewing technology that merit consideration. And if so, it begs the question if it's morally acceptable to keep the technology to ourselves."

Schwartz is going to say something again, so I take the chance to finish my food.

"Okay, this complicates things even further. But let me suggest that we, at least for the time being, ignore the medical benefits—the potential medical benefits, and focus on the intelligence benefits. So, let's paint the picture for the first scenario, scenario 1. We try to keep the mind-viewing technology to ourselves. We get hold of the remaining LarSal agents and either re-recruit them or deactivate their mind-viewing ability. We find Steed and Kulak and figure out who else is involved. We might enroll the LarSal agents in identifying who in Congress was behind the 46+ movement. We continue with existing and or new mind-viewing agents and deploy them at strategic locations or for specific purposes, such as interrogations."

Schwartz pauses and looks at me. "Now, if we add to that what Symphony mentioned. We could view that as an evaluation of medical benefits. After all, we don't know what the long-term effects of this extra chromosome are, do we? The same goes for the LarSals. So, we keep this whole business to ourselves for a couple of years—and it might not even be that long before it somehow spreads across borders—while we're evaluating the long-term effects of the extra chromosome on human health and how the mind-viewers can be employed for medical purposes, while we at the same time are reaping the intel benefits. I would have no moral qualms about this."

"So, after a couple of years, we would go public is that what you figure?" I ask.

"I honestly don't know what to think. But it gives us a few years to ponder."

"And talking about the public," Barbara McCarthy says, "are we planning to keep this secret from our own citizens, the U.S. public? If we don't, there's no way we can keep it from spreading like wildfire around the globe."

Schwartz is bracing himself for a comment, which we now know will take close to a minute. Seeing this, Soros interjects. "Unfortunately, I think that's the only way. My recommendation from this meeting would be to agree with Lionel's suggestion, that is, scenario 1."

"Is this a consensus?" Sanderson asks. She looks at Bryce.

"I tend to agree," he says.

It seems like everyone else, including me, agrees as well. I don't know if that's because we genuinely feel this is the best way forward or because we, by now, are so exhausted and bleary-eyed that we just want the meeting to end.

Sanderson looks around one more time. She then adjourns the meeting.

"You will all get a copy of the transcripts. If you could review it and send me any edits or comments the day after tomorrow, that would be appreciated. I will then talk to Secretary of State Keaton. Bryce, I know you have an early meeting tomorrow morning with Alex and Lionel. I would appreciate it if you could let me know as soon as possible after your discussion of any additional thoughts that we might attach as an addendum to the transcript."

————

As I walk back to the Waldorf Astoria—once upon a time, the Trump International—I keep thinking about what we agreed on an hour ago. With mind-viewers covertly operating on behalf of the U.S. Government, the chances of keeping this a secret from the general population seem slim. I was too tired to voice my concerns at the meeting. Anyhow, I'm not sure what we would have decided on instead. The obvious alternative would have been for the President to present the status quo in a public announcement, something I think is forthcoming at some point anyhow. Such a message would be better received if it came before people started to become aware of it independently through the jungle telegraph.

Well, *que sera, sera*. Now, I'm going to bed and continue reading P.G. Woodhouse, arguably the most widely read humorist in the English language. I read most of his books a long time ago, and I've started to re-read some of them. If you're anything like me—but then, of course, you're not, but if you were—you'd really enjoy Woodhouse's characters: the affable and wealthy but dimwitted and idle Londoner, Bertie Wooster and his super-intelligent and highly competent valet, Jeeves; Lord Elmsworth of Blandings Castle; and the dandy Etonian Rupert

Psmith, to mention a few. What I find most astounding in Woodhouse's writing is the way he plays with words; he's a wordsmith second to none.

But I realize I'm too tired to read. If I hadn't been, I would have opened my book app and continued with *Right Ho, Jeeves.*

CHAPTER 38

Spring 2028. Not as planned.

George Steed and Randolph Kulak were never found. At least they haven't been found yet, a little over a year since last year's congressional hearing. The members of Congress who purportedly were involved in the 46+ movement have not been identified. Of course, this is based on information I have, so you might want to take it with a grain of salt. I think it's correct, though, since Bryce would probably let me know otherwise. Thanks to Paul Fischer, four people with connection to 46+ and or the FutureGenome Lab have been charged with conspiracy to overthrow the U.S. Government. They are currently incarcerated while fighting legal battles where they claim their role was to provide aid for intelligence gathering, not in a plot against the Government.

Speaking of Paul Fischer, you may wonder what happened to him. Well, thanks in large part to Bryce, Fischer is still the Director of the GIC. The role of the GIC—now with enhanced congressional oversight—remains the same as before: to initiate and identify projects in genomics research of potential importance for U.S. national intelligence. The BLUEgenes project with chromosome design and delivery continues as a top-secret program at a new location and now also includes human genome editing with the Crex-OR constructs. It's assumed that other constructs will be added to the custom-made chromosomes in due course. And no, I don't know where this new location is. Well, Bryce told me it's in Texas, so I know that much. And I know that the PI leading the research team is from Rice University. So, I know that the location is in Houston. But where in Houston, I don't know. Other than that, it's in the Central Business District. And that it's a ten-minute walk from the Toyota Center.

The final recommendation to the National Security Council from the meeting on April seventh last year, now famously, albeit secretly, known as the 7@7 meeting—I'll leave it to you to crack that one—was along the lines we agreed on to keep the mind-viewing genes and technology as classified material. This was also the advice the Council gave to the President two weeks later, on April twenty-first, at the beginning of Passover. So, it was decided that the U.S. Government covertly continue to explore the Mind-Viewing project with appropriated funds to DARPA. In other words, to use the Crex-OR gene construct for human genome editing with the extra pair of chromosomes.

Since the Mind-Viewing project was classified, the legal and ethical guidelines were largely left on the wayside while preauthorization clauses were drafted. This was also rationalized by the fact that mind-viewing human individuals had already been produced in the hundreds. New mind-viewing agents have been generated and deployed for intelligence gathering at various locations. I'm not privy to any details. Almost all I know about this comes from Bryce—I make him talkative by letting him win in chess. One medical trial has been performed so far, and it was as emotional as it was successful; A blind man, injected with the Crex-OR construct, was able to see his eight-year-old daughter for the first time through an assistant viewer. All parties involved signed confidentiality clauses. Similar experiments are in the pipeline. Studies with mind-viewers capturing images from spy dogs have been initiated.

Efforts to apprehend the estimated two hundred fifty remaining LarSal agents were unsatisfactory. As I explained at the 7@7 meeting, we have resources to apply for spotting Crex-ORpossessing people, but that only led to the identification of fifteen LarSals. This means that more than two hundred former LarSal agents are still unaccounted for.

Would you be surprised if I told you that things didn't work out as planned? Didn't think so. Claims that the U.S. Government was using "telepathic spies" to steal personal information from its citizens started to pop up on social media and other outlets last fall. The culprit seemed to have been disgruntled LarSals who were under severe emotional stress because of their mind-viewing abilities and wanted to report themselves to the authorities with the hope of getting rid of the Crex-OR constructs. Excision kits for removal or disruption of the Crex-OR mini-chromosome had been developed, but no infrastructure or process for handling these cases had been put in place. Obviously, no public announcements for LarSals to turn themselves in could be posted as the whole operation was classified. It was also unclear what effect a partial deletion of the chromosome might have on the cells. Additionally, some LarSals went rogue and sold their services as private spies to the best bidder.

So, the situation was dire. Not only because of the unrest that spread from the Capitol to the rest of the country. But more importantly, because of the potential interactions between LarSals and emissaries from terrorist groups or hostile governments.

In mid-March, Bryce calls me to a meeting with DARPA. Secretary of State Lucas Keaton will be there. As will Dr. Sheila Wright, Deputy Director of DARPA, Stanley Wiley, program manager from DARPA overseeing the BLUEgenes project in Texas, and Professor James Lindquist from Rice University and the lead for the BLUEgenes project. When I arrive at the meeting at nine in the morning, there is still snow on St. Elizabeth's campus and heavy rain splatters on my umbrella. Very dismal indeed!

"Couldn't you at least have arranged for better weather?" I ask Bryce as we meet in his office. "It's a torrential rain out there." I'm the first invitee to arrive. I'm early; the meeting is set for ten.

Bryce looks at me with his pleasant, warm brown eyes and takes an orator pose, with his right hand towards the sky and raised index finger. Then he declares:

"Be still, sad heart! and cease repining;
Behind the clouds is the sun still shining;
Thy fate is the common fate of all,
Into each life, some rain must fall,
Some days must be dark and dreary."

"Wow," I say. "Impressed. Where's that from?"

"It's by Henry Wadsworth Longfellow. Didn't you learn that in school?"

"For some reason, American poets were not front and center on the literature curriculum when I was a kid in Sweden in the seventies."

I hear the rustling and flapping sound of shaking umbrellas, and the rest of the folks are arriving.

"Yuckee, it's raining cats and dogs out there. I hate this bleak weather," says Sheila Wright, and the others produce supporting murmurs.

"Into each life, some rain must fall, as Longfellow reminds us," I say casually, ignoring Bryce's look.

"It's nice to hear that poetry is still alive and well," Wright retorts with a warm smile as we shake hands.

I nod gracefully and look out the window, trying to assume a humble stance before greeting the others.

While we get seated, Bryce gives me a mild tackle. "Contemptuous punk," he whispers, but with a smile.

Right after the short introduction, an admin comes in with a cart and sets up coffee and tea, a tray with sandwiches, and two platters with scones—blueberry and banana cream, by the look of them. I glance at Bryce and give him a thumbs up. Now I feel bad. I'm not sure why; I haven't done anything wrong; I just showed that I'm a good student of poetic wisdom.

"As you know from your briefs, we have a situation on our hands." Bryce's voice is serious, and, for once, there's no jovial smile on his face.

"Symphony and I have had a long relationship with this issue from the start. And obviously, Symphony is the one who discovered the Crex-OR genes and their function. I know he has some questions for James that we believe are at the crux of devising countermeasures to handle the situation we find ourselves in. So, I'd like to start there. Symphony?"

I put down my scone (banana cream). "Yes, there's one burning question we need to have answered to understand the likelihood of the mind-viewing technology ending up in the wrong hands. So, James or Stanley, am I assuming correctly that the complete information for the Crex-OR genes not only being introduced into the cells but also be packaged into chromosomes with a centromere and telomeres, and recruited histones and RNA into a euchromatin state, are all encoded in the injected constructs?"

James, an almost bald but bearded gentleman in his upper fifties, nods emphatically. "Yes, that's absolutely correct."

"So," I continue, "all instructions needed for the Crex mini-chromosome to be formed in the nucleus of all targeted cells, for the genes to be expressed, and for the receptor proteins being synthesized and inserted into the plasma membrane are included in the construct?"

James nods again. "Yes, you are correct."

"The reason I'm asking," I say, "is because DNA synthesis, of even extremely long sequences, these days is commonplace and fairly straightforward to set up in your garage or get online. So, if someone gets hold of a full sequence for the injected Crex-OR construct, he or she could relatively easily obtain the constructs. Is that right?"

"Right, and there are so many biohackers these days that have set up shop, so getting DNA constructs, even complex ones, delivered to your door is more or less routine."

"And, injection is not an issue, I presume?"

"No, not at all. I know the FutureGenome used IV injection to get results as quickly as possible. But a simple subcutaneous injection with a syringe or a prefilled pen works just fine. The content will eventually get into the bloodstream."

Bryce asks, "So it's a fair assumption then that biohackers or other suppliers with access to the Crex-OR construct will be able to provide syringes or syringe pens prefilled with the Crex-OR constructs for anyone who wants to pay?"

"I'm afraid so."

"But," I say, "how would you get access to the genome sequence for the injected Crex-OR constructs? The information for DNA delivery and chromosome formation and packaging is not retained in the sequence you get from a blood sample."

James nods. "That's right."

"From rumors I hear," Bryce interjects, "it seems as if the Genie is already out of the bottle. I guess there could have been leaks in the former DARPA-FutureGenome collaboration. Or, some LarSals might have gotten hold of the sequence. How about your current BLUEgenes project? Any chance of accidental slip-ups?" He looks at James and Stanley.

"We're as vigilant as we can be," James says. But, of course, I can't say with hundred percent certainty that information doesn't somehow seep out from our project."

Stanley, a tall guy with an uncanny resemblance to a young Samuel L. Jackson—or Samuel R. Jackson, depending on your vantage point—nods. —Sorry, that's a bad inside chemist joke. It only makes sense if you know about chiral molecules. If you don't, don't fuss about it; it's kind of silly anyhow.

Yes, Stanley; he's around the mid-forties, I would think. With a dark complexion and a tall and gangly frame. "I think it's more likely that the sequence for the Crex-OR constructs was obtained by people working in the FutureGenome lab or the VitaMin clinic, most likely after Steed and Kulak bolted."

"Thank you, guys. Now, Lucas," Bryce turns to Secretary of State Keaton, "you're here as the Secretary of State, obviously. But, more relevantly, you're a member of the National Security Council. What are your thoughts when you hear these statements?"

Keaton sighs. "Well, we're in a critical part of the presidential primaries. Dropping this in the topic soup will certainly add some spice. It's bound to be the hottest issue in the debates, not necessarily along party lines, all the way up until the presidential election. But, that aside, it becomes painfully clear that we must act and act swiftly. First off, we need to state legislation that criminalizes the use of these gene constructs outside of the government Mind-View program. As much out of necessity as courtesy, our allies need to be clued up about the circumstances; we need to inform them and set up policies in preparation for tracking the illegal use of the genes. And, I think the President needs to address the nation about the situation."

Keaton takes up a laptop from his briefcase. "Let me show you something. As a junior senator, I was part of the IC (the U.S.

Intelligence Community). In a threat assessment we wrote in 2016, we singled out genome editing. We wrote, and I quote: 'Research in genome editing conducted by countries with different regulatory or ethical standards than those of Western countries probably increases the risk of the creation of potentially harmful biological agents or products.' I assume that the irony here is not lost on you?"

CHAPTER 39

Fall 2028. A different world. Life is good.

No, the irony that Secretary of State Lucas Keaton alluded to in the meeting at Bryce's office in March is certainly not lost on me. Here, it is the U.S. that has introduced a potentially harmful product in the hands of anyone who wants it, including non-allies and terrorists. And I'm ultimately responsible for the whole scenario. Makes you wonder, doesn't it, if we'd been better off if I'd never mentioned anything about what John Smith revealed to me. We would then most likely have published some interesting data about extinct olfactory receptors in early hominins. And the science community would work on trying to find out the function of these receptors. All the while, I would be one of very few (John, Julie, and myself) who knew the truth. — No, I wouldn't have told Bryce since he would feel obliged to act on the information. But I'm working for the DHS, so withholding the potential importance of the Crex-ORs for U.S. national security would have been questionable at best a felony at worst.

So, I'm sitting here in the lilac grove in our backyard, drinking coffee and nibbling on a huckleberry scone. It's fall, a beautiful and warm Saturday morning. I'm wearing a yellow shirt—so far stainless—that pairs well with my tan. I see robins picking worms on our lawn by the Columbia, and I hear the frantic call of killdeers from the front yard by our long driveway. Jupiter is by my side, dissecting an artificial bone with salmon flavor. Julie is playing Bunco with some neighbor ladies.

I'm pondering life. I decide it's good—notwithstanding my qualms about letting the proverbial cat out of the bag with the

Crassus Project and despite Bryce winning more than his fair share in chess. Confusing but good. The current state of affairs is quite different compared to when we started our journey together five and a half years ago. For starters, you have to assume that you unknowingly will encounter mind viewers on a daily basis almost everywhere. A black market has sprung up for "Crexing"; to get micro-syringes with Crex-OR constructs for self-injection or find outlets where you can get it administered. Crex trafficking has become a lucrative business on par with some drug cartels. You can also "Crex out" by getting excision syringes that delete most of the Crex mini-chromosome and disable the mind-viewing ability. People who get Crex do so for a multitude of reasons. They might want to try their powers at the Black Jack or poker tables. Or they want to find out what their boyfriend or girlfriend or other friends think. Or they want to improve their scores on tests or games such as chess. Or, they are in it just for the exhilaration. When you get tired of your mind-viewing gift or become emotionally stressed by it—which is quite common—you can Crex out. Many repeat this cycle several times.

As with many other kinds of substance abuse, Crexing can lead you down a dangerous path with dependence, emotional and physical stress, financial distress, and extortion. The financial burden from Crexing is manifested in all ages, but most prominently among teenagers, who are increasingly targeted by Crex dealers. A Crex syringe can cost anywhere from two thousand to five thousand dollars, and many Crexers end up in debt to Crex dealers and may also resort to criminal activities to repay debts.

Ever since the President's address to the nation on April first—a poorly chosen date, as it turned out since half of the nation thought it was a joke—the U.S. Government has frantically been on a multipronged course of proactive and reactive activities to deal with the many aspects of the mind-viewing landscape.

The U.S. Government and the CDC (The Centers for Disease Control and Prevention) have issued warnings for Crex use. In addition to the risk of ending up in dire financial straits, the long-term effects of injecting Crex-OR constructs are unknown, especially for repeated Crex injections. The same thing applies to Crexing out. Partial deletion of the Crex chromosome leaves remnants in the cell that might lead to deleterious effects. Again, the risks are exacerbated by repeated cycles of Crexing and Crexing out. You see warnings posted on social media streaming platforms, as well as in grocery stores, schools, and hospitals. You also see and hear prompts to mind viewers to turn themselves in in exchange for dismissal of charges and medical attention and evaluation. Many have done so, but it's just a fraction of all mind viewers out and about today. The NonPhen technology we devised at OMICS—one of my many brilliant ideas, remember— is still used at airports and other security checkpoints to expose mind viewers and has turned out to be quite successful as far as technologies go, but the number of identified mind viewers remains modest. We're also using our own mind-viewing agents to covertly recognize foreign mind viewers.

Injecting yourself with genes or drugs is not illegal; you're allowed to experiment with your body if you accept the risks. However, the Crex-OR gene construct is a regulated substance, so Crexing is a crime. The jury is still out on whether or not Crexing out should also be considered a crime. You can apply for permission to get Crex; for example, a blind person might get Crex approval if he or she has an assistant that will function as a guide. Another example is a pediatric diagnosis of toddlers and young children with engulfing anxieties expressed as bodily pain. Yet another is veterinary studies on dogs suffering from frequent nightmares to find out what they experience in their dreams. The way I see it, the employment of mind viewers for clinical applications will be a growing field.

The transmissibility of the Crex virus from mind viewers to non-mind viewers is high, and the symptoms, as we know, are horrible. But the infectious period is only three days or less after Crexing. The CDC has arranged for a vaccine to be administered at all major pharmacies. To avoid being tracked by contaminated people, some Crex users self-quarantine for three days after Crexing before going out in public.

Meanwhile, the U.S. Government continues to expand its mind-viewer force with new agents and officers. Some of those are equipped with nanobots (nanorobots) that circulate in the bloodstream and report on any potential long-term effects Crexing might have. As part of the new BLUEgenes project, DARPA has asked the research team to devise a way to control the Crex-OR genes remotely. For example, optogenetically, to be able to turn off or on the genes with infrared light or some other wavelength, or audiogenetically, with a distinctive sound wave. Once implemented, it would offer the ability to shut down the mind-viewing ability in those who possess it.

Specialized divisions of K9 units, consisting of mind-viewing handler/dog teams, are also under development.

I know only a little of what's happening in other countries; most of it I hear from Bryce. I understand the U.S. is negotiating with our allies to form an alliance against mind-viewing terrorists and selected countries. A U.N. resolution has been drafted and will be the topic of a NATO meeting in Geneva in early December. Crexing, being a global issue, is manifested in many unpleasant ways. Like, the lines at airport check-ins, which nowadays are excruciatingly long. Luckily, I'm one of many who have received a Crex-preapproval pass.

Remember the recording of the interview Bryce and I had with early LarSal agents two years ago? One of them said that the FutureGenome and 46+ folks wore hard-plastic helmets to protect themselves from being viewed. DARPA had continued from the initial observations we made of olphons and their transmissibility back in the OMICS Lab. This research is ongoing. Nowadays, you can buy headgear, such as caps, visors, or bandannas with thin protective plastics. Banks, pharmacies, and many other service centers have set up protective covers to shield staff from customers.

Workplaces are routinely screening staff and visitors for Crex by swab samples. If you decline, you may be let go. I had OMICS screened early on. Of the close to eight thousand personnel, eleven never showed up for screening. Three of them could not produce a legitimate excuse and were terminated with immediate effect.

All these precautionary activities might soon be moot, however. As judged by the tone and public responses during the primaries, it's expected that whoever becomes the President in November, a first swift move will be to legalize Crexing. Steps towards decriminalizing Crexing are already underway in Canada, Australia, New Zealand, Scandinavia, and Germany.

There is one major caveat: the U.S. Government and all other nations that participate in the dialogue on the legal status of Crexing stress that employing the Crex-OR genes in reproductive engineering—targeting the germline—is illegal. As I informed NSA Deputy Chief Sheryl Barnes at the 7@7 meeting, the Crex-OR constructs are used in somatic engineering. That is, the mini-chromosome containing the Crex-OR genes—chromosome twenty-four—is only located in the neurons of the vomeronasal organ. A human's complete set of chromosomes (the karyotype) is forty-six. Inserting the Crex mini-chromosome in the germline would result in humans with a karyotype of forty-eight chromosomes. A man and a woman who both have forty-eight chromosomes would very likely produce fertile children with the potential to fix mind viewing as a permanent trait throughout generations. If either of them instead had the standard karyotype with forty-six chromosomes, they would be genetically incompatible and not able to produce normal, fertile children. Despite the ban on reproductive engineering, there is likely to come a time when couples who plan to have children will want to reassure themselves by taking compatibility tests to ascertain that they are of the same karyotype.

As I said, life is confusing. We're living in a new reality compared to just a few years ago.

———

Bryce and Lucy came over yesterday around noon. Bryce had a meeting in San Francisco, and Lucy came along. As usual, Victor, their son—and d4c4 developer—and his wife took care of Bryce's and Lucy's two dogs (female Labs) and one cat (male Norwegian Forest Cat). After lunch—barbecued Chinook from the Columbia with citrus pesto and garlicky mashed potatoes—Julie and Lucy went for a kayak ride while Bryce and I took to the porch upstairs to play chess. We could see Julie and Lucy paddling away upstream the river. Then, they will let go and effortlessly coast back downstream. We could hear them laughing. They probably talked about Bryce.

Bryce had won the last two games we played in person, on two separate occasions in July, while I won our last game on the app.

"Before I play another match with you, I request a Crex test," I told him when we sat down. There's no way you could have won the games in July the way you did without some help."

"I didn't need any help; I'm the eagle on the fence post."

"Wow, are we in a witty mode today? While you're setting up the pieces, I'll go and get my Crex visor." I'm kidding, of course.

Bryce won again. But it took over two hours and was close despite the fact that I made a stupid mistake, not noticing that my queen was in peril. Bryce offered to let me reverse my move, but I'm too much of a gentleman for that. Well, there's always next time.

———

That was yesterday. I'm still in the lilac grove. I've finished the first scone, and the second is in dangerous proximity. I've promised myself that, starting next year, I'll limit myself to one scone per day as a max. As I consider this significant move in my lifestyle, I decide to test myself by not eating the second scone in front of me. But I can have more coffee. As I go inside to get a second cup, Julie comes home and joins me in the lilacs. I tell her proudly about my decision. She is very encouraging and says she'll be by my side and support me whenever she can. She goes inside to get herself some coffee.

Jupiter looks up from her bone. *"There's no fucking way you're not going to eat that scone before the end of the day. I know you, man."*

"There is, too. You should have more faith in me.

"Ha, that's very funny. Well, let's wait and see."

"We can wait till the cows come home. It won't matter; when I make a decision, I stand by it. I have character!"

Jupiter rolls around on her back making hissing noises as if fighting for air. Julie comes out with her coffee.

"What's with the canine?" She asks.

"She's just having a fit."

Of course, as you may know, a stale scone is not worth devouring. And, I'm not going to say anything more about this other than that a golden rule among scone aficionados is that if you have a freshly baked scone, you either eat it there and then or not at all.

When I bring bottles and glasses out to the lilac grove for wine time at five p.m., the scone is gone. Jupiter is with me. She looks at the table and then at me.

"The raven took it," I say.

———

After dinner and an evening walk with Jupiter, Julie goes inside to prepare for church tomorrow. She's reading the texts at the liturgy. I go back to my favorite outdoor rocking chair in the lilacs. I consider the many mysteries of life I have on my plate. Like, why do the squirrels in the oaks at the OMIC's courtyard keep running around with walnuts in their mouth when there are no walnut trees around? Walnuts don't grow on oak trees last time I checked.

Then we have the olphons. What are they made of, and what happens to them if there are no receptors around for them to dock to? Do they just fade away? And how many animals emit olphons? We know that dogs and cats do. How about cows? I've often wondered what goes on in Rosy Boyd's brain. But seriously, it would be fascinating to find out what kind of mental images cows produce all those hours spent regurgitating their food.

Then, there are the conundrums relating to the 13QT parchments. If you remember, one phrase read, "The progression of mankind was intervened long after the words of the mouth succeeded the images of the mind…" This makes sense in light of what we now think we know about the evolution of communication in hominids, right? But there was also another rendition of the same message; it read, "…the time to intervene with the progression of humankind on Earth after they started using their tongue and viewing of the mind was recessed to the background." Did you pick up on that? I did, but I haven't given it much thought until recently. "Viewing of the mind was recessed to the background," what does that mean? Does it mean that humans still have some kind of mind viewing? Not with Crex-ORs, obviously, but maybe modern humans have a legacy remnant of Fat Man's faculty, part of the signal transduction pathway downstream of the Crex-ORs. I'm thinking of Ronda Trueblood at Berkeley and her studies on human pheromones and the involvement of the vomeronasal organ. As I said before, there's most likely a whole lot more chemosensory signaling within and between humans than what we're aware of.

How about the intriguing reference that evolution was instigated not only on Earth but also in other places? Where are these places? Does it mean other planets? And why don't we hear anything about the 13 QT excavation from the Israel Museum? And, maybe, the biggest mystery of all: why does Bryce keep winning in chess when I'm so much better than he is?

So, as you see, I have a lot to wrestle with.

———

Okay, did the raven take the scone, you ask with great anticipation. Well, I'll say this: last summer when I left the lilacs for a short while to adjust a sprinkler head, I saw the raven—we know him; he often hangs out in a big birch nearby—dive bomb and snatch my remaining scone (blueberry) by the coffee cup. So, there's that. It points to a plausible scenario, right? But, then again, if you've read Edgar Allan Poe's poem about the raven, and you know what the raven said, then maybe…?

Well, I leave it to you to parse that one. Meanwhile, I shoot off *Nxg7+* in the d4c4 app. Perhaps this time…? Then I lean back and ponder life. From a rocking chair's perspective, overlooking the Columbia at seven thirty in the evening on a warm August day, and despite the new world we're living in, I decide it's good.

"What do you say, Jupiter? Life is good, right? And for once, try to polish your language."

She gives me a patronizing glance as if assessing my yellow shirt and reclining position.

"Are we having a walk later tonight after you're done slouching in the chair like a giant banana?"

"Sure, we can do that."

"Okay, if so, I concur with your appraisal."

Well, so there you have it, folks; life is good. Very good, indeed.

And, "tomorrow is another scone," as Scarlet O'Hara said. Well… something like that.

The End

ABOUT THE AUTHOR

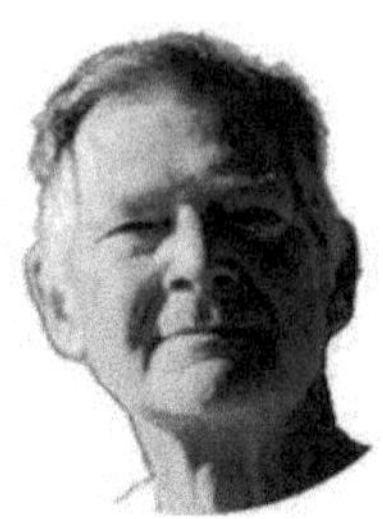

Christer Jansson is a retired scientist turned fiction author. He was born and raised in Sweden and currently lives in the United States. He has extensive experience in scientific writing, including journal articles and book chapters. In writing fiction, Christer draws from his expertise in biochemistry and molecular sciences research from his previous positions as Professor and Department Head at the Swedish University of Agricultural Sciences in Uppsala, Sweden, and as a Senior Scientist at the Department of Energy's Lawrence Berkeley National Laboratory and the Pacific Northwest National Laboratory. His research ranged from studies of the molecular basis of photosynthesis to genetic engineering of plants for enhanced drought tolerance and productivity. When he's not writing, Christer spends much time in the kitchen, cooking or baking. He's partial to vegan food and sourdough bread and likes to explore new recipes and restaurants. He enjoys playing chess, hiking, and spending time with his children, grandchildren, and his wife's parents. He lives with his wife, a dog, and a cat in Berthoud, Colorado, on the Front Range of the Rocky Mountains, where he works on his second novel.